THE HEALTH INSURANCE
FACT & ANSWER BOOK

Also by the author

Health and Lifestyle
The Medicare Answer Book
Never Too Old: A Complete Guide for the Over-Fifty Adult

Energy
Total Warmth: The Complete Guide to Winter Well-Being
Fireplace Stoves, Hearths and Inserts
The Wood-Burning Stove Book

Gardening and Cookery
Cash Crops for Thrifty Gardeners
The New College Cookbook
Grow Your Own Chinese Vegetables
The Salad Book
Summer Garden, Winter Kitchen
The College Cookbook

THE HEALTH INSURANCE FACT & ANSWER BOOK

Geri Harrington

A Harper Colophon Book

1817

HARPER & ROW, PUBLISHERS, New York
Cambridge, Philadelphia, San Francisco
London, Mexico City, São Paulo, Singapore, Sydney

FIRST EDITION

Library of Congress Cataloging in Publication Data

Harrington, Geri.
  The health insurance fact & answer book.

  Includes index.
    1. Insurance, Health—United States—Handbooks,
manuals, etc. I. Title. II. Title: Health insurance
fact and answer book.
  HD7102.U4H288   1985   368.3′82′0029   84-48602
  ISBN 0-06-015447-0   85 86 87 88 89 MPC 10 9 8 7 6 5 4 3 2 1
  ISBN 0-06-091258-8 (pbk.) 85 86 87 88 89 MPC 10 9 8 7 6 5 4 3 2 1

Contents

Acknowledgments

This book could never have been written without the encouragement and help of the entire health insurance field; from the many individual companies who willingly provided policies, to the associations who furnished me with position papers prepared for congressional hearings and other special occasions. Among those who patiently answered my queries, sent me voluminous material, or submitted to lengthy interviews, I would especially like to mention Mory Steinbok, Marlene Z. Bloom, and Diane M. Orvos of the Health Insurance Association of America; Lee J. Feldbinger, director of insurance information, Insurance Federation of Pennsylvania; Mavis A. Walters, senior vice-president, Insurance Services Office, Inc.; the Blue Cross Association and the Blue Shield Association, and Pat Brassil, Blue Cross/Blue Shield of Connecticut; Walter Buzzwitz, American Council on Life Insurance; Robert Felder, American Can; Michael Zipp, director of marketing and insurance relations, Connecticut Business and Industry Association; William T. Berry, Benefit Communications, Aetna Life & Casualty; R. Kippin James, director of marketing, Aetna Life & Casualty; Joan Mooney, Greenwich, Connecticut, office of The Equitable Life Assurance Society; Mary Gray, president, Women's Equity Action League; Elizabeth Morrison, Herger & Co., Baltimore, Maryland.

As always, I found legislators an important resource, particularly Representative James J. Florio and, in his office, Grey Staples, who referred me to many invaluable people in the field and made me aware of special conferences and meetings. Also helpful were Senators Robert Packwood and Frank R. Lautenberg; Burt McChesney, Assembly Committee on Elections, Reapportionment and Constitutional Amendments, and Assemblywoman Maxine Waters, committee chairwoman (California); Carole Ward-Allen, chairwoman of the California State Commission on the Status of Women, and Susan Cowan Scott, the commission's public affairs manager.

A word of special appreciation goes to Hannah Leavitt, chief of litigation, Pennsylvania Insurance Department, who patiently walked me through the Mattes case, with the help of copies of her brief for appellee; and to J. Robert Hunter, president, National Insurance Consumer Organization, who was always available when I had a question and who vetted part of the manuscript for accuracy.

Understaffed and overworked as they all are, the insurance departments of the states were cheerfully helpful. Among those who gave most generously of their time, expertise, and copying machines, I would especially like to thank the following:

Alabama, Paul E. Wallace, CFE, deputy commissioner; **Arizona,** Andrea S. Lazar, assistant director; **Arkansas,** Audrey Fields, health policy analyst, Compliance Division; **California,** L. I. Engriquez, associate insurance policy officer; **Colorado,** Bud Hay, insurance analyst; **Connecticut,** Danny Albert; **Delaware,** Kenneth M. Heck, director of Actuarial Section; **Florida,** Bill Gunter, commissioner;

Idaho, David B. Pittam, policy analyst; **Illinois,** Walter H. Minch, insurance analyst; **Indiana,** Margaret E. McAllen, CLU, consumer consultant, Consumer Services Division; **Kansas,** Fletcher Bell, commissioner of insurance; **Louisiana,** Sherman A. Bernard, commissioner of insurance; **Maine,** Thomas M. Record, attorney, legal services specialist; **Maryland,** Sidney A. Green, chief, Life/Health Insurance Division; **Michigan,** Donald J. Koch, complaint analysis officer, Consumer Assistance Division; **Montana,** E. V. "Sonny" Omholt, state auditor; **Nebraska,** Walter D. Weaver, director; **Nevada,** Ingrid E. Barbash, assistant supervisor, Life & Health; **New Mexico,** Adrienne Diamond, supervisor, A&H Policy Forms Division; **New York,** Deborah A. Kozemko, JD, insurance policy examiner and Raymond A. d'Amico, JD, CLU, CPCU, chief, Health & Life Policy Bureau; **North Carolina,** Ronald Raxter, staff attorney, Administrative Law Division; **North Dakota,** Irv Smith, deputy insurance commissioner; **Pennsylvania,** Monica O'Reilly, press secretary; **South Carolina,** Douglas A. Boome, chief actuary; **Texas,** Evelyn F. Ireland, director, Research & Information Services; **Vermont,** Roger L. Lever, rate & form analyst; **Washington,** Whittier Johnson, director of public affairs; **Wisconsin,** M. E. Van Cleave, assistant deputy commissioner.

I

THE INFORMED
CONSUMER

Neither the author nor the publisher makes any representations with respect to the contents hereof and specifically disclaims any implied or express warranties of merchantibility or fitness for any particular usage, application, or purpose.

This publication is designed to provide accurate and authoritative information in regard to the subject matter covered. It is sold with the understanding that the publisher is not engaged in rendering legal, accounting, or other professional services. If legal advice or other expert assistance is required, the services of a competent professional person should be sought.

1

Improving the Odds—The Health Insurance Gamble

In 1982 health insurance premiums in the United States totaled $111,186,000,000—an expensive gamble by the American people. These premiums were paid on the chance that health care costs would be so much higher that even this staggering amount would pay off. And there actually was an 80 percent payoff; in the same period benefits totaled $88,210,000,000, the amount paid out for health care by insurance companies, Blue Cross/Blue Shield, and other plans in 1982.

Of course, as in any gamble, these figures don't mean you have an 80 percent chance of collecting once you have paid your insurance premiums. The man who broke the bank at Monte Carlo didn't benefit the thousands of other players who lost that same night; what he did was make the odds look better. In the same way a person who collects $70,000 for a heart transplant (supposing he or she is fortunate enough to have a policy that covers such a procedure) improves the statistical picture, even though thousands of his or her fellow workers may not put in more than a $100 claim all year.

What these statistics illustrate is that in their intrinsic nature, insurance companies have more in common with

Monte Carlo and Las Vegas than with General Motors or IBM—the big difference is that consumers buy peace of mind for the chips, even if they don't win. They also get a fairer shake most of the time and, unlike with other gambles, they really hope their bet won't pay off. If, instead of a gamble, a health insurance policy were a guarantee that you wouldn't incur any serious or costly illnesses, you wouldn't begrudge paying even a high premium.

Another difference is that casinos set the house odds, making fairly sure, barring an occasional mathematical genius, that they will pay out only exactly as much as they intend to. An insurance company tries to do the same thing (with its estimated loss ratio) but may be hit by a once-in-a-hundred-years natural disaster that can wipe it out. This latter contingency has to be taken into account along with the statistical average and experience record and, not unnaturally, leads to a tendency to increase the margin of safety beyond what statistics alone would seem to justify. A nervous (or greedy) company will allow what is considered an unreasonably wide margin; a better company (from the standpoint of the consumer and of regulatory agencies) will cut a little closer to the bone. Thus you have companies that pay back thirty cents on the premium dollar, as compared with companies that pay back ninety cents. (The latter figure will be found only among the nonprofit companies, since no commercial company could stay in business with that small a margin.) A good commercial company will pay back sixty-five to seventy cents.

Here again, however, it will not necessarily be *your* premium dollar that gets the return; knowing the loss ratio and knowing it is high improve the odds that you will get a fair shake on your claims. From your standpoint, it will be even better if you are so healthy that you have no claims and, therefore, collect no benefits.

In the long run, if you belong to a healthy group, all of whom have a low claims record, you will benefit through lower premiums. This is the rationale behind the lower premiums of group policies. A large pool of healthy workers in low-risk occupations with a goodly number of young men would be your best bet.

When you play the horses, poker, or dominoes, there is not much you can really do to improve the odds unless you are a professional. Health insurance is different. When you buy a policy, you make a conscious choice. Even with on-the-job health insurance (as we will see in later chapters), you are asked increasingly to pick and choose (and sometimes your choice of job may be swayed by a difference in benefits). You don't have to be a professional to choose wisely, but you do need to be an informed consumer. The more you know about health insurance, the better your odds. That's what this book is all about.

2

Don't Get Sick in America— Without Health Insurance

The title of this chapter is taken from Daniel Schorr's well-known book about the sorry state of health care delivery in the United States. In the book he tells of a Dutch family living in the United States who, though far from indigent, found themselves about to be bankrupted by the expenses of a chronic illness of the breadwinner. Fortunately for them, they were still Dutch citizens and were able to return to their native country, which took care of them with no more ado. In saying good-bye to Mr. Schorr, they said they were sorry to leave the many good things they had found here. It was a great place to live, they said, "but don't get sick in America."

Since the book was written, the pendulum has swung for many workers, with health care coverage one of the major fringe benefits now offered by large corporations. Unfortunately, the pendulum is now swinging again; even the best-protected workers are facing increased out-of-pocket costs. For the millions of uninsured Americans, the picture is increasingly dismal; without insurance, even a minor illness can be financially devastating.

This urgent need for health insurance is peculiar to Americans. Unlike other industrial nations, we are unique in not having a national health plan. In Great Britain, for example, 93 percent of the nation's medical costs—about $20 billion a year—are paid for by the government. The closest thing we have to that kind of coverage is found in varying degrees in Worker's Compensation, Medicare, and the health care plans that cover members of Congress, the White House staff, our chief federal executives, and members of the armed forces.

Even where national health plans exist, old habits die hard. Approximately 4 million Britons still own private health insurance, and the wealthy have a tendency to go to expensive, private, Harley Street physicians for treatment of minor ailments. In the case of a high-cost illness, such as major surgery, however, even the rich Briton often turns to National Health.

Since the overwhelming inflation in health care costs in the United States is blamed primarily on the effect of third-party payments, the question arises whether Britain's much wider third-party system has led to the same sky-rocketing costs. Ask any American tourists who have recently had to have medical care in Britain. Invariably they will tell you they paid less for an office visit in England than an American hospital has been known to charge for a spoonful of cough medicine. And if they had surgery, they are still amazed at how low the total bill was.

The difference between American and British third-party payments is that Britain not only covers the cost of health care, it delivers it. British health care providers, unless they elect to retain their private status, work for the government. And the British government is so efficient that it spends less—5.5 percent of its gross national product—on health care than any other industrial nation. The United States, on the other hand, spends almost 10 percent, the second highest in the world.

"Okay," you may say, "but what about the comparative health of the British citizens?" Unfortunately for American consumers, they are paying more and getting less. Among ten Western countries rated for the health of its citizens, Britain ranked fourth, America ninth.

THE ROLE OF HEALTH INSURANCE

Americans have no choice; only those with health insurance can be sure of access to the excellent but costly medical technology available in the United States. How costly it is is indicated by recent figures compiled by the Health Insurance Association of America (HIAA). According to the HIAA, "the average cost to the hospital per patient day was $38.91 in 1963, $327.40 by 1982—a 741 percent increase." Or more than three times the consumer price index, which rose 215 percent during the same period. But whereas it may be easy to see why you need health insurance, it is not so easy for you to get it. For one thing, there are literally thousands of policies to choose from and there is almost no one to give you unbiased advice. Publications like *Consumer Reports* do their best with a difficult product and persist, in spite of criticism that pours in when they make a mistake in their analysis of policies, in trying to inform the consumer. But no single article can touch all bases or speak to the special problems of each consumer. Insurance policies are not absolutes, black or white, good or bad. What is good for one individual may be totally unsuited to another; to be an informed health insurance consumer, you need a broad understanding of health insurance per se, and guidance in relating it to your special needs.

To begin at the beginning . . .

It will probably come as no surprise to you that in this world of euphemisms, *health insurance* has practically nothing to do with health and everything to do with the lack of it; you buy health insurance to protect yourself against the high cost of being sick or injured. If there were insurance that covered preventive health care—the costs of, for instance, jogging, vacations, staying moderately thin, and getting occasional routine physicals and check-ups—that could properly be called health insurance. Unfortunately, that is just the coverage it is all but impossible to buy.

What health insurance actually covers is part of the costs of hospitalization, dread diseases (the insurance companies' term, not mine), elective and emergency surgery, accidents of almost every description (with some exceptions, such as injuries arising from acts of war), and most of the various ills that the flesh is heir to. An area easily overlooked by those who have no immediate need of it is the mostly meager coverage usually available for any illness that can be termed mental. Neither can you buy stress insurance until the stress has resulted in a recognizable illness, such as ulcers or a heart attack.

Unfortunately, health insurance—and other American third party payment systems—has created a no-win situation for the consumer; health care costs have risen beyond the means of any but the very wealthy. In addition, health care providers are increasingly focusing on the bottom line, taking only those patients who can pay.

ESCALATING HEALTH CARE COSTS

You may dismiss the rise in health care costs as just part of overall inflation, but actually, as we have already seen, these costs bear little relation to annual inflation rates. In fact, inflation seems to be a less important factor than where you live. A 1984 study by the HIAA showed that the daily charge for a semiprivate room in a hospital in the District of Columbia was more than double the lowest rate, $108, in Mississippi. If you are thinking of relocating, you might like to know that southern states are usually the lowest, northeastern and western the highest. And even within a given state, you can do better in one locality than another. In Pennsylvania, from 1977 to 1981, for example, the cost of a hospital room in McKean County rose 130 percent. In the same period hospital room rates rose 123 percent in Chester County, 135 percent in Dauphin County, and 122 percent in Montour County. The smallest increase, in Northumberland County, was still a whopping 30 percent, where the actual cost in 1977 was $83 as compared to $108 in 1981.

These figures don't even tell the whole story: hospital charges have gone up far more than a perusal of semiprivate-room rates would seem to indicate. Today hospitals routinely charge for many items that were heretofore supplied without charge; you won't find charges for cough medicine, tissues, sutures, Band-Aids, and the various parts of IV equipment on old hospital bills. Now they are not only billed for, the charges for them are frequently enormously higher than what you would have to pay at your local pharmacy (which is selling at retail, with a pharmacy service charge tacked on).

The inflation in hospital costs is further hidden by administrative changes. An anesthetist on the hospital staff is covered by your basic hospital insurance, but when was the last time you heard of a staff anesthetist? Now most anesthetists are outside the hospital and render their bills separately, along with the surgeons. And they have so taken advantage of this new status that a recent study showed that anesthetists' average annual income is higher than the very comfortable income of surgeons. (Surgeons are both horrified and shocked by this situation and often complain bitterly that they have to undergo a far more rigorous training than anesthetists, whom they do not consider their peers in the medical hierarchy.)

Given these continually escalating costs, it is little wonder that consumers look for a way to protect themselves against possible bankruptcy in the event of a serious illness. In the United States the only source of protection available is private health insurance, and Americans have gotten the message. The Health Insurance Association of America (HIAA) reported in their 1982–83 sourcebook, "At the end of 1981 more than 188 million Americans—84 percent of the civilian noninstitutional population—were protected by one or more forms of private health insurance. These included nearly 173 million persons under sixty-five—representing 86 percent of this age group." And these included, also, the five out of six Americans age sixty-five or older who had bought private health insurance in spite of having Medicare coverage. By the end of 1981 over 1,000 private U.S. insurance companies were writing individual and/or group health insurance policies.

Of the approximately 188 million persons with health insurance, most of them were covered for hospital expenses, an increase of 16 percent since 1971. It is no accident that this is the most common coverage. First of all, it is obvious to anyone who has been hospitalized or has a relative or friend who has been that the daily room and board rate is just the tip of the iceberg, and that a stay of only a week can run up charges of thousands of dollars. In addition, hospital coverage is widely available and comparatively easily obtained.

Surgical-expense coverage runs a close second, with similar growth; in 1981, 177 million persons had this kind of insurance. Hospital-related insurance, such as for the cost of an operation, is often offered in a package, along with coverage of in-hospital expenses; it is only when coverage is sought for out-of-hospital expenses, such as doctors' office visits, that coverage is both more meager and more expensive. There is, of course, a perfectly good business reason for this: hospital stays, on the average, are of fairly short duration; doctors' office visits, especially for certain treatments, can occur over and over and run up all sorts of laboratory, X-ray, and other similar charges. While most people will not land in the hospital with any frequency, they may have frequent occasions to visit the doctor—and it is assumed that these occasions will be even more frequent if the insurance company rather than the individual is paying the bill.

As health care costs have risen, the cost of protecting oneself against these costs has risen, also. As a result, not only is health care out of reach of many, but so is health insurance. Among the studies that have been done to determine exactly how many Americans are without health care insurance, the figures do not always tally, but they are all large enough to cause concern. The Social Security Administration, for example, estimates that in 1976, 24 to 25 million persons, or 12 percent to 13 percent of the under-age-sixty-five population, had neither public nor private hospital or surgical cost protection. The Congressional Budget Office (CBO), in a report on the uninsured population, found that 11 to 18 million persons were without coverage in 1978. The CBO found, also, that young adults are almost twice as liable as other age groups to be without coverage; although they are only 11 percent of the population, they represent over 20 percent of the uninsured. And lest you doubt that the expense of health insurance is related to failure to purchase it, the CBO reports also that among persons earning less than $10,000, 55 percent are without health insurance protection. With the result, of course, that those least likely to be able to afford the uninsured costs of illness are those most liable to incur them. As far as I know, no studies have been done on what percentage of those on welfare and Medicaid have been put there by the devastating financial effect of an illness, but this possibility is of concern to all, since in the end it is the taxpayer who foots the Medicaid bill.

The seriousness of the unprecedented rise in the cost of health care has finally filtered up to Congress and to the business community; presently many efforts are underway to restrain hospital costs and to educate the consumer to a more efficient use of health care services. Legislation aimed at rewarding hospitals for greater efficiency has now been implemented, and business is taking a hard look at group health insurance policies that it is finding an increasing burden.

THE BUSINESS OF GETTING INSURED

Granted health insurance is a necessity; how can you get the best coverage for your money? First and foremost, you must understand that insurance is strictly a business, albeit one that depends more than most on the application of statistics to reduce risks. And since insurance companies (with the exception of nonprofit groups such as Blue Cross/Blue Shield) are naturally in business only to make money, they should not be faulted if they are no more altruistic than any other business.

The insurance industry's product is, however, somewhat different from a box of detergent. In recognition of this, the industry benefits from certain privileges and incurs certain obligations that are not expected of soap companies. It also sells its product somewhat differently from merchandise (although it is now possible to buy insurance at Sears stores and other retail outlets).

Almost all health insurance companies work in much the same way. For a consideration (the premium), they

Health Insurance for Pets

Inflation in health care costs may change the way we live in more ways than one; the family dog and cat may have to go. America's pet owners, confronted with the rising cost of veterinary care, have created a growing market for a new kind of health insurance; now you can insure small animal pets, such as dogs and cats, against the many accidents and illnesses that are liable to befall them. Policies similar to those offered for humans are usually available through literature found on pet-related premises—animal hospitals, pet shops, grooming services, veterinarians' offices, and pet-product departments of stores.

These policies are limited to the small menagerie usually found in households, rather than offering coverage for a million-dollar racehorse, for instance. If you are interested, remember the laws protecting humans against the fine print in the policy do not apply to pet insurance. Examine pet policies carefully for the usual loopholes, such as exclusions, pre-existing conditions, and the like.

Should you buy one of these policies? J. Robert Hunter, president of the National Insurance Consumer Organization, thinks not. "This is in the junk coverage category. . . . It's not an accident that pet insurance in some instances has been created by veterinarians, who are probably a little jealous of what Blue Cross has done for the doctors and are trying to emulate that."

agree (the policy) to pay out money in the event of certain contingencies (the covered benefits). If you buy a homeowner's policy, you will be paid (according to the terms of the policy) when your house burns down, when someone throws a ball through your window, or when any number of similar untoward events take place. You will probably also be protected to a limited extent if you are sued by the mailman who has slipped on your icy walk when delivering the latest batch of junk mail. Likewise, an automobile policy will protect you against the usual hazards of automobile ownership, including broken windshields (though these are sometimes excluded), theft, and the need for a tow.

Statistically, the frequency with which these happenings occur is fairly easy to predict. Auto accidents, the nature and extent of resulting injuries, engine breakdowns, and auto thefts are all well documented every year. So for insurance companies to realize a profit on paying you when these things happen, all they have to do is charge a high enough premium, based on their experience as to average frequency and cost, to leave a comfortable profit margin.

In the early days of the industry, insurance margins were very wide indeed. Although statistics were not as extensive and there was no track record, consumers were even more inexperienced and had little idea of probabilities. Half a century ago premiums were pennies—fifty cents paid to a man who came around regularly to collect—but often the coverage was for such an unlikely contingency as "loss of a leg while riding on a train, boat, or airplane." (Some modern policies cover contingencies that are equally unlikely, but for a considerably higher premium.) As the insurance industry grew, it gathered more statistics and was able to assess the odds somewhat more scientifically.

How successfully this was done is indicated by a quote from Thomas J. Finley, Jr., president of The Insurance Federation of Pennsylvania. Writing in a brochure, *The Insurance Industry's Role in Pennsylvania's Economy,* he says:

> The American insurance industry possesses assets that are 2½ times the assets of the American oil industry, 60 times the assets of the auto industry, and, indeed, ⅔ the assets of the entire combined *Fortune* 500 companies. Last year, Americans paid out 235 billion dollars in insurance premiums, equivalent to $1,000 for every man, woman, and child in this country. Countrywide, nearly 12% of our annual disposable income goes to the cost of insurance. The insurance industry now employs nearly two million people in the United States, up from only 800,000 in 1950.

In 1981 the health insurance premium income of all insuring organizations was $84.9 billion (adjusted for duplication); $49.0 billion to insurance companies, and $45.2 billion to Blue Cross/Blue Shield and other plans.

The industry is, furthermore, working on expanding its market. To attract those who have resisted buying insurance, companies have sharpened their pencils and come up with benefits for special groups, such as women (who have traditionally been "underinsured"). The best and most convincing way to do this is through the application of statistics, but it must be done carefully to achieve the twin goals of offering more favorable insurance to special groups while increasing the insurance company's profit.

Auto insurance is an example of how this has been done. In order to make their predictions more accurate, and to attract the desirable low-risk consumer, automobile insurance separates the good guys (women, married people over thirty, residents of low-crime areas, owners of typical American cars) from the bad guys (young men under thirty; residents of high crime areas; people who have put in more than three claims within the year; and people who drive compacts, sports cars, or luxury cars) and adjusts the premiums accordingly. (As we will see in the discussion of sex discrimination, these statistics, as well as those for life insurance, are sometimes used somewhat selectively, with only part of the benefits passed on to the favored group.) This system has worked well for auto insurance for many years and has only recently been put in jeopardy by the accelerated rate of car thefts. (It is difficult for the statistics on car thefts to stay up to date.) Inflation has also been a problem, since the cost of parts and repairs has gone off the charts.

Health insurance, however, is complicated not only by inflation and the inflated cost of parts and repair, but also by the number of variables and the lack of clear-cut, up-to-date statistics in many areas. The insurance company has to consider many more risk factors for health insurance than for auto insurance—whether you are male or female, your age, your occupation, your health record to date, the part of the country in which you live, and many other personal statistics, all of which may be a guide to how likely it is that you will get sick and cost the company money. In addition, it must determine how to pay you: by paying the health care provider or by sending the check directly to you; by paying a lump sum for certain specified illnesses and procedures or by paying a percentage of the (more or less) actual cost of the same. It has to weigh family coverage against individual coverage (how old do the children have to be not to be "family" anymore), single women against spouses, and what to do when you reach age sixty-five and probably become eligible for

Medicare. And they have to do all this in a highly competitive marketplace.

As if that were not enough, they have to wend their way through the maze of the fifty United States, which regulate insurance on a state-by-state, rather than the federal, level. Each insurance company must be approved to sell policies in each state in which it wants to do business and must conform to at least the minimum standards that state mandates for each type of insurance. If the company wants to sell in several states, it ends up writing a policy that will pass muster in most of the states. This creates the kind of problem that Medicare supplemental policies encounter, as in the case of the AARP policies discussed in the chapter on Medicare supplemental insurance. Here the company had to point out in its brochures that half of its policies could not be offered in (in this instance) Connecticut. It is noteworthy that the company chose not to take the easy way out of the dilemma; it would not have had to make this disclaimer if it had not called its policies *Medicare supplemental* but had instead simply called them health insurance policies for seniors.

In addition, the federal government sometimes throws the industry a curve, as it did in 1984 when it made Medicare the secondary payer and all other health insurance (including the personal injury part of automobile policies) the primary payer. This, of course, added a new factor to the equation of policy pricing and meant increased costs to the beleaguered over-sixty-five consumer. It must have created a statistical nightmare for the insurance companies, which probably built in a higher than usual margin to cover all the new unknowns.

All this has led to confusion and complexity; the consumer has not known what to buy or where to turn to find out. No sooner has the consumer studied the market and settled on a policy than he or she finds that it is no longer available and has been replaced by three others. For those comparatively lucky members of large unions, this has not, until recently, been an overwhelming problem. The union hires trained health insurance analysts to determine what companies under their jurisdiction should have in the way of benefits; if the union is strong enough, the employer picks up all or the lion's share of the cost. This, however, as we will see in a later chapter, is changing; the worker will no longer be spoon-fed health care coverage but will have to take an increasing share of financial responsibility for that choice. Needless to say, the average worker, who will have had little or no experience with making health insurance decisions, may have to learn the hard way—from a hospital bed—about the weaknesses in his or her coverage.

For the nonunion white-collar worker in a large company, there is still usually on-the-job health care coverage, although the benefits may not be as good and will definitely be more expensive than what the union worker can get.

For the self-employed or the small businessperson, there is much less to choose from and all of it is almost prohibitively expensive. For the over-sixty-five retired person on Medicare (an already inadequate program that is being steadily eroded), supplemental health insurance is simultaneously becoming both increasingly essential and unaffordable, and catastrophic coverage (especially if not purchased in younger years) may be an impossible dream.

If you are one of those people who turns purple at the thought of a national health plan, don't complain the next time your health insurance premium comes due, uncovered charges use up your cash reserves, you are outraged at the price of a new car (which includes several hundred dollars' worth of health care coverage for automobile workers), or you hesitate to have necessary dental work done because your policy doesn't pay for it. Console yourself that although the United States is the only one of nineteen industrial nations (including Holland, Denmark, France, England, West Germany, and Belgium) that doesn't have such a plan, that is the way you, the American citizen, want it, and you can change your mind and vote for different policies anytime you get fed up with the status quo.

3

Getting Your Feet Wet
—A Short Course
in Health Insurance

When it comes to buying health insurance, knowledge isn't power, but it helps. It is important to know right from the start that no policy exists that will cover all your health care costs; the closest you can come to this ideal state is the group insurance coverage provided by some large corporations or the restrictive but comprehensive coverage of a health maintenance organization (HMO). What you are more liable to have to deal with is the fragmented and patchwork coverage of various types of policies.

Policies differ in two ways: what they cover and how they make payments. They may cover a large proportion of your health costs or only a small fraction. A policy may pay the health care provider directly, or it may pay you. Generally speaking, a policy that pays the provider offers more complete coverage. A policy that pays you directly is more liable to pay a flat sum only for very specific items, without reference to actual costs.

TYPES OF POLICIES

Medical Expense Insurance

The kind of policy sometimes called medical expense insurance or reimbursement type pays all of, or a percentage of, the actual charges of hospitals and medical care, and sometimes includes coverage for physicians' charges and related services. In examining this type of policy, note what it does not pay for—prescription drugs, well-baby care, and dental care are three areas that may not be covered. (Look carefully—a policy may also exclude all nonhospital-related charges or even all charges not billed directly by the hospital, such as anesthetists' charges.)

Medical expense insurance comes in many guises, from the most limited to the most comprehensive coverage. It can usually be found to cover one or more of the following expenses:

hospital charges only
hospital and surgeons' charges
hospital, surgeons', and in-hospital physicians' charges
hospital, surgeons', in-hospital physicians', and in-hospital private nursing charges
physicians' charges
comprehensive in- and out-of-hospital charges
major medical charges

Policies are not always clear in indicating what they do and do not cover and can be hard to follow. It pays to make a checklist for each policy under consideration so you can immediately spot uncovered areas and make instant comparisons. It is also a good way to avoid unpleasant surprises when you file claims. If you have any questions or are not absolutely clear about any point, ask the agent or the company to explain it to you.

If you are not sure what you need and what is a frill, talk to someone who has recently been hospitalized. Private-duty nursing used to be considered a luxury, a prerogative of the rich, but with the present state of hospital care, many middle-income people would not think of going in for surgery without having a private-duty nurse for at least the first two days after the operation. And round-the-clock private nursing does not come cheap.

Hospital Indemnity Insurance

Another basic category of policy is generally called hospital indemnity insurance. This is not directly tied to health care costs. Although it is always grouped with other health care insurance, it really, as the name indicates, is insurance to augment your income, but since it pays during hospitalization, it is properly called health insurance. Do not confuse this with disability insurance, which has a much broader function and replaces part of your income without requiring hospitalization.

Service Type Insurance

There are types of health insurance that do not quite fit into either of the previous categories, for instance, that offered by Blue Cross/Blue Shield; this is called service type insurance. For instance, Blue Cross negotiates contracts with "participating" hospitals to purchase their services at below the going rate. This practice has long been a source of irritation to private insurance companies that have had to pay the full rate.

At present most Blue Cross/Blue Shield organizations are nonprofit, although that is gradually changing. The Blues operate on a state-by-state basis, with coverage varying widely. If you have been happy with a Blues plan but move into another state, do not assume you will automatically have the same coverage; chances are there will be differences.

You should also be aware that Blue Cross and Blue Shield are not one company but two entirely separate ones, although they generally interface. In combination they offer essentially the kind of coverage found under medical expense insurance, sometimes—though not invariably—somewhat less expensively. Traditionally, they never offer hospital indemnity or disability insurance (but this may change as they give up their nonprofit status and move into the general health insurance field).

Disability Income Insurance

Disability income insurance is not, strictly speaking, health insurance, because it is not directly related to health care costs. Neither, unlike hospital indemnity insurance policies, is hospitalization a prerequisite. Its function is to protect you against loss of income due to inability to work, generally because of illness or accident. Because it is thus related to the state of your health, it is thought of as at least a kissing cousin to health insurance.

The amount of disability insurance you can buy will be limited by the amount of your salary. Obviously the insurance company must guard against providing you with an incentive to malinger, such as paying you benefits that are greater than your regular salary; actual benefits will always fall considerably short of that.

Disability income insurance is routinely offered as a job-related benefit but can be purchased by the individual directly from an insurance agent. Each policy differs as to conditions, limitations, and requirements for eligibility. There is also a big difference in length of coverage; some policies cover you only for a short period, others for several years, others for life. Waiting periods before benefits start may also vary considerably.

An important feature may be whether coverage is for both partial and total disability or only for total. In the latter case, the definition of *total disability,* as set forth in the policy, could be critical.

In addition to private disability insurance, there is Workmen's Compensation and, in the event of total disability lasting more than twenty-four months, the possibility of qualifying for Medicare coverage. It is well to be generally familiar with the existence of these programs so you will know where to look if the need arises.

Benefits from private disability income insurance are always in the form of cash income directly to you, to be spent at your discretion.

HMOs—Health Maintenance Organizations

An entirely different kind of health insurance coverage is provided by HMOs—the only coverage in the United States that in any way resembles the national health care plans of other countries. Unlike a national health care plan, however, membership in one HMO does not automatically entitle you to care nationwide; it is primarily a local service, limited to residents of a specific geographical area. Obtaining health care when you are away from your HMO area may be difficult and is, at best, available only in the event of an emergency.

Medicare

Medicare does not fit into any of the previous categories (although a Medicare beneficiary may elect to join an HMO). It is health insurance provided by the federal government to the totally disabled, to those with end-stage renal disease, and to those over age sixty-five who are eligible for Social Security. (It may be purchased even if you are not eligible but the cost is so prohibitive as to make that option an unrealistic one.) Unfortunately, as with other health insurance, Medicare coverage is far from complete and is getting increasingly costly. Even those who have both Medicare Part A and Medicare Part B coverage are well advised to buy supplemental insurance as protection against some of the charges not covered by Medicare. As with all health insurance, it is impossible for Medicare recipients to achieve complete coverage, even with supplemental policies.

Medicare Supplement Insurance

Over the years this has been referred to variously as *supplement* and *supplemental* insurance; nomenclature in this field seems to be a problem for everyone concerned. Either term used in describing a policy is your assurance that you are getting at least the minimum basic coverage. It should be prominently displayed on the cover of the booklet you must be given that outlines the policy's benefits and limitations.

This type of policy is available only to those who are qualified for Medicare. It is supposed to fill the gaps left by Medicare coverage, but it leaves plenty of gaps of its own. If you buy this, get the most coverage you can.

COMPARISONS OF POLICY TYPES

How They Differ

As we have seen, the type of insurance known as medical insurance comprises not one but many kinds of policies. There is the *hospital expense* policy, which covers, at a minimum, all or a percentage of room and board in the hospital and related charges, such as use of the operating and recovery rooms, drugs administered while in hospital, staff nursing care, and similar charges. It will not cover TV rental or other optional expenses. The *service-type* policy (the Blues) will pay actual hospital charges, either 100 percent or some other percentage (usually 80 percent, often for a lower premium than private insurance calls for). Other types of policies will pay only up to a specified maximum. There are usually limitations, for example, a time factor, such as benefit periods, or maximum number of days covered, and there are various ways in which this can be expressed—by each illness, by actual in-hospital time, by out-of-hospital time between admissions, and so on.

Many hospital policies are combination policies; the most common combination is hospital plus surgical expense coverage. In other words, you are covered both for your hospital stay and for the charges of the operation that put you there. Do not confuse surgery coverage with broad physician coverage; often postoperative office visits will not be covered (if they are charged for); neither will your own family doctor's visits be (when he "looks in on" you in the hospital for five minutes every day and sends you a bill for each "visit"). In addition, since many surgeons often routinely have assistant surgeons present, and since these assistant surgeons often render a separate bill, note whether your policy includes or specifically excludes payment for this additional surgeon.

Another type of combination policy includes coverage for your family physician's in-hospital visits. Those charges, based on daily "look-in," can add up to a sizable sum. Often, however, even if covered, the specific amount your policy will pay is so much less than the actual bill that it may not be worth your while to take on the higher premium for this type of coverage.

The most comprehensive hospital policy will cover all the costs just mentioned plus private-duty nursing. As it happens, private-duty nursing coverage, when it is available, is usually good. The best coverage is offered in a policy that pays a percentage of the actual costs rather than a flat hourly rate or for a limited number of hours.

Medical expense insurance with good coverage of out-of-hospital charges is available but harder to find and more expensive. If you buy this, be sure it includes coverage for laboratory tests, diagnostic X-rays, EKGs, and so on, no matter where obtained.

Dental expense insurance is more widely available than it used to be, but mostly through the group policies of large companies. Even when it is available, it is often strictly limited in the procedures it covers. After people reach about thirty-five years of age, most of their dental problems involve the gums rather than the teeth, so coverage that does not include this area is not so useful for the older worker. Most dental insurance will cover root canal work, but only under specified conditions. Payment for braces and other orthodonture work is important coverage because of the considerable expense involved.

Many people set great store by nursing home coverage but fail to understand its limitations. Short-term coverage is available only in the type of nursing home known as a skilled nursing facility (SNF). There are comparatively few of these in the United States. Long-term coverage is generally not available under any circumstances; custodial care (which is what a long-term nursing-home stay usually involves) is never covered. Nursing homes other than SNFs are not covered, and most of the facilities thought of as nursing homes are not SNFs.

Hospital indemnity coverage will pay a specified amount of cash directly to you (rather than to the hospital)—daily, weekly, or monthly, depending on the policy, while you are actually in the hospital. You won't get as much as your salary (or anywhere near it); there may be a waiting period of approximately a week before payment starts (most hospital stays last less than a week); and there will be a specified maximum amount of money or days covered.

Who Buys What?

A study by the HIAA in 1980, "A Profile of Group Medical Expense Insurance," found that among 21.8 million employees, 99 percent of those with hospital expense coverage had a level of 80 percent or more coverage of the average semiprivate room-and-board rate in their local area. Since, as we have seen, this is the most common type of coverage, it means that those hospitals could be sure a large proportion of their patients were sufficiently solvent (through their insurance companies) to meet the high cost of hospitalization. In turn, the patients themselves had no financial worries in connection with their hospitalization and were hardly aware of the costs. Given this situation, it is hardly to be wondered at that hospital costs and insurance premiums are being priced out of reach of the average consumer who works for a small company or is self-employed.

The study found also that Medicare coverage is most comprehensive in Part A—the part that covers hospital expenses. Yet even there, in 1981, 15.6 million Medicare beneficiaries found it necessary to purchase private health insurance also; 7.2 million of these had policies that specifically covered hospitalization. It should be noted that of the 7.2 million, 3.1 million had bought the hospital indemnity type of coverage. The elderly, with their more limited income, are keenly aware of the peripheral charges associated with illness and tend to be receptive to plans that appear to augment their income at such a time. Whether this is a wise choice is another story.

The HIAA found that Medicare recipients with supplemental private insurance broke down into the following categories:

TYPE OF COVERAGE	NUMBER OF PERSONS 65 OR OVER COVERED
Hospital indemnity	3,078,000
Medicare Part A co-insurance coverage	4,097,000
Medicare Part B co-insurance coverage	2,655,000
Prescription drugs	1,319,000
Nursing home care	2,177,000
Private duty nurse	1,559,000

If you are not yet sixty-five or over, there is a message for you in those figures: Get your health insurance coverage up to date and anticipate your old age. Many policies stop at age sixty-five—even group policies—and those that continue for your lifetime cannot be purchased after a certain age. Health insurance should be an integral part of retirement planning and should not be left to the last minute.

Major Medical

Since even the most informed consumer cannot buy complete coverage, what is the solution? The best answer is to buy as basic insurance one of the types just discussed, then—if you can afford it—get major medical insurance in addition. Major medical is a fail-safe policy that picks up where the others leave off.

Major medical is comparatively new—available only

since 1951—and it helps fill the void created by rising health care costs. In 1981 over 107 million people had major medical policies from private insurance companies. And another 149 million had the equivalent through the Blues and other independent plans. Major medical coverage is broad and much less picky than basic health insurance. It typically has a high maximum benefit—either per year or for life—and a stop-loss feature that limits out-of-pocket costs. There are several types, including one that supplements the typical hospital-surgical-physician coverage, and another more comprehensive policy that includes basic coverage and extended-care benefits.

According to the HIAA, in 1980 nearly 90 percent of 21.8 million employees in the HIAA profile study had major medical policies, 46 percent of them with a maximum benefit of $1 million or an unlimited amount.

You can quickly recognize a major medical policy: it will have a high deductible because it is not expected to pay ordinary expenses (which are presumably covered by other health insurance). Major medical traditionally is bought to protect you from total financial disaster in the event of a serious or long-term illness.

TIP Once you understand what types of policies are available and how they differ from one another, you will be less liable to become overinsured through the purchase of duplicate coverage. Don't count on your broker for this kind of analysis . . . some brokers (not yours, of course) deliberately load you up with policies they know are duplicating your coverage.

THE GROWTH OF HEALTH INSURANCE

It is interesting to compare the number of persons with health insurance policies in 1940, 1960, and 1980.

Persons with Health Insurance Protection
by Type of Coverage in the United States
(000 omitted)

	1940	1960	1980
Hospital expense	11,962	122,500	189,000
Surgical expense	4,900	111,525	178,223
Physician's expense	3,000	83,172	169,529
Major medical		32,590	155,192
Disability income			
short-term	N.A.	42,436	65,400
long-term	N.A.	[a]	21,093
Dental expense		N.A.	80,528[b]

N.A. = not available.

[a] Included in "short term," with the possibility of some duplication.

[b] Estimate.

SOURCES: Health Insurance Association of America, Blue Cross Association, Blue Shield Association, U.S. Department of Health and Human Services.

4

Insurance ABCs—How to Read a Policy

Both the federal and state governments have been working hard over the past few years to encourage the insurance companies to write their policies in simpler, clearer language that is able to be understood by any reasonably literate person and to set their policies in a reasonably large size of type (no more small-print clauses you have to read with a magnifying glass). The improvement has been considerable, but even so, policies are hard to understand because many of the terms are either not used in everyday life or have taken on specialized meanings. Before we get into a discussion of actual policies and coverage, therefore, I thought it would be a good idea to familiarize you with some of the basic terms you will encounter. In later chapters we will see what to look for under these terms, but for now they will serve primarily as an introduction to health insurance trade talk.

Premium. The premium is the amount you pay for the policy. (If you are covered at work, your employer may pay all or part of it.)

TIP You may pay a premium semimonthly, quarterly,

semiannually, or annually; sometimes you have a choice and sometimes you don't. If you have a choice, the more frequently you pay, the more it usually will cost you. With this type of policy an annual payment, if you can swing it, is generally your best buy. An employer that offers health insurance coverage may pay all, part, or none of the premium. The premium you pay in a group policy (like the one you get at work) will be the same, for the same coverage, for all workers at the company (unless the contract the company has with the union allows for certain special instances, such as a higher premium for high-risk occupations). The premium you pay for an individual policy (one you buy yourself, unconnected with your job or any group) will be higher. And if you are in an occupation that is considered dangerous, you may not be able to get coverage at all. There are various other factors that may make you more of a risk than the "average" person; if any of them apply to you, both your premium and your difficulty in obtaining good coverage will be greater.

With some policies the premiums go up every year as you get older. Group policies don't tend to (though some do if they are not on-the-job contracts), but you will encounter this in individual policies in unexpected places, such as in some Medicare supplemental policies and some Blue Cross/Blue Shield comprehensive policies. It may sound like a good deal if you are in your twenties, but the increases come fast, and soon you feel locked in to the spiraling premium costs. It's better to get a policy without this feature; in the long run, you will benefit.

Most premiums go up annually due to "inflation." On the other hand, it is sometimes possible to reduce a premium by settling for less coverage (fewer benefits).

Most policies cannot increase premiums on an individual basis but only for all those who have the policy. (Do not buy a policy that says it can increase your individual premium on the policy's anniversary or at any other time, unless it specifies it will do so only when the increase applies to everyone who has that policy.)

TIP If you would like a policy that won't increase its premiums and can't be cancelled by the company, look for the words *noncancellable and guaranteed renewable.* If you can't find this clause in a policy you like, make sure it is at least *guaranteed renewable* so the rug can't be pulled out from under you if you get really sick or old. Of course, any policy can be cancelled by you at any time and by the company if you fail to pay your premium.

A policy that is noncancellable and guaranteed renewable usually specifies that coverage extends either to a certain age or for life. A policy containing this clause must be renewed by the company at the same rate at which you took it out. A policy that is guaranteed renewable cannot be cancelled but the premiums can be increased, provided they are increased for a particular class, such as for everyone in your geographical area who has that policy. Some policies are *guaranteed renewable for life,* which sounds more reassuring than it is, since those policies can (and often are) so easily be changed or discontinued for the whole group.

Loss ratio. The loss ratio is the percentage of premiums that is paid out in benefits. Many states specify that health insurance group policies must have a 70-percent loss ratio, and individual policies, 65 percent. This is an "anticipated" figure, but theoretically the states check each year to make sure the company is meeting the estimate. It is possible, in states with more lax regulations, to buy policies with a loss ratio as low as 40 percent. This is stacking the odds even further against yourself than they already are, and you can do better than that.

TIP   If the company or salesperson won't tell you the loss ratio, and you think it's a pretty good policy in spite of that, call your state insurance commissioner and ask what it is. (That's also one way of making sure the policy is approved for sale in your state. Of course, if you live in a state that doesn't police these matters, you have a problem.)

Do not assume that the policy automatically has a high loss ratio just because it is from a good company. I have seen health insurance policies from Equitable—a good company—with a loss ratio as low as 50 percent; you ought to be able to do better than that.

Benefits. These spell out your coverage. If the policy doesn't specifically and clearly state that it covers something (ambulance, private-duty nursing, etc.), assume that it doesn't. (Occasionally it will turn out, especially with a group policy, that it does, but it's better not to count on it since it is unlikely.) Remember, it's not the job of the policy to point out what it doesn't cover.

Note carefully any coverage that is subject to limitations and restrictions (which may be explained on an entirely different page from the description of benefits); they could be so extensive as to effectively negate the coverage. Be especially wary of the areas covered by key phrases such as *pre-existing conditions* and *exclusions and limitations.*

States that care about this sort of thing generally lay

down guidelines and may even set minimum requirements for various types of policies. These requirements can be very specific, including the size of type used in the policy and the placement of certain basic information.

Benefits can be paid in one of two ways: directly to you or directly to the health care provider. The amount can be arrived at in different ways—according to a schedule set up by the insurance company, according to Medicare's approved charge, or according to the actual bill. The company pays a percentage or a fixed amount of the basis they use. If the amount is based on the insurance company's schedule of rates, you have no way of knowing how good the policy is unless you can compare the actual schedule against actual costs in your area. How much does the policy schedule allow for a fracture? Maternity care? A gall bladder operation? Are these charges realistic compared with what your own doctor charges? Are they adjusted annually for inflation (health care costs have been rising faster than inflation rates, but some sort of adjustment should be built in or even the best schedule will soon be obsolete.)

TIP A percentage benefit schedule is better than a fixed amount. Fixed amounts, especially these days, go out of date rapidly and leave you with yesterday's coverage for tomorrow's bills.

If the policy pays a percentage of the "reasonable charge" for a service, look in the policy for the definition of this term. (Also see Reasonable and Customary Charge, p. 45.) It wouldn't be sensible for the insurance company to agree to pay any wild charge the health care provider may come up with; usually the "reasonable charge" is fair if it is based on local charges—a reasonable charge in Mississippi would be a drop in the bucket in the District of

Columbia. Some doctors will accept what the insurance companies allow; some will bill you quite a lot more and expect you to pay the difference out of your own pocket. If this happens with your doctor, you may find his or her charges way above average for the area and decide to shop for a new doctor ... or a new policy.

Deductibles. Deductibles are amounts you pay before the policy's coverage will take over. Usually you have a choice of amounts, from low to high, so that you can tailor the deductible to your financial situation.

The higher your deductible, the lower your premium should be. It is considered good practice to pay as high a deductible as you can afford. Beware, however, of high deductibles combined with high premiums and long waiting periods. You must compare policies so you can spot the especially greedy ones.

Major medical or catastrophic illness policies usually have deductibles ranging from $1,000 to $5,000. Given the purpose of that type of policy—to protect you against the very high costs of major illness or injury—it makes sense to go for the highest deductible you can handle. Major medical insurance is not meant to cover run-of-the-mill illnesses. Statistically, the chance that you will need this kind of coverage is very low, so you play the odds by choosing a high deductible; and the company, using the same odds, can charge you less and still come out ahead (even if that means having to pay out $50,000 or more occasionally).

Co-insurance. Read this part of the policy carefully; it will set forth the extent to which you share the costs with the insurance company. Co-insurance takes over when the deductible leaves off and may be expressed either as a percentage or simply as whatever is left after the company's benefit payment. (See also Lifetime Stop-Loss, p. 46.)

A Bankers Life and Casualty Company's policy brochure describes its co-insurance feature as follows:

> Co-insurance is a way for you and Bankers to share the payment of your medical bills; you pay a percentage of the bill and we pay the rest. You pay 20% of the covered expenses (we'll pay 80%) until your share reaches $1,000, including your deductible. After that, we'll pay 100% of the covered expenses. If more than two family members are in the hospital in a year, we'll pay 100% of expenses after the deductible, for those family members after the first two. By you sharing the cost, your premium is lower.

While the grammar leaves something to be desired, the meaning is fairly clear. But you have to read very carefully if you are not used to this type of policy or you will get the impression that with this policy, you can never incur more than $1,000 in out-of-pocket costs. Unfortunately, that is far from the case. Where it says, for instance, "we pay the rest," you have to understand that this does not give your providers a blank check. On the last page, under "These are the Exceptions," the brochure says, "We Do Not Pay ... Costs which are more than the rates approved by the Commission on Hospital and Health Care, or are more than the reasonable and customary charges, or are not medically necessary, or are for services or supplies which the individual or institution is not licensed or certified to supply." This means, for example, that if your surgeon charges $4,000 for an operation for which Bankers determines the "reasonable and customary charge" is $2,000, Bankers will pay, after you have met your deductible, 80 percent or $1,600 and you will have to pay 20 percent or $400 *plus* the $2,000 that is over the "reasonable and customary charge." So Bankers will pay $1,600 and you will end up paying $2,400. This is spelled out in the brochure, but you have to know where to look and what to look for in order to arrive at the whole picture. And, of course, you have to know what the schedule of "reasonable and customary charges" actually is before you can determine how much your payment will be for any given procedure.

Also, where the brochure says, "After that, we'll pay 100% of the covered expenses," you must realize that that means the company, in the example just given, would pay the entire $2,000 referred to above (if it were incurred "after that"), but would never pay anything over and above the allowed amount. This is the usual way health insurance policies work but can result in unpleasant surprises at difficult times if you don't understand what you are reading.

Pre-existing conditions. This is one of the trickiest areas in your policy. You cheat only yourself if you don't tell the truth on your application, but it's almost impossible to tell whether the company is going to be as honest as you are unless you have friends who have had some experience with a similar policy from the company.

Simply put, a *pre-existing condition* is "a current health problem which you had prior to becoming insured" (an HIAA definition). In other words, if you had diabetes before taking out the policy, that could be considered a pre-existing condition, depending on the policy's specific definition. This is such an important and complicated feature of health insurance policies that I have dealt with it in some detail in chapter 17.

Exclusions. We have already noted that a policy does not cover anything unless it says it does—in spite of possible assurances to the contrary from your salesperson or insurance broker. In addition, there are specified items not covered, and these are usually listed under a section in the policy called "Limitations and Exclusions" or one or the other.

Standard exclusions common to most health insurance policies include:

- Treatment in a government hospital, such as Veterans' Administration hospitals.
- Suicide or intentionally self-inflicted injuries.
- Cosmetic surgery, including sex change operations.
- Health care while on active military service.
- Injuries resulting from an act of war.
- Expenses payable under Worker's Compensation.
- Illness resulting from the use of controlled drugs, unless otherwise specified.
- Custodial care, whether in an institution or at home.
- Eyeglasses, hearing aids.
- Personal comfort items while in the hospital, such as television rental.
- Bills covered by other health insurance. If you have two policies that duplicate coverage, only one will pay. The insurance companies work out between them which one pays what. In 1984 Medicare, normally the primary payer, arbitrarily positioned itself as second payer when any other coverage exists. The general rule otherwise is that the policy you have held the longest is the primary payer.
- Care not medically necessary or not prescribed by a doctor.
- Expenses you are not legally obligated to pay.
- Charges above those that are "reasonable and necessary," a term that is usually defined somewhere in the policy.

Some exclusions are worth looking out for, since they are not universal and can presumably be avoided. Some of these are:

- Pregnancy. The kicker is that a woman may want a policy that covers pregnancy without reference to her marital state or whether she is a spouse or a worker. Some group policies provide this; it may be harder to get in individual policies. Group policies may try to limit this coverage to female workers (not extending it to wives of workers). Check your policy; assume nothing. The laws affecting pregnancy coverage are in a state of flux (see chapter 19 on sex discrimination for a detailed discussion of this); they are being challenged and sometimes overturned as fast as they are passed. If this coverage is important to you, check your policy for exactly what is and is not covered. If you have a disability policy, check it especially carefully for coverage of length of leave (at least six weeks minimum), retention of pension benefits without penalty for leave, and whether or not an employee gets her job back when she returns from leave.
- Dental treatment is an important benefit, but one that is comparatively recent. You probably will not be able to get it in an individual policy.
- Treatment for alcoholism. This is a benefit that keeps appearing and disappearing. If it's not important to you, don't worry about it.
- Specific illnesses. If you have had previous treatment (but not necessarily for a problem that falls under the "pre-existing condition" umbrella), the policy may have an exclusion added to it in the form of an attached "endorsement" or "rider" that does not provide coverage for any costs relating to this illness. This is strictly a heads-the-insurance-company-wins,

tails-you-lose proposition. You are being denied coverage exactly where you are most liable to need it, and the insurance company is still making you pay the full premium—just as if you were getting full coverage. If you run into this situation, you might want to look into some fairer policies.

Waiting period. Waiting periods occur only when you first take out a policy. A policy can be nonspecific, simply stating that coverage will not begin until a stated time after you have signed the policy. Or it can be specific, such as a one-year waiting period before pregnancy is covered. Often a pre-existing condition will lead to a waiting period being used as a form of exclusion. In other words, the policy may set a waiting period for an illness such as cancer, heart trouble, or digestive disorders. If you unfortunately discover one of these conditions before the waiting period is up, you will never be covered for it under this policy. Since waiting periods can be as long as a year or even more, this is a serious limitation. Hold out for as short a waiting period—like thirty days to six months—as possible.

Elimination period. This is something like a waiting period, but it is found primarily in hospital indemnity and indemnity income policies. Your payments, for instance, may start on the first, the seventh, the twelfth, or an even further off day of hospitalization. Here the insurance company has the advantage of knowing the statistics and thus being able to pick the most advantageous length of time. You, on the other hand, may not realize that most hospital stays are comparatively short, so the low premium for an indemnity policy with a longer waiting period may seem like a good buy. Chances are it isn't; if you chose a period of a week or more, you may never collect a penny for that coverage in your whole lifetime.

Benefit maximum. No policy is going to go on paying you indefinitely, regardless of how large your bills are. The benefit maximum stated in the policy tells you the most you will be paid. It may limit the dollar amount or the number of days of hospitalization or nursing home care that is covered. The best kind starts all over again after you have filled the qualifications for a new benefit period or started a new calendar year.

A sure sign that health care costs have gotten out of control is the total amount policies will pay in a lifetime. Until recently the benefit maximum was $500,000, and the first-time policyholder was usually really impressed with this. Now newer policies routinely offer a benefit maximum of $1 million.

Entrance age. Most policies, except those especially designed for seniors, cease coverage at age sixty-five. The federal government, however, now requires that group policies continue if you have membership through your job and if you continue to work after age sixty-five. In any case, take a look at your present policies to see where you stand. At the very least, it may alert you to the need for additional health insurance.

While there are policies that can be bought at any age, some that continue coverage after sixty-five can be bought only years before you actually reach that age. If you haven't reevaluated your health insurance coverage by the time you are fifty, you should do so at that time.

Family policy. If you have a spouse and/or children, you may want a policy that will cover all of them. Even if both husband and wife work, this is still important for a number of reasons: one policy may be better than another; the policies may complement each other, filling gaps in one with coverage from the other; in case of a job loss, you will still have coverage. Since most on-the-job coverage comes with the job, paying two premiums (if the employers don't pick up the tab) shouldn't prove too burdensome. If, however, you don't have job-related coverage, you should get only one policy—with very complete coverage—that includes the whole family.

Reasonable and customary charge. If this term is used in a policy to indicate the basis on which the policy will pay covered charges, the law requires that it be defined somewhere in the policy. The definition may read like this one from an Equitable policy:

> Covered charges will not exceed the regular and customary charges for the services, supplies, and treatments in the locality in which they are provided or rendered.
>
> Regular and customary charges means the usual and reasonable charges for services, treatments, and supplies, based on such factors as the following:
>
> 1. the nature and complexity of the services and treatments;
> 2. the usual charges made by other doctors, facilities, agencies, or institutions for similar services, supplies, and treatments in the same locality.

Policies that don't pay according to reasonable and customary charges may specify "inside limits," which means they will pay up to a fixed amount for your hospital room or surgical expenses, regardless of the actual cost. You have to pay the difference, whatever it may be. If the inside limit is unrealistic in terms of charges in your area, the policy may be of little use to you when you need it; meanwhile you will be paying premiums, possibly for many years, during which time you will not have occasion to collect any benefits at all.

Lifetime stop-loss. Most policies, as we have seen, require you to pay deductibles, co-insurance, and other out-of-pocket expenses. To keep these from becoming overwhelming, many policies now have a stop-loss provision that puts a cap on these expenses. To quote from a Sentry policy, "The Lifetime Stop-Loss then takes over (after you have paid out a maximum of $1,000—including the deductible—for each ailment) and pays 100% of the employee's covered expenses up to one million dollars for each accident or illness as long as the employee remains insured." This policy requires 20 percent co-insurance up to the stop-loss of $1,000. Not every policy offers exactly this particular stop-loss feature—the actual amounts will differ—but it is available in both individual and group policies.

Illness vs. accident. There used to be a sharp difference between these two conditions, but recent laws tend to require that they be treated as one. Of course, if you go out of your way to buy just an accident policy (like the ones sold in airports), no one can protect you against yourself. Look for policies that don't differentiate—the size of your hospital bill will not depend on how you got the problem that put you there.

Option. No one who has ever purchased a car is liable to be confused about the meaning of this term. It invariably costs more for whatever the option is, even if it is actually something you must have. Many health insurance options, however, are easily done without and may not be worth the extra cost.

TIP Don't be discouraged about the difficulty in absorbing all the information in this chapter. It is meant to give you markers and guidelines to help you wade through a policy, but the job has been made easier for you in several ways. First of all, either federal or state laws require that certain terms be defined in the literature and in the policy itself. When this occurs, you can be sure the insurance company and you agree on what the terms mean. This usually involves crucial areas of coverage, such as "reasonable charge," and it is comforting that your government is policing it. In addition, where there is a good state insurance commission, certain coverage is mandated in certain types of policies, such as the state of Connecticut's refusal to approve Medicare supplemental policies that do not meet its requirements for specified wording, graphics, and coverage. In this event some of your work has already been done for you, and you can take it from there.

Once you have settled on a policy and bought it, check regularly to be sure it doesn't need updating. This is especially important with policies that pay specified amounts rather than percentages of actual costs.

II

WHEN NUMBERS COUNT—GROUP INSURANCE

5

How Group Health Insurance Is Changing

Until fairly recently only union negotiators and employers concerned themselves with the details of worker health care coverage. The rank and file accepted their benefits as one of the perks of the job and thought no more about it; chances are most workers didn't even know what their insurance covered until they got sick. Employers generally bit the bullet until it occurred to them to pass on part of the added cost to the consumers (who aren't even aware the high cost of the products they buy includes their involuntary contribution to the workers' health care insurance).

In the early days, health insurance premiums were manageable and represented a comparatively modest part of overall manufacturing costs. Today group health is big business and big bucks. The Departments of Labor and Health and Human Services estimate that the annual health insurance premiums paid by corporations in 1984 have more than doubled since 1977—from $28 billion to $58 billion. According to the United States Chamber of Commerce, this comes to an average per employee of $2,000 a year. The C of C estimates, further, that health care represents 11 percent of the average payroll, a figure that is liable to increase markedly; from January 1982 to September 1983, a time when overall prices rose 6.38 percent, medical care costs rose 15.3 percent.

Employers find themselves having second thoughts about picking up health care premiums when their bottom line begins to be seriously affected by this escalating fringe benefit. Employees, however, are understandably reluctant to accept less than they have been getting.

Health insurance as a fringe benefit first came into the corporate picture during the Depression. At that time many workers, unable to meet what were then comparatively modest medical expenses, welcomed corporation offers to shoulder this burden. Insurance companies, enabled to sell hundreds and thousands of policies at one fell swoop, were delighted to work out low-cost package deals employers could live with. Today job-connected health care benefits are a fact of corporate life; 97 percent of American workers have on-the-job health insurance, most of which covers 75 percent or more of physician office visits, not to mention even more extensive coverage of hospital and other health care costs.

The situation has, however, gotten out of hand. The corporations find themselves locked into providing these now costly benefits at a time when unions are powerful enough to demand, also, regular wage increases and increased fringe benefits in other areas. The result is increased inflation and increased costs in consumer goods. Joseph A. Califano, a director of the Chrysler Corporation, speaking before the Economic Club of Detroit in April 1983, said Chrysler's $373 million annual health insurance costs were adding $600 to the price of each Chrysler car. Additional costs that affect every consumer include the overall inflationary effects of these third-party payments, the rise in health insurance premiums, and the spiraling increase in out-of-pocket health care expenses, even for those with several health insurance policies. Only recently, with the advent of high unemployment, has the employer had the clout to take back some of the benefits offered in previous years.

In an effort to gain some control over health care costs, large corporations are now trying to reduce their role in a number of ways, including passing on more of the expense to the worker who is the beneficiary. Ironically, a fringe benefit that arose during one depression could be lost, or at best greatly eroded, in the event of another.

There are already rumblings. In September 1983, several large corporations approached the bargaining table with the suggestion that employees pick up a greater portion of their premiums and pay higher deductibles. For example, the Quaker Oats Company of Chicago doubled the amount of the monthly health insurance premiums its employees paid, from $3 to $6 per family, plus an additional $2 for each child. Citing an increase of 58 percent since mid-1981 in its $12 million annual health care costs, Quaker asked employees to pay up to $750 for hospitalization and offered incentives rewarding lower utilization of health services, such as a bonus of up to $300 tax-free for a reduction in the number of doctor-office visits. Currently the Quaker Oats plan includes a $300-deductible policy that pays 85 percent of costs over the deductible to $5,000. Although the union received a guarantee that this plan would include an approximate wage increase of 8 percent, the company considers it is still ahead, since under the old plan its costs would have risen an estimated 20 percent.

At about the same time, Citibank moved to reduce its share of premium payments from 90 percent to 80 percent, with the employees picking up the difference.

W. R. Grace & Company, whose plans had no deductibles or co-insurance, added them for the first time in

1983, as did the Ford Motor Company in overhauling its basic hospital care program.

As might be expected, the unions have successfully resisted many of these changes; when they do, the burden falls primarily on the nonunion white-collar workers who have no one to go to bat for them. The result has been an increase in white-collar costs; for example, at Ford alone, the changes added $250 in deductibles and $750 in other health expenses for that group. The unions' resistance to these changes is not just natural cussedness. They contend that who pays the costs is not the point; the point is to control the costs, and even to reduce them to a more sensible level. The corporations agree but say the way to control the costs is to make the worker, who is the health care consumer, pay more of the bill, because, the reasoning goes, people paying their own bills will be more careful about how they spend their money. The theory is apparently based on the belief that lower utilization of health care services will eventually force health care providers to charge less in order to try to maintain the volume of their business. In a world in which electric companies maintain their profit levels by increasing rates whenever business falls off in order to end up with the same amount of money in spite of selling less of the product, this would not seem to be a realistic solution.

INNOVATIVE GROUP PLANS

Cafeteria Health Plans—How Aetna Does It

The insurance industry has responded to the employers' desire to get out from under by developing some creative new approaches to group health insurance packages. An interesting example is a plan developed in December 1983 and underwritten by Aetna Life & Casualty for the Connecticut Business and Industry Association (CBIA). The principle of the plan is to provide cost-effective health care by doing away with a comprehensive package and instead offering employees a number of options—a cafeteria of benefits in which they can pick and choose those that they want. If they choose correctly (from the employers' standpoint), they are rewarded. The rewards are usually either cash savings or actual cash bonuses.

The way the rewarding reimbursements function is shown by a few examples of choices the employee can make.

1. If the employee agrees to have presurgical testing done outside the hospital rather than after hospital admission, he is not required to pay a deductible and the charge is covered 100%.
2. Since entering a hospital on Friday or Saturday is inefficient—little lab work and few tests are done over the weekend, but the hospital still charges its usual rate for room and board without granting full access to hospital services—limiting one's admission to Monday through Thursday means more efficient use of the hospital, and weekday admissions are rewarded accordingly. (This is becoming a common cost-containment measure; if it keeps gaining in popularity, hospitals may have to join hotels in offering special low weekend rates and attractive perks like an extra-nice Sunday brunch.)
3. Generic prescription drugs, which cost less, are covered 100 percent; brand-name drugs are covered at a lower level.
4. Obtaining a second opinion before surgery is covered 100 percent.

5. Outpatient surgery is covered 100 percent, compared to 80 percent for in-hospital surgery. Without home health care coverage (which this particular plan has), this option may be a little hard on the beneficiary, especially if the worker lives alone and has no one to take care of him for the first 48 hours after general anesthesia. At the very least, someone is needed to drive you home from outpatient surgery (such as for a broken leg or a cataract operation; a cabbie who deposits you on the curb is not much help).

R. Kippin James, director of marketing at Aetna's Employee Benefits Division, says of this plan that it "incorporates the best of the best." It includes coverage for many features often not included in standard group policies, such as home health care, hospice care, and in-hospital alcoholism treatment. Most health care costs are 80 percent covered. In 1984 the employee paid, per calendar year, a $200 deductible for a single person or $600 for a family.

While cost-cutting options of this sort were designed primarily for the benefit of the employer, they are generally also beneficial for the employee. The little inconvenience and advance planning required to make use of them is minor compared to the continued benefits and lower costs that they confer on the worker.

Cafeteria benefit policies are gaining acceptance nationwide as more and more corporations turn to them for employee-acceptable cost cutting. But now they are beginning to go beyond cost-efficient options.

More and more policies utilize flexible reimbursement plans, and these may lead to possible problems. When the health insurance benefits are tied in with other fringe benefits—when an employee can, for instance, choose more vacation time and less health insurance coverage, or even actual cash—he or she may not be able to resist the sure benefit of a longer vacation compared with an "unlikely" illness.

The most extensive cafeteria plan offered covers basic benefits and then such a tempting variety of options that health care coverage is relegated to the sidelines. This type of plan can be offered only by companies with a minimum of 100—and usually many more—employees; Aetna, for example, offers cafeteria plans only to companies with 1,000 or more employees; too many options plus too few employees results in too few people in each group plan and brings costs up to an unacceptable level. Even if these plans were offered to small companies, they couldn't afford them; the computerization required to implement this type of plan within the company means start-up costs of as much as $250,000 to $500,000. The payback period becomes impracticable for any but the corporate giants.

Modular Version

A simplified version of the option package is the so-called modular version. Here the options are grouped into various packages; employees may choose freely among the various plans but cannot design their own. Because the options are limited by the number of packages offered, setup and administrative costs are considerably reduced.

John Diriam, of Towers, Perrin, Foster & Crosby, a management consultant firm in Boston, characterizes the modular plan as "cafeteria compensation with a fixed price menu." Employees can choose the coverage that suits their personal needs, over and above the usual single-vs.-married option. For instance, a young male unmarried worker might take a high deductible on dental and medical insurance (for which his age indicates he wouldn't have much utilization) and get in exchange extra vacation time and cash reimbursement. A senior employee might prefer to forgo the extra vacation time and cash in favor of more dental and medical protection.

Reimbursement Account

An even more innovative approach is the totally flexible reimbursement or spending account. It comes in many variations, but the basic idea is the creation of a cash reserve against which employees can draw. The use of the funds is not limited to health care costs; the money can be used to cover other out-of-pocket expenses, including financial counseling, legal fees, college tuition, and child care costs—sometimes even homeowner's insurance. The money in the cash reserve comes from either the employer or the employee, or both. In the event of the money coming from the employee, it is taken in the form of a salary reduction. The result is that the employee receives the same amount of money as before, but part of it becomes a tax-free benefit. If, as is highly probable, this option is ruled taxable by the IRS, it may no longer be viable. Until that happens, however, an employee offered this type of plan could elect to put, say, $3,000 into the cash reserve and, as a result, get a $3,000 reduction in taxable income.

The IRS is not at all happy with the tax-free aspect of this type of plan. In 1984 it ruled that cash reserves are taxable when disbursed, whether as rebates or as any other form of cash. Since this includes the portion the employee might chose to spend on health care, it means previously nontaxable health care benefits are suddenly taxable. Certain restrictive regulations might confer exemption from this tax status, but the whole area is gray at present. Meanwhile the government feels it is involuntarily subsidizing this type of health care benefit because income tax is reduced when the salary is reduced. According to a *New*

York Times article of May 25, 1984, John E. Chapoton, assistant secretary of the Treasury for tax policy, "says the plans could deprive the Government of $11.6 billion in revenue over five years." And Bruce Steinwald, acting director of health policy at the Department of Health and Human Services, echoes this sentiment: ". . . It is a bit unfair to expect Uncle Sam to bear such a high proportion of the freight."

There are a number of other aspects of these plans that need to be carefully considered. Obviously it would not be to the employees' benefit for the reduced salary to be used as the basis for disability income insurance or pension; neither would it look as good on a person's employment record in the event of a job change. The employer, therefore, would need to keep both a gross and a net salary account for each employee, thereby incurring increased accounting costs. This, in turn, is further liable to focus IRS attention on the untaxed area, especially since actual cash is involved. In addition, the nature of the plan somewhat negates the idea of health insurance, which is to provide protection against the high cost of illness. A healthy employee faced with many places to spend this reserve cash may gamble on staying healthy and may, accordingly, divert health insurance money to day care, a vacation, or a down payment on a second home. An unexpected accident or illness could prove this to be a poor decision. It appears that once again the problem of high health care costs is not being tackled at the source.

RAMIFICATIONS

Although these plans are already in effect in some companies, they cannot be considered to be in their final form until the IRS has ruled on them; there will undoubtedly have to be some changes. Bob Felder, benefits director at

American Can Company in Greenwich, Connecticut, is enthusiastic about the cafeteria idea but he cautions, "If a company puts in a cafeteria plan just to slash the cost of benefits, I think the program will flop." As to employee reaction, Felder points to the Yankelovich, Skelly & White study conducted in 1983 among 4,000 American Can employees. Of the employees surveyed, 90 percent said they liked selecting new benefits each year, and 74 percent rated their benefits program either "very good" or "excellent."

On the other hand, cost cutting is clearly a large part of the appeal of this type of plan to the employer. In Mendocino County, for example, seven participating school systems provided employees with Blue Shield of California policies calling for a $500 deductible. The school system undertook to set aside this amount for each employee, on a use-as-needed basis. Any money not used by the end of the year accumulated in the employee's account and was paid out when the employee left or retired. In the four years during which the plan has been in effect, 23 percent of the employees have not drawn any of this fund. This experience record has resulted in lower premiums for Mendocino; the superintendent of schools there estimates the savings in premiums to be as high as $250,000.

The enthusiastic attitude toward this type of plan is not always shared by union officials. Karen Ignagni, deputy director of the A.F.L.-C.I.O's Department of Occupational Safety, in a *New York Times* interview, said, "We think it [this type of plan] creates a perverse economic incentive for employees to use fewer health care services. That could actually increase costs. If health problems are ignored, they only become more expensive in the long run." Certainly encouraging employees to delay seeking medical attention can often result in long illness that might have been prevented if diagnosed early. More and more diseases, from shingles to cancer, respond much more favorably to early detection and treatment. Such plans also discourage preventive medicine, which HMOs have shown to be a much more effective way of reducing health care costs.

On the other hand, unions themselves are often tempted by these plans, which offer benefits that the workers seem to want. A 1984 contract negotiated by the Aluminum, Brick and Glass Workers with Alcoa and Reynolds provides $700 for each of 17,000 workers, the money to be disbursed at the end of the year if it is not used for health care. The union is happy, and Alcoa, which estimates it will be saving up to 10 percent in premiums, is equally pleased.

Regardless of the way the IRS rules, it is clear that group health insurance in the future will be very different from what most workers have today. Cost containment will be the number-one priority for the employer, and flexible packages, with emphasis on individual needs and wants, will put the burden of choice on the individual employee. Conceivably, two-income families could end up with incredibly comprehensive coverage if they pick their options carefully between them (American Can even pays up to $2,000 for the charges an employee incurs for an adoption). On the other hand, freedom of choice also carries with it responsibilities and dangers. Unwise choices and emphasis on short-term gratification could be disastrous in the event of an unexpected calamity (and what calamity is expected?). If the options offered are not carefully selected and basically serious, the insurance package could easily take on the aspect of a TV game show.

The flexible health insurance package, like the breakup of AT&T, gives consumers a job they aren't trained for and have no expertise in. It means that in the future it will be essential for consumers to know much more about buying health insurance—even group insurance—than they do at present.

6

What to Look for in a Group Policy

Group insurance is insurance offered to groups of people who are able to form an entity recognized by insurance companies as eligible for "group policies." While insurance companies humor the understandable desire of nongroup individuals to obtain the undeniable benefits of group insurance, they tend to draw the line at groups organized solely for the purpose of qualifying for group health insurance; some additional common ground is required in order for a group to be recognized as bona fide. Associations such as professional or trade organizations may qualify under this definition.

The easiest way to qualify for a group policy is, however, as a worker with health care as a fringe benefit. Any company or union with twenty-five or more employees is eligible for true group insurance; the larger the number of employees, the better the policy. Insurance companies do not, however, rule out the possible market to be found among smaller businesses; those with under twenty-five employees, and even those with only three employees or even one (the proprietor) will find that a "group" policy may be available to them. Generally speaking, the smaller the group, the poorer the coverage and the higher the premium.

Group policies for under twenty-five employees are simply not in the same category as those negotiated by AT&T, General Motors, or other large corporations. Their policies are tailor-made, written especially for them and to the requirements of both the corporation and the labor union involved. They may—but generally do not—extend the same coverage to nonunion white-collar workers as they do to union members. Smaller companies usually have a choice of standard plans, with benefits and premiums that are not negotiable. The one-to-three-employee companies may or may not be able to get a better deal than a person buying individual insurance.

Your employer may offer you a group policy that is not a true group policy but what is called a *franchise* policy. This is actually an individual policy sold through the organization; it may or may not be better than a policy you can buy yourself on the open market. The employer will not pay any part of the premiums of franchise policies.

If you are self-employed or work for a company that does not offer this fringe benefit, it is, as we have seen, possible to make yourself eligible for a group policy by joining a group that offers one. Religious groups, trade associations, special-interest organizations (such as women's groups or professional groups) are all possibilities. Some of the policies they offer are not especially good because the insurance companies are not generally impressed with groups of this sort and do not give them a real group policy break. I would imagine, for instance, that the American Association of University Women (AAUW) could not command the best basic policy simply because its membership is all female (though passage of the unisex bills would rule out discrimination on that basis), and it may be that the group also has an older average age than insurance companies consider optimum. On the other hand, the AAUW does offer some highly specialized policies with quite unique features that I have not seen anywhere else. In any case, if you belong to or can join a group, it is worth looking into. Some groups belong to HMOs, and that sort of coverage may suit you very well (see chapter 16 on HMOs).

All further discussion in this chapter will be limited to policies available to groups of twenty-five or more employees.

DISADVANTAGES—AND WHAT TO DO ABOUT THEM

Since it is generally understood that group policies offer vastly superior coverage compared to individual policies, I am reversing the usual order of things by considering the negative before the positive; it might be supposed that group policies have no disadvantages, and that is not the case.

1. *Involuntary loss.* It's bad enough to lose your job; it could be devastating to lose your health insurance at the same time (since the insurance provided by your employer is a job benefit, it may cease when you are no longer employed). There is sometimes a provision to continue the policy for a specified length of time after you are terminated or retired. Some policies cease completely on the date of your job termination; some extend coverage for the next thirty or more days. If this provision is not spelled out, coverage will cease completely on or shortly after the date of termination. Examine your policy for an "extension of benefits" provision to find out where you stand.

TIP Of the companies with 25 to 499 employees, 83 percent have some provision in their policies for continuation or conversion of coverage "upon retirement or upon termination other than retirement," so chances are yours does, too. Here is what you need to know.

Group policies that offer the option of *conversion* allow you to convert the group policy to an individual policy. You will not, however, necessarily get the same coverage you had on the job. Of the policies offering conversion, only 29 percent offered conversion or continuation privileges under the original group plan. A converted policy will generally cost more and cover less; it may or may not be your best deal, so compare it with other options.

If you think you might want to convert, you have to work fast; the conversion privilege is usually contingent upon your filing an application to do so within thirty days of your job termination date. The main advantage to converting a policy (providing it meets other criteria for a good policy) is that you usually are accepted without regard to prior health problems, with no preexisting exclusions or limitations, and without a waiting period.

Conversion and Your State

Some states—Kansas, for one—have laws that require group policies to continue coverage for up to six months after termination, with conversion privileges available after that. If your state has a similar law, this gives you ample time to either get another job or look into a good individual policy. Check with your state insurance commission if you aren't satisfied with your conversion benefit.

TIP   If you have reason to believe you will get a new job
fairly quickly, or if you get a new job but under the
new policy have a waiting period before you are
completely covered and an even longer waiting period
before your family is taken under the policy's wing,
you may want to take out *temporary health insurance.*
This type of policy is written for different periods,
such as sixty days, six months, etc. Many of the larger
insurance companies, such as Aetna and Travelers,
offer this type of policy. As soon as you get your on-
the-job policy or certificate, look up the coverage on
conversion so you won't have to fumble around at a
time when you may have a lot of other things on
your mind.

2. *No shopping around.* A group policy goes with the
job and does not present the choices of the open
marketplace. Its quality depends on the skill of the
company's or the union's analyst and negotiator, as
well as the clout the buyer can bring to the bargaining
table. Since employers have traditionally picked up a
good part of the tab, they have to consider what the
policy will cost them as well as what benefits it covers.
If you are a member of a union that is negotiating
with a large corporation, you are also dependent on
the strength and wisdom of your union. If bargaining
gets tight, insisting on additional health care benefits
may mean sacrificing part of a salary increase or some
other benefit. Which tradeoffs are desirable will be
decided by executives and may not be the choice the
individual worker would make. Of course, in a union
you will have a chance to vote on the package, but it
is unlikely you will have the knowledge to make a
completely informed choice.

This is a minor problem and need not concern

you, except that you may want to purchase an individual policy if coverage is lacking in areas in which you want it. The advantages of a good group policy more than outweigh any disadvantages. Your responsibility is merely to determine whether your group policy has any serious gaps and, if so, to buy outside insurance that will cover or at least mitigate them.

ADVANTAGES YOU SHOULD GET

1. *Lower premiums.* Compared to any policy an individual can buy, a group policy premium will be much lower. In addition, your employer may pay part of the premium. This varies; some employers pay nothing, some pay up to 50 percent; a few may even pay 100 percent, but this is becoming less and less common.

2. *Higher benefits.* Because group policies usually cover large numbers of young, healthy, low-risk males— people who might not ordinarily buy health insurance at all and need it comparatively infrequently—insurance companies can safely offer a wide range of benefits. They could safely offer the same benefits on an individual basis to the young, healthy, low-risk person who worked but did not have on-the-job health care benefits, but that would require the expense of screening each policy applicant.

3. *No medical screening.* Group policies do not require a physical or any sort of screening. Here, again, the statistics say you'll probably be a comparatively low risk (after all, you looked healthy enough to get the job), so the insurance company doesn't worry about the occasional diabetic or other chronically ill employee. An exception to this is a company with

predominantly female employees; it will not be able to get as good a policy.

4. *Security.* You can't lose a group policy because of illness or too many claims. Neither will you find that the company suddenly refuses to renew it. The only way you can lose a group policy is to refuse to pay your share of the premiums or to leave your job.

5. *Experienced buyers.* Insurance is so complicated that the average person is usually not qualified to buy his or her own health insurance. (Though I hope this book will serve as a guide through the maze and help the reader to a more informed choice.) You could probably say the same thing about the expertise of the average car buyer, but there's a lot more at stake when you're buying health insurance. If you're a member of a union, you have the employer and your union analyst putting together the package, both highly experienced people. This doesn't mean you shouldn't take a careful look at the end result; they may have left benefits out for reasons other than your welfare or made choices that omit benefits important for your particular situation. Keep in mind that many group policies should be backed up with the purchase of individual insurance.

IF YOU HAVE A CHOICE

While you can't go shopping in the open market for an on-the-job policy, employers are more and more often asking you to make a choice among options. If a company has twenty or more employees and there is one in the area, an HMO will be one of the options. The HMO is a prepaid medical plan known as a health maintenance organization. It is so different from a health insurance policy that it is discussed separately in chapter 16.

The choice you will be offered among options is fairly clear-cut in one respect: You get what you pay for. The higher the premium, the deductibles, and the rate of co-insurance, the more coverage. Whether you need that much coverage is another story, and whether any of the policies will totally fill your health insurance needs is something you will want to determine. If you are a civilian and your employer is the federal government, the post office, or the District of Columbia, you have over fifteen plans to choose from, several of which are HMOs. Private industry employees do not have quite such a French pastry tray of choices, but whenever you have a choice, make it carefully.

Making a choice may be difficult even if your employer picks up 100 percent of the cost. As we have seen in the cafeteria system, choosing one plan means doing without some of the features of another.

Keep in mind, also, that you may be incurring retro-active tax liabilities. In May 1984 the IRS took an especially hard look at zero-balance reimbursement accounts (Zebras), which represent approximately 10 to 30 percent of all flexible-spending plans. If, as it is considering doing, the IRS bans Zebras, participants will have to pay back taxes on money reimbursed (with pretax dollars) under the plan during the last three years.

MAKING A DECISION—SOME GUIDELINES

If you have a choice of policies, get a good-size pad, make a column for each policy, and down the left-hand margin write the following possible benefits:

Possible Benefits—What to Look For

HOSPITAL COVERAGE

Percentage or dollar amount covered. Percentage is better because it goes up as costs do.

Number of days of coverage (at least up to a year). This may be expressed by benefit period, by year, or in some other way—be sure you understand any limitation.

Miscellaneous hospital expenses, including hospitalization for diagnostic tests. These should be spelled out somewhere in the policy. Among the items included should be anesthesia, operating room charges, diagnostic X-rays, lab tests, blood tests, etc.

MEDICAL COVERAGE

Doctor hospital visits.

Doctor office visits.

Surgery, inpatient, outpatient, and ambulatory care.

Diagnostic lab tests, EKGs, X-rays, etc., out of hospital. Maternity care, including complications. Should cover women in any category—married or single, wife or worker. Most policies say coverage same as "for any disease," not the most graceful way of putting it, but it does tell you what you want to know.

Newborn care from day of birth. Look out for this one. Birth defects and many, many expensive problems can arise in the first few days of life. A short waiting period can be a financial disaster.

Prescription drugs. An increasingly costly item—a good policy will cover you for these costs.

Plastic surgery. Not for cosmetic reasons but when necessary after an accident or certain dental procedures.

Dental care. A benefit that is offered more than it used to be. About 50% of plans now offer good coverage; some include your child's braces.

Possible Benefits—What to Look For (Continued)

Eyeglasses, hearing aids, routine examinations for same. You may not get this, but at least know if it's missing.

Mental health and psychiatric care. Coverage for these items is improving, but is usually more limited than for other illnesses.

MISCELLANEOUS COVERAGE

Deductibles and co-insurance. If you pay deductibles and co-insurance—and more and more employers are requiring this as a cost-containment measure—in 1953 they were, on the average, about $100 for individual policies, $300 for family policies, with possibly an additional $50 and $150 respectively for a dental option. This provided major medical as well as basic coverage. By 1984, with innovations in health insurance plans, deductibles averaged $200 for an individual and $600 for a family, but adherence to cost-containment guidelines would allow the employee to raise company participation to 100% for some charges. After the deductible, the co-insurance is usually 20%, with the employer picking up 80% (see p. 38 for an explanation of co-insurance).

Stop-loss. If you are not familiar with this term, see page 00 for an explanation. Stop-loss is often mandated by state law. If offered as an option, the additional cost to you is usually under $100 a year. Lifetime maximums now commonly are $1 million. Policies offering this try to make a big thing of it—and it is mind-boggling that health care costs have gotten so out of control—but it is not at all unusual, so do not be unduly impressed. It would be a much healthier (no pun intended) state of affairs if lifetime maximums could be realistically set at around $10,000 instead of $1 million, but the over 150,000 Americans who had bypass surgery in one year alone know only too well that that would be completely inadequate. Even 20% of the overall costs of a single bypass operation can run to several thousand dollars.

Possible Benefits—What to Look For (Continued)

Pregnancy. The federal government only rarely steps in to legislate insurance, since it is basically the states' prerogative. Recently, however, it did pass a law mandating medical benefits for pregnancy, including normal birth, complications, sick leave, etc., in certain types of policies. The original law applied only to employees and did not include the wives of employees, but many policies include them anyhow. In examining this portion of the policy, make sure pregnancy is fully covered; some policies exclude the expenses of normal birth and cover only complications. Group coverage should be more comprehensive than anything you can purchase in an individual policy, so if good pregnancy coverage isn't included, ask why not.

Pre-existing conditions. Be sure you understand your coverage in this area. Insurance commissioners tell me it is the cause of most of their health-insurance-related complaints. Here again a group policy is much more lenient than an individual policy. The two key areas are the policy's definition of *pre-existing* and how long a waiting period is required before coverage begins. A waiting period of six months is reasonable, but many policies require a year. Any longer than that is unreasonable.

Exclusions. See page 41 for a list of the most common exclusions.

The most important exclusion, and one you can do nothing about, is custodial care—the help a beneficiary may require for daily living, such as eating, dressing, washing, getting in and out of bed. There is no policy that will pay for this, even though lack of such care may be life threatening, as in the case of a person who cannot eat without help. As long as your condition is subject to improvement, it is usually possible to get some kind of care, but if you develop a chronic illness, as so many elderly people do, and if the prognosis is that your condition has plateaued and will not improve, you will

Possible Benefits—What to Look For (Continued)

find that insurance coverage disappears. You should be aware of this—even though it cannot be helped at the present time—if for no other reason than that whenever you can, you should speak up for custodial care being included in all health insurance, including Medicare. At present only the very wealthy and the very poor (those who are poor enough to qualify for Medicaid) can be sure of receiving custodial care.

Exclusions are often stated in the form of riders. Unlike individual policies that may tack on riders to exclude all the conditions for which you especially need coverage, most group policies tend to overlook individual idiosyncracies or physical problems and work on an average group health statistic. Naturally there are some exceptions, such as hazardous occupations, but generally a person in less than excellent health will benefit from being lumped as part of a basically healthy group.

Dependents. All members of your immediate family should be covered. Children should be covered from birth until age 19 or 21 (23 for full-time students).

SUPPLEMENTING GROUP INSURANCE

Once you have analyzed your group policy and discovered its strengths and weaknesses, you will probably want to take out individual supplementary insurance to fill in the gaps. If, for instance, your group plan covers basic hospital costs but limits payment for surgery to a schedule, the schedule may be inadequate. For example, a heart bypass operation for which the surgeon bills $10,000 may be 80 percent paid for by one policy, or you may be entitled to the scheduled amount of $1,000 on another policy. Your out-of-pocket expense with the latter policy would be $9,000—an amount well worth insuring yourself against. Even the $2,000 left for you to pay if you have the first policy may be more than your budget will stand, especially since there are bound to be other out-of-pocket expenses connected with this type of operation. So, in this example, you may want either a policy that will pick up the co-insurance of 20 percent or a policy that will pick up major medical expenses. The major medical policy will have its own deductible that you will have to pay, but you should not ever expect to totally make up for poor coverage in your primary policy, unless you are willing to duplicate coverage at a comparatively high cost.

PAY AS YOU GO—A DISTURBING NEW DEVELOPMENT

There is a rapidly growing perception on the part of the health-care consumer that doctors are becoming more interested in making money than in taking care of the sick. This feeling is exacerbated by a new development in which certain doctors try to get their patients to pay the bill as they are leaving the office. Aside from the insensitivity and callousness that is shown by the failure to recognize that someone who has just been to the doctor is quite possibly somewhat shaky and not in the most cheerful state, and that no one, sick or convalescing, is helped on the road to recovery by being reminded of the extraordinary rise in doctor bills (and is often embarrassed by the fact that her or his checking account contains funds insufficient to pay the bill then and there), it introduces an element of crass commercialism into the doctor/patient relationship. Many consumers tell me it makes them feel as if they have just purchased a pair of shoes or a head of lettuce, and the image of the doctor as shopkeeper is not one they find reassuring. Certainly it is contrary to custom among professionals; neither lawyers, writers, nor those in other professions require payment on a cash-on-the-barrel basis.

The excuse usually given by doctors with whom I

have discussed this is that collections are so poor, they are simply looking for surer ways of getting their money. While no doubt the inflated cost of health care and the decreased ability of many of the ill, especially if they are elderly, to meet these costs are reflected in slow payment practices, the figures that are released each year of doctors' incomes do not indicate that they are suffering unduly. Since at the same time they are complaining of collection rates of less than a third of their bills, they often refuse to accept Medicare assignments, which would guarantee payment for 100 percent of their Medicare patients, and prefer instead to pay collection agencies, it is difficult to accept this excuse for adopting such a distasteful and unprofessional practice. Under these circumstances physicians should not wonder that consumers repond by applying the same criteria to medical care as to any other purchase and complain, through a malpractice suit if necessary, when they feel they have been sold shoddy merchandise.

Not only individuals but society as a whole pay a penalty for this practice. If health-care consumers are expected to pay cash for medical services, their utilization of health care is bound to be unfavorably affected and the delivery of health care to be different for the rich and the middle-class consumer, regardless of the cushion of group insurance. An article on the Op Ed page of the December 31, 1983, *New York Times* by Toby Cohen, ex–project director of the Medical Practice Task Force, New York State Assembly (although written for another purpose) addressed this problem.

The article used as an example two men, both working for the same company and covered by the same insurance, who required psychiatric treatment. The group policy they held provided for up to 180 office visits a year, with 85 percent reimbursement of the actual charges (a generous coverage, more than you may be able to get). According to the writer, the more visits such treatment requires, the more the psychiatrist is liable to require that the patient pay cash, so that the psychiatrist does not have to wait until the end of the treatment for payment from the insurance company.

Psychiatrists are not inexpensive; $100 a session is quite usual, so even paying just the co-insurance of $15 a session at four times a week would mean a tab of $60 a week out-of-pocket. If, however, the psychiatrist wanted the whole fee up front, that would mean a payment of $400 a week. In the example given, one employee earned $10,000 a year and could not advance $400 a week, even though he would be reimbursed for $340 of it eventually. The other earned $60,000 a year and could afford to advance the cash.

The result was that the psychiatrist took on the wealthier patient and referred the less affluent one to a younger psychiatrist, who was willing to wait for payment from the insurance company but who hedged his bets by seeing the patient only once or twice a week.

The moral of the story was that two employees, paying exactly the same group insurance premium for (theoretically) the same benefits, were actually receiving a very different level of medical care. The affluent employee was able to incur actual psychiatric bills of $16,320 annually, while the less affluent employee cost his company only $4,896. The level of care was not comparable, and the poorer employee was, in effect, subsidizing the wealthier one. Aside from the difference in the experience and professional standing of the psychiatrists, there was the considerable difference in the frequency of visits, a very important factor in psychiatric care. Mr. Cohen had an interesting solution to this problem. He suggested that doctors should be paid directly by the insurance companies and not be allowed to collect from the patient. The insurance company would then bill the co-insurance to the patient, from whom the insurance company would probably be able to collect more easily than would the doctor, since an arrangement could be made to deduct the money from the paycheck.

Change is in the wind. As I write, the federal government is considering requiring doctors to accept Medicare payments from all Medicare patients, according to a schedule of fees set up by the government, and the state of Connecticut is working on legislation in the same area.

It appears that the actions of a few doctors are liable to make life difficult for the many dedicated physicians who look at patients as people rather than as dollar signs. But they have only themselves to blame for not speaking up before matters got out of hand. If medical care is denied to those Americans who need it, the health and productivity of the nation will suffer, and so will the economy of the country. If we are not to be at a disadvantage against other countries, we must find a way to deliver at least an equally high level of health care to all our citizens.

7

Group Policies for Federal Employees

If you are employed by the federal government, you are in an elite group when it comes to health insurance benefits and have some of the best group insurance available in the United States today. It is still necessary, however, to know what health insurance is all about, because you have over fifteen plans to choose from. Neither is it a comparatively simple matter of choosing among various policies; these plans include private insurance from such companies as Aetna, plans from the Blues, plans that are administered through HMOs (and even here, several are available), and plans available from associations, such as unions and the Government Employees Hospital Association (GEHA). If you like an association plan best and are thinking of joining one for that reason, add the cost of annual dues to your premium cost (though dues are usually nominal and confer other benefits in addition to the insurance package; in addition, they are often tax-deductible).

The watchdog that oversees federal health insurance plans and protects the workers' interests is the Office of Personnel Management (OPM). It not only administers the program but sets minimum standards for plans and mandates the format of the brochures that explain plan benefits. Before you make your own personalized comparison chart, you might want to get the Plan Comparison Chart that OPM offers free. (I'm assuming that as a federal employee, you already know of the various informational brochures OPM publishes, such as *Federal Employees Health Benefits Program.* If not, ask at your personnel office.)

The process of evaluating the benefits of these plans is similar to what you must do to evaluate plans in the private sector. Making a list of the benefits you would like to receive, with a column for each plan you are considering, will quickly give you an at-a-glance comparison. If you don't know where to start, use the Blues' most expensive high-option plan as a basis; it is usually the most comprehensive. If it is too costly, at least you will be able to go down the list and determine what you feel comfortable doing without. This pared-down list should conform fairly closely to the much less costly Blues low-option plan. Unless you or your family have special health problems, this may be the most cost effective list of benefits for you to work with. In most instances it is not absolutely critical if you choose a plan that you later have second thoughts about; you can switch plans fairly easily, providing you keep track of when this is permitted. Usually any change in your marital or familial circumstances automatically allows you to switch at that time (for example, your present plan may not offer maternity coverage, and marriage may suddenly make that a more desirable benefit). The OPM brochures aren't always up to date regarding state laws, so you may be entitled to even more benefits than are listed if you are working in a state that mandates them.

Which plan you choose will determine not only what benefits you receive but also what those benefits will cost you. The government, like most employers, will pick up part of the tab, but your share of the cost, including premiums and deductibles, can range from about $120 to $800 a year for an individual policy, to about $1,700 for a family policy. Like private-sector policies, there are lifetime maximums and similar limitations. And just as scheduled payments in nongovernment policies vary geographically (being higher in affluent areas), so will your premiums be higher in those areas. A general understanding of group policies in the private sector will help you through the maze of government health care benefits, so if you turned to this chapter first, you may want to go back and read chapter 6.

The benefits you will find most poorly covered are well-baby care, other preventive medicine such as physical checkups and shots, and routine dental care. (Note that HMOs do include coverage for some of these.) In addition, the usual exclusions, such as cosmetic surgery, glasses and hearing aids, charges above "reasonable and customary," and custodial care, are not covered.

Since this is the era of the two-income family, be sure to coordinate your government coverage with your spouse's coverage; you may be needlessly duplicating benefits and increasing your costs without improving your coverage. Since it is so easy to change plans, a change in your spouse's job situation (such as unemployment) can be taken care of by updating your coverage during the next open admission period.

One feature you do not have to check is the conversion privilege. The government requires that all plans offer this if you leave your government job; it even includes mandatory coverage for your children until the age of twenty-two. This is a good hedge, but since you will no longer be partly subsidized by the government's contribution, your converted government plan may no longer be your best bet or it may be beyond your financial resources; check it out. Unlike other plans, HMO benefits will usually stay the same, though the cost will go up considerably.

All in all, you may consider yourself lucky if you have access to federal government health insurance plans, but to make the most of this opportunity and to do so at the lowest possible cost, you will still have to do your homework.

8

How Does Your Policy Compare?

If you have a group policy, you probably take it for granted that your health insurance needs have been taken care of or, at the very least, are out of your hands. As we have seen in previous chapters, this is not necessarily so. If your company has one of the new employee-option plans, it will be up to you to determine your own health priorities. And if you are not given an in-house choice (or even if you are), you still ought to look over the policy with an eye to supplementing it if it is not adequate for your needs.

You may have much more say than you realize about the health insurance plans offered by a company. If you belong to a strong union you can speak up in meetings about areas in which you feel the negotiated health care package is wanting or inequitable. And at the bargaining table something always has to give on both sides; union management is liable to give in more easily on those benefits it feels the workers do not feel strongly about.

In addition, you may sometimes be offered two jobs simultaneously. Confronted with this happy dilemma, be sure to compare the health insurance package offered in each instance; good benefits may outweigh a difference in salary.

Everything else being equal, you will get a better deal from a large company than from a small one. This is not a matter of greater generosity on the part of the larger company; it is due mostly to the insurance company being able to put together a better package for a bigger customer.

In looking for a good on-the-job insurance package, what can you reasonably expect? Here are some figures from studies done by the Health Insurance Association of America. They are based on companies with 25 to 499 employees. Companies with fewer employees will probably offer benefits on the low end of the scale. Companies with over 499 employees should be able to come close to the top and may even offer some of the innovative plans discussed earlier. See how your policy compares with these percentages; if you fall in the less-than-50-percent category (see below) for any benefits that the majority of workers are receiving, and if you are with a large company, you might want to ask, "How come?"

Group Policy Benefits—Who Gets Them?

BENEFIT	PERCENT OF EMPLOYEES RECEIVING BENEFIT
Comprehensive medical:	
Deductible	58%—$100 deductible; 7%—$100 deductible, except for hospital or hospital and surgical expenses
Benefit maximum	88%—$100,000 or more; 83%—$1 million or more or no limit
Mental illness	87%—some coverage
Stop-loss	68%—out-of-pocket limits of $1,000 or less

Group Policy Benefits—Who Gets Them? (Continued)

BENEFIT	PERCENT OF EMPLOYEES RECEIVING BENEFIT
Supplementary major medical:	
Deductible	75%—$100 deductible
Benefit maximum	94%—$100,000 or more, or unlimited
Mental illness	99%—some coverage
Stop-loss	61%—out-of-pocket limits of $1,000 or less
Basic expense:	
Semiprivate hospital room	89%—100% coverage
Miscellaneous hospital charges	94%—100% coverage for $500 or more
	77%—unlimited coverage
Basic surgical costs	90%—maximum benefits of $1,000 or more
	49%—no maximum
In-hospital private physician	79%—$10 or more maximum per visit
Diagnostic X-ray and lab	88%—maximum $100 or more
	26%—no limit
Intensive care:	
Hospital room and board	49%—coverage equal to daily room-and-board rate
	18%—unlimited coverage
	15%—limited to reasonable and customary charges
Nursing home:	
Daily room and board	68%—$30 or more, or coverage for semiprivate room
Number of days of confinement	95%—60 or more days
	53%—120 or more days

Group Policy Benefits—Who Gets Them? (Continued)

BENEFIT	PERCENT OF EMPLOYEES RECEIVING BENEFIT
Home health care:	87%—100% coverage
Cost containment benefits:	
Generic drug prescriptions	79%—some coverage
Second opinions on nonemergency surgery	76%—some coverage
Outpatient surgery	85%—100% coverage
Preadmission testing	85%—100% coverage
Paramedical services	32%—100% coverage
Hospice	3%—100% coverage
Dental:	
Comprehensive benefit maximum	85%—some coverage
	72%—annual maximum of $1,000 or more, or no limit
	89%—some coverage for themselves or dependents (excluding employees with dental coverage only, or disability income and dental coverage only)
Dependents:	
Maternity	91%—some benefits
	90% with maternity coverage had 100% coverage
Continuation and conversion:	
Some provision for continuation of coverage at retirement or upon termination other than retirement	83%—some coverage

Group Policy Benefits—Who Gets Them? (Continued)

BENEFIT	PERCENT OF EMPLOYEES RECEIVING BENEFIT
Continuation under group plan for employees with continuation or conversion privilege	29%—covered under ongoing group plan
Medical supplemental for employees with continuation provision	90%—had coverage

Disability:

Short term: benefits mostly for up to 13, 26, or 52 weeks	76%—from first day of disability due to accident; no later than eighth day of disability from sickness
13-week benefits	20%
26-week benefits	76%
52 or 104 weeks	4%
50% predisability income	98%
66⅔% predisability income	69%
Long term: benefits from 2 years to age 65 to life	
After 6 months' disability	76%
After 3 months' disability	15%
To age 65 or older	87%
Average monthly benefit $700 or more	67%
At least 60% predisability income	93%

Cost ... Who Pays?

Primary coverage:	
100% paid by employer	67%
Part paid by employer	27%
Dependent coverage:	
100% paid by employer	29%
Part paid by employer	46%

If you work for a small company, its package may not compare favorably, but these figures still will indicate which are the most generally offered kinds of coverage and which are comparatively new—and not so widely offered— benefits. If your company has an old policy that has not been updated, it is more liable to be lacking in coverage. If there have recently been a number of high-cost claims, such as an unusual number of heart bypass operations, the company's risk may have been reassessed and the policy as a whole may no longer offer as much or, at best, may offer the same benefits as previously but for higher premiums. If a large number of workers at a company are engaged in high-risk labor, the benefits will be less than average. In many cases you may want to take the job anyhow, but when there is a choice, hold out for the all-around best deal.

NEW HOPE FOR PREVENTIVE CARE

As employers explore ways of lowering their health-care costs, they are discovering that healthy employees cost the company less than sick ones do. This has led them to the long overdue conclusion (known for decades to the Russians and Japanese) that paying for preventive medicine is cost effective. According to recent studies, 100 out of 1,000 employees will be found to have two or more risk factors (high blood pressure, obesity, elevated cholesterol) or be smokers. If the company can induce 25 of these employees to significantly reduce the high-risk factor, health-care costs will go down 10 to 15 percent. If just one smoker kicks the habit, the company can save approximately $200 a year in medical costs; it can save $260 if one individual has a lowered blood pressure.

Companies that have already instituted preventive

care programs include New York Telephone, with 80,000 workers. It found that running the program for one year cost $2.8 million, while the amount saved in health-care costs was $5.5 million—a clear gain of $2.7 million. More and more companies are instituting these programs and realizing similar benefits; the future of preventive medicine looks encouraging indeed.

III

ON YOUR OWN—
INDIVIDUAL HEALTH
INSURANCE

9

The Individual As Health Insurance Consumer

Any individual who must get health insurance directly from a company or an agent instead of as a fringe benefit is at a tremendous disadvantage in the marketplace. Not only will he find that no one is particularly interested in his business, he will also soon discover that the policies that are offered to him are fewer, vastly inferior in coverage, and far more costly than those offered to groups, especially to large groups.

THE DIFFICULTIES AND THE NEEDS
OF THE INDIVIDUAL CONSUMER

The discrimination against the individual purchaser extends even to the government; most laws, including the pending unisex bill, that regulate health insurance apply only to group policies. The one ray of hope is the fact that insurance is mostly regulated on the state level—a smaller pond where it is easier for an individual to get together with others who are similarly situated and to make waves that will extend to the state capital.

Even such companies as the formerly nonprofit Blue Cross and Blue Shield (now becoming for-profit companies), once the bastion of individual policies, are now increasing their group policy business and offer many special breaks, such as the Wrap-Around Physicians' Benefits in New York City, that are available only to groups. And HMOs, which once welcomed all individuals with open arms, now have limited enrollment periods and are often closed to new individual members because they have been filled by group memberships.

Faced with these difficulties, it is not surprising that millions of Americans do not have a single health insurance policy. Since it is more difficult to gather statistics on individual policy owners, estimates as to just how many people are completely out in the cold vary widely. For instance, a 1974–75 study by Pracon, Inc., for LaRoche Laboratories estimated that 12.2 million persons or 6 percent of the total population had no private or public health insurance coverage. The Social Security Administration estimated in 1976 that 24 to 25 million persons or 12 percent to 13 percent of the under-sixty-five population had no hospital or surgical care insurance (the most commonly held insurance). And in 1977 the National Center for Health Services Research apparently concurred with this latter figure. In 1978, however, the Congressional Budget Office (CBO) concluded that from 11 to 18 million or 5 percent to 8 percent were without health care coverage. Young adults are least liable to be covered, as are those persons earning less than $10,000 a year.

With so many millions of people without health insurance, the individual may wonder whether he or she really needs to spend hard-earned money on premiums. After all, few families have catastrophic medical expenses during any given year. The CBO found, for instance, that in 1982 only 23 percent of all families had medical expenses exceeding $1,130; 11 percent exceeded $3,000, and only one-half of 1 percent had more than $20,000 in medical expenses. To be sure, this study did not include the poor or the elderly, presumably because the poor are taken care of by Medicaid and the elderly by Medicare. (Though this is a somewhat optimistic viewpoint, it is true that Medicare provides some coverage even though it is woefully inadequate.)

Another view of the odds that you may not need individual health insurance coverage are the statistics related to frequency of large health insurance claims; only a comparative few are for claims exceeding $25,000. A 1976 survey showed that out of 7,600,000 persons with group health insurance contracts, only 478 incurred expenses of $25,000 or more, which comes to 63 persons out of a million. The average of such claims was $43,000. For claims of $50,000 or more, the frequency was only 15 per million, and only 9 persons incurred expenses of $100,000 or more. It should be pointed out that the over-sixty-five age group is poorly represented in this study, since it was based on employer-employee groups, and at a time when Medicare was still the primary payer if an older person continued working.

If these figures convince you that the odds are in your favor and that the chances are good that your own personal financial resources will be adequate, take a look at what could happen in a worst-case scenario. It is impossible to predict what expenses you will incur, but here are some possibilities.

Heart transplants presently cost about $70,000.

The average hospital stay (1982) is 7.6 days, at a daily cost (in community hospitals) of $327.40, a total of close to $2,500. And even this cost figure is almost mythical, because it covers only room and board. If all you needed was room and board, you could stay home or at a Holiday Inn for a lot less. Include the other usual charges, from laboratory fees to operating room and recovery room charges, an occasional X-ray, EKG, pharmacy charges, "routine special service," anesthesia, and so on, and you will find your actual hospital charges more than double or triple. Also, remember these are 1982 figures, which represent a 741 percent increase over 1963 costs (when the cost of living rose "only" 215 percent).

Having a baby, providing it was an uncomplicated delivery in a hospital delivery room in 1982, cost on the average $1,615.80 in the rural West to $2,312.50 in the urban Northeast. Of course a cesarean is higher; the U.S. average cost is $4,340.30 (compared to $2,092.70 for an uncomplicated normal delivery). And that doesn't include possible loss of income on the part of the mother during the six weeks of pregnancy leave, well- or sick-baby care, or other peripheral costs.

If you're accident prone, consider that $11.2 billion in medical costs were incurred through accidents in 1981 alone. And this figure doesn't include lost wages, motor vehicle property damage, or other personal expenses.

One way the individual can fight back is to join a group. As group policies become the only game in town, more and more groups are offering their own health insurance policies; they must be examined carefully, since there is great difference in quality among them.

The best way to get group health insurance is, of course, to get a job that offers it as a fringe benefit. The purpose of this section, however, is to help those who do not have on-the-job coverage and must fend for themselves.

WHERE TO FIND OFF-THE-JOB GROUP COVERAGE

1. Small Business Groups
   a. If you have a small one- or two-person business, you may find to your surprise that you are still eligible for a "group" policy. It won't bear much

resemblance to the one you could get if you worked for General Motors, but it may be somewhat better than buying an individual policy as a single or family person.

b. Blanket or franchise group insurance is not true group insurance, but it may appear so since it may be offered by an employer or an small organization. It has certain advantages over individual policies, such as not requiring individual applications, but it is regulated under different laws from those regulating other types of health insurance policies, so you need to examine the coverage even more carefully. Franchise and blanket group insurance (they are not the same but are often discussed in tandem) are usually more limited than other types of policies. An example of a blanket disability insurance policy that most parents have encountered at one time or another is that which covers sports-related injuries of public school children. Anyone who has tried to collect on this type of policy is liable to have found that the coverage wasn't quite what they thought it was, especially if surgery is required some time after the injury was incurred.

2. Many other types of organizations—fraternal, industry-related, religious, or professional—including such diverse groups as the American Association of University Women, the American Association of Retired Persons, the Authors Guild, B'Nai Brith—that you may already belong to or may join for a small membership fee, offer policies of various kinds. Often both under-sixty-five and Medicare supplement policies may be purchased in this way. If you do not have any health insurance, be careful not to invest in some of the more specialized offerings; many of them are suitable

only if you want that coverage in addition to your primary policies.

All things considered, it would seem better to put in the homework required to get at least standard basic health insurance coverage rather than play Russian roulette with your financial future. You may not be able to get as much or as good coverage as you would like, but at least be an informed consumer and learn to tell a good policy from a poor one.

10

Making the Best of It—How to Shop for an Individual Policy

The first question to ask yourself is, "How old am I?" Fortunately, it is a question for which you will have a ready answer; other questions will not be so easy. Insurance companies are very concerned with your age and will be more helpful if you are under rather than over fifty. If you are over sixty-five, you can thumb your nose at them to some extent; you are eligible for Medicare and are not dependent on private insurance for basic coverage.

The ideal age, from the insurance company's standpoint, is around thirty to thirty-five. At that age the level of your general health is fairly apparent (have you let yourself go? are you still trim and fit? are you addicted to anything—drugs, cigarettes, alcohol?), and your occupation is to some extent stabilized (most people do not become steeplejacks, test pilots, or deep-sea divers for the first time after 30). Your mental health is also capable of assessment; nervous breakdowns, therapy, and institutionalization would all be a matter of record and would have to be itemized on your application. It is surprising that your mental health is all that important, since in most instances the coverage you will be able to obtain in this area is so meager as to be practically nonexistent. In spite of this, a record of mental illness, no matter how long ago or how mild, turns insurance companies off.

If you are under fifty and do not have a major medical policy, put getting one on the top of your list. The older you get, the fewer policies will be available to you. This is simple common sense from the industry's standpoint, since the older you are, the more liable you are to incur long, expensive illnesses, which are less profitable to insure than short, inexpensive illnesses. The big claims that are filed are not for the common cold.

Once you are in your sixties, getting a major medical policy that is worth your premium is almost, if not actually, impossible. Since old policies disappear and new ones are constantly being offered, it is difficult to make a positive statement about what is and is not available, so look anyway; you may get lucky.

Once you have established your ratio of desirability (to the insurance company) on the basis of age, your next question is, "What sex am I?" This is not an invasion of your privacy but a simple question that should be simply answered according to the notation on your birth certificate (unless you have had a sex-change operation in the meantime).

If the answer is male you are in luck. If the answer is female, and something like the unisex bill for the individual has not been passed, you will be discriminated against in that your premiums will be higher and your coverage possibly less broad than for your male counterpart.

The insurance industry, as we have seen in their arguments against the unisex bill, point to lower automobile premiums for young women than for young men, as well as lower life insurance premiums. The industry does not brag about its higher health insurance premiums for the fair sex. When pressed, however, their justification is tables of statistics showing that women, on the average, have more illnesses than men and, therefore, consult their doctors more. According to the National Center for Health Statistics, women make 43 percent more doctor visits than men. Even when gynecological visits are excluded, their visits to doctors are 24 percent more frequent.

This is not to say that women are not healthier than men (after all, they do live longer). They are admittedly less liable to heart disease, cancer, strokes, and accidents. On the other hand, they are more liable to respiratory problems, digestive ills, infections, and parasitic diseases, ailments that lead to all those extra doctor visits and that cause them to stay in bed 46 percent more often than men. In addition, these sickly, long-lived creatures are more aware of their symptoms and may be more liable than men to curtail their activities. If the picture thus painted sounds faintly Victorian, with the lady of the house reclining on a chaise lounge in a darkened room while she recovers from a sick headache, don't blame me; it's all based on statistics. And if it seems at odds with other statistics, particularly those about the number of working mothers, the busy schedules of the heads of matriarchal single-parent families, and the profiles showing that in families in which women work, she does more rather than less of the housework when she takes a job— talk to the statisticians.

The answer probably lies in statistical correlations. It may be that breaking down the statistics for men by income, job classification (boring vs. interesting, for instance), hours in a day spent at work (including housework and child care as well as on-the-job), stress, etc., would show a pattern that was not sexually related and more similar to that of women. That is only a theory, however; the reality is that a woman will not be able to get as good a health insurance policy as a man, purely and simply because sex-related statistics say she is a poorer risk.

CHECKING OUT A HEALTH INSURANCE POLICY

As with any purchase, do not buy any policy without comparing it with the competition. Since you are buying direct, you will probably be dealing with an agent. One good way to evaluate a policy is to study the first one you see and then use it as leverage against all the others. Ideally, you should make a chart that shows at a glance a comparison of the various benefits the policies offer. This makes it easy for you to say to an agent, "Yes, your policy pays such-and-such for so-and-so, but Policy X from Company Beta pays half again as much and has a much higher cap."

To elicit the proper response, do this in a slightly puzzled tone of voice, with your body language conveying that you think the agent you are talking to is more knowledgeable than you and will be able to help you explain this apparent weakness in the company's policy. Do not under any circumstances sound argumentative, accusative, or too bright. (Women are better at this than men, but then they have had more practice.) What you hope to elicit is an unguarded answer that will tell you trade secrets about other companies ("Yes, but you'll never collect from them." "Well, their claims record is good but you'll notice they are much more expensive." "Oh, I don't think you'd be happy with them . . . look at this clause."). A few conversations like this and you will know more about the various companies' policies than many of the agents do. Most agents don't know much about other companies' policies, but they usually know their own and can at least provide the rebuttal they have been trained in.

Your biggest problem will be finding an agent who deigns to take seriously a customer who isn't in the market for a big group policy. Most agents will try to steer you into a situation in which you are at least eligible for some sort of "group" policy. "You're self-employed? Well, then, you must have a business. Now, we have a policy for companies with just one employee—the owner. Let's see if you qualify for that." If you have three employees, you're even better off. If you do qualify, examine the "group" policy and compare it with a simple individual policy. The most important thing you can do to get yourself the best possible policy is to shop around. It's tedious and time consuming, but essential. Say to yourself, in the words of a well-known advertising slogan, "I'm worth it."

POLICY CHECKLIST IF YOU'RE UNDER 65

Get the broadest possible coverage. Look for coverage in two areas: basic and major medical. Basic coverage should include hospital and medical; major medical protects you against the catastrophic illnesses the costs of which could bankrupt you (like bypass surgery). Until recently it took two policies to cover all this ground, but it is now possible to find combination policies. Only a comparison of specific policies will tell you whether getting two separate (and complementary) policies or one combination policy is the better buy.

TIP You will probably find that buying two separate policies will give you a wider choice and more flexibility. For instance, if you are in a financial situation in which you could in a pinch lay out $10,000 for health care costs without hurting too much, buying a major medical policy with that much of a deductible should mean a really low premium. On the other hand, if all you can see yourself paying for is $1,000, the major medical policy with a $1,000 deductible is going to cost you more. The general rule is to spend as much as you can for broad basic coverage and take as large a deductible as you can when buying major medical.

Get a policy that is at least "guaranteed renewable." This does not protect you against rises in premiums, but it does mean that your policy will not be canceled because you have made too many claims. The only way the company can cancel this type of policy is if it does away with it entirely, either for the geographical area or for subscribers as a whole (unless, of course, you fail to pay your premiums, which lets the company off the hook).

The premiums should not increase with your age. As we have seen elsewhere in the book, many policies have a system whereby premiums automatically increase as you move into another age group. This reduces the spread of risk to the company, and you lose the benefit of having a spread over younger as well as older subscribers. If you are young, you will benefit temporarily, but as the years pass, the policy will become increasingly less of a good deal. Unfortunately, some otherwise good policies have this system (including some Blues policies for individuals), so you may decide to take one in spite of it. If you are tempted by such a policy, be sure to include the age-related premiums in the minus column when comparing it with other policies. The time to think about it is when you buy the policy; by the time you are in the older group and paying the higher premiums, you may no longer have the wide choice you had at the younger age.

Preexisting conditions should be as limited as possible. Ideally, a six-month exclusionary period prior to the effective date of the policy and six months after are all you should accept. Beware of policies worded so that the preexclusionary period extends back to your birth. Present policies often go as far as a combined two years (before plus after); give such a policy a minus.

Avoid policies that are too specific as to what they will cover. The insurance company knows better than you do what diseases you are most liable to get. Experts generally advise against "dread disease" policies, which primarily play on people's fears of cancer. There are many more illnesses and diseases than you can possibly imagine, and you should increase your odds of the policy being of some use to you by being protected for all of them. Obviously the only way you can do this is by buying a policy that covers the expenses of all illnesses and diseases without specifying which ones.

If you have a medical history that includes certain unpopular illnesses (the kind that tend to be recurring and expensive), you may find coverage for them excluded for life (see *pre-existing conditions,* p. 40) or excluded in your policy by means of a rider.

Avoid riders. (See previous paragraph.) Not only do riders reduce your coverage in just the areas in which you are liable to need it most, they also discriminate against you as compared with other subscribers to the same policy because you are being deprived of full coverage with no compensatory reduction in premium. It's as if you sat down to a prix fixe menu costing $150 a person and were the only one at the table not allowed to choose caviar for a starter. The big difference is that the money involved is much more liable to be in the thousands than in the hundreds.

When comparing policies, give any with riders a minus.

Policies that continue some sort of coverage, preferably supplemental, over age sixty-five are more desirable than those that stop at that age. Of course, you then have to examine the coverage to determine whether it is adequate, but at least you are not left high and dry. With this option, you can shop around when you get closer to sixty-five to see whether a better policy is then available, but you will be in a better position to be picky.

Look into HMOs. See Part Six on HMOs for a full discussion of this possibility. If you are interested and if there is one in your area, check into it promptly as to open enrollment period . . . it may be full.

Check the loss ratio. A policy that has good benefits but seldom pays off on them, or only pays after a hassle, is not a good policy no matter how enticingly presented. If no one else will tell you, ask your state insurance commissioner. Loss ratios below 60 percent are not your best buy; Blues policies have traditionally had loss ratios of 90 to 95 percent (when they are nonprofit).

Get illness and accident coverage. Health-care costs are just as financially debilitating no matter what their cause. Policies that differentiate between illnesses and accidents are not considered as good as those that pay your hospital and medical expenses regardless of how you incurred them (with the usual exceptions, such as acts of war). Given a choice of comparable policies, avoid the ones that differentiate.

Be sure coverage is expandable. It should include you and any family you have or may acquire in the future, whether spouse or children. You may think you will never want any kids, but don't bet your health insurance policy on it.

Carefully note and compare waiting periods and any other limitations with other policies. If your coverage doesn't start until after you have been hospitalized for a week, remember that statistics show that most people don't stay in the hospital much longer than that. When comparing premiums, correlate them with waiting periods; you should pay a much smaller premium for a policy that doesn't pay for most average-length hospitalizations.

Trends in the way insurance is written change, sometimes due to changing life-styles, sometimes to the company's experience in that area. What you want is the best deal you can get, and only a comparison of current policies can tell you what that is. Until recently, for instance, dental coverage was not available no matter what. Now most group policies include some sort of dental coverage. Naturally, individual policies lag far behind the benefits of group policies, but if dental coverage becomes generally offered, you want to buy the up-to-date policy that includes it. (This is only an example; the new gimmick might be some sort of coverage I haven't even encountered.)

Deductibles and co-insurance. Deductibles are what you pay before the policy pays anything; co-insurance is what you pay when the policy is picking up part of the tab. Experts feel that it is best to pay as high a deductible and as much co-insurance as you can afford. That's all very well if the premium for that policy compares favorably with those offering low deductibles and co-insurance. If you get less and pay more (or the same), it's a heads-they-win, tails-you-lose proposition. Also be careful the statistics aren't against you (as with a long hospitalization waiting period).

Compare the caps. Policies usually specify how long you will be covered and/or how much (the cap), in maximum dollars, you can collect. *How long* may be expressed in terms of benefit periods. *How much* is usually a dollar amount that may be applied annually or for a lifetime.

If benefits are expressed in dollar amounts (so much a day for a hospital room, for instance), get an update on costs in your area to see whether the policy's benefits would be a drop in the bucket or a real help. Policies that pay percentages are more related to actual figures and keep up with increases in costs. (Of course, premiums will also have to rise in that case.)

Does the policy give you any breaks? You pay more and get less buying an individual rather than a group policy; is there any way you can benefit? There is if your policy distinguishes between a healthy and an unhealthy life-style. For instance, you may qualify for a lower premium if you are a nonsmoker. Look for the policies that, all other benefits being equal, recognize your individual assets. After all, many policies do so to your disadvantage through exclusions, riders, and preexisting conditions clauses; it's only fair if there is some return the other way.

COMPARING SPECIFIC BENEFITS

The best comparison you can make is with the list of group benefits in chapter 8. You may find comparing what group policies offer with your individual policies is depressing; or you may decide to get a job with some large, generous company; or you may at least join something. Just keep in mind that the individual purchaser of health insurance has lost the game before starting to play it and can only hope to come in a good second. How well you do within that limitation depends on how hard you work at it. With possibly thousands and thousands of dollars at stake in the event of an expensive illness, buying a good health insurance policy is a better gamble than a lottery ticket and worth its weight in peace of mind.

IF YOU'RE 65 OR OVER

See Part Four.

IV

WHEN MEDICARE IS NOT ENOUGH—MEDICARE SUPPLEMENT POLICIES

11

The Medigap Safety Net—How to Keep from Falling Through

WHO NEEDS TO KNOW ABOUT MEDICARE?

Many people think they need not concern themselves with Medicare because they are nowhere near sixty-five years of age. They forget, or do not know, that Medicare is also available for the totally disabled (after 24 months of total disability) and to those with end-stage renal disease (kidney disease). Even a young adult may have occasion to use Medicare under these circumstances. In addition, a sick or elderly person is often not able to cope with the machinery of Medicare and fails to get what is due because he or she does not know how to file claim forms, how to follow up on incorrect payments, or how to motivate uncooperative health-care providers to accept the assignment. In cases like these a friend or relative is often saddled with the job of straightening out the mess, without a clue to where to begin. It is a good idea to have at least a smattering of knowledge of the subject, and to know where to go for more complete information (your Social Security office, for starters). Once you find out what Medicare doesn't cover, you will begin to understand why there are Medicare supplement policies.

SUPPOSE YOU'RE STILL WORKING

It's possible that in that case you don't need to think about a Medicare supplement policy.

Since 1983 employers with twenty or more employees who have job-related health plans must give employees age sixty-five to sixty-nine the option of staying with their employer's health plan. If they do, and they sign up for Medicare too, Medicare will pick up some of the gaps in the employer's plan, but the employer's plan will be the "primary" coverage. In other words, it must pay its usual benefits first, before Medicare enters the scene. Check with your employer; the company must provide you with written information that will enable you to make a decision. If you don't sign up for Medicare Part A, the federal government will penalize you (presently 10%), increasing your Part B premium for each year in which you were eligible to sign up and didn't. In such an eventuality, when you finally do go on Medicare, you will then have to pay an inflated monthly premium for the rest of your life.

ISN'T MEDICARE ENOUGH?

When you become eligible for Medicare, you quickly discover that it will cover considerably less than half—some say less than a third, and the percentage is dropping every year—of your actual health care costs. (From 1981 to 1984, nearly $10.5 billion of previously Medicare-covered health care costs have been dumped into the laps of Medicare beneficiaries to add to their out-of-pocket costs.) This gap in coverage can amount to a staggering amount of money in a very short time. In 1984 it was possible, with complete Medicare coverage, to run up out-of-pocket hospital expenses of about fifteen thousand dollars in the first five months that you became eligible for Medicare. When you realize that that does not take into account additional charges from physicians, consultants, tests, and therapy (especially from providers who do not accept the assignment), it is not hard to understand why it is a good idea to take out a policy that picks up some of these uncovered costs.

No matter how high a premium you can afford, however, you cannot buy a policy that will pay for all the expenses you will have in connection with your health care. The best you can hope to do is get the most complete coverage available and be clear about its limitations. The type of policy to look for is called Medicare supplement. The federal government is so aware of the inadequacy of Medicare coverage and of the necessity of supplementing it that even though it has sharply reduced the number of publications offered to consumers, it offers a slim brochure on Medicare supplement policies. In addition, both the federal and state governments have passed laws protecting consumers against some of the more blatant questionable practices by some insurers in this area.

Medicare supplement polices are sometimes referred to as Medigap policies, but this is really a misnomer; it would be more accurate to call these policies Medicare gap helpers. The government calls them Medicare supplement policies, but even this name does not put the prospective purchaser on notice that many gaps will still not be plugged. In thinking of safety nets, it is important to keep in mind that nets have holes and they are often big enough to fall through.

It is an unpleasant fact that all Medigap policies are expensive. Until the runaway inflation that prevails in the health provider industry is brought under control and health care costs become more rational, insurance that commits itself to covering some of these costs will be equally overpriced. Many seniors who currently have Medigap policies are being forced to cancel them because they can no longer afford them. Let us hope that Medicare itself is not—as presently appears possible—also priced out of their reach.

With the cards so obviously stacked against them, what are Medicare beneficiaries to do? At least be sure you are getting the best value for your premium dollar. As with many other purchases, price is only a rough guide to quality; only a detailed comparison of the benefits offered and the gaps to be filled by two or more policies will show whether a policy is fair or a rip-off.

YOU'RE NOT ALONE

The creation of Medicare made Americans health-insurance conscious. It also, however, created runaway health care costs; today the average senior pays more for health care, with full Medicare coverage, than in the good old days when Medicare did not exist. I should really say Medicare and other health insurance policies, since it is primarily the third-party payment system, in which the patient's insurance, rather than the patient, pays the bill, that has allowed costs to rise far beyond the point where the average American can afford them.

As costs rose and seniors found that costs not covered by Medicare could bankrupt them, the insurance industry developed policies to insure against this contingency. Unfortunately, this market was so lucrative due to the fear of seniors, on their limited incomes, of finding themselves destitute as the result of the costs of even a minor illness, that unsavory insurance practices soon ran rampant in the industry. Medicare beneficiaries were preyed upon by unscrupulous salespeople and companies that knowingly sold duplicate policies—sometimes as many as thirty to a single person. They even sold policies the buyer clearly could not afford, for which the premiums alone totaled more than the buyer's annual income. They coaxed the buyer into canceling a perfectly good policy for a "better" one, with a new waiting period and more stringent preexisting clauses. Every con and scam that had ever worked in other industries was applied to this new market, until finally the situation grew so scandalous that the federal government stepped in to investigate.

Senator Lawton Chiles and Representative Claude Pepper (both Democrats from Florida) were leaders in the fight to clean up the industry. In 1978 at a hearing before the Special Committee on Aging, which was looking into the abuses of Medigap policies, Senator Chiles detailed some of the practices that had led to the hearing. Among these were "oversale and misrepresentation," company directives that set quotas, routine denial of claims, and other questionable behavior.

As a result of the investigation, the government came up with standards that say so-called Medicare supplement policies should provide certain minimum benefits, the cost of the policies should be "reasonable," and consumers should be given certain specific rights, such as a "free look" at the policy for ten or more days, during which the policy can be canceled, with a full refund of premium.

MINIMUM BENEFITS IN SUPPLEMENT POLICIES

Here are the minimum benefits for Medicare supplement policies, according to the federal law that went into effect July 1, 1982; forty-three states have adopted these standards.

1. The policy should supplement Medicare Part A and Part B, including some coverage for skilled nursing

home (SNF) care. For instance, the policy must pay what Medicare doesn't for eligible hospital expenses (Part A) from the sixty-first to the ninetieth day of hospitalization in any benefit period. It must also cover co-insurance for your lifetime reserve days, when used. It does not require Day-1-to-Day-60 coverage (Medicare charges a hefty deductible for Day 1).

2. When you have used up all your hospital benefits, the policy should pay 90 percent of Medicare-eligible expenses for an additional 365 days. (Many policies that go along with this benefit pay 100 percent.)

3. The policy should adjust the amount of any payments for deductibles and co-payments whenever Medicare's amounts increase (not to be construed as requiring coverage of Part B deductible).

4. Medicare supplement policies should pay up to at least $5,000 a year for Part B benefits. Basically the policy is supposed to pick up the 20 percent of the reasonable and allowable charge that Medicare never pays, but it is allowed to set a $200 deductible (including your Part B deductible) before coverage begins. Plan One and Plan Two of the AARP policies, for example, do this. (See detailed discussion of these policies in next chapter.)

5. Length of pre-existing-conditions exclusion should be no more than six months.

6. A "free look" at the policy should be allowed, with cancellation permitted within 10 days, for a buyer-initiated sale, or within 30 days otherwise.

7. There should be no less than a 60 percent loss ratio for individual policies, 75 percent for group policies.

8. The policy should be written in clear, simple language, with no provisions in small, "invisible" type.

9. The company should give you a buyers' guide.

Unfortunately, these federal standards require only voluntary compliance, but they act as guidelines to the consumer as to what to look for in a policy.

An even better consumer aid is the fact that the states, which can pass laws regulating the insurance industry, have taken action to protect the buyer. Some states have done better than others, but almost all states have established certain minimum requirements that a policy must meet if it is to be sold within the state as a Medicare supplement policy. Many states have simply taken the federal guidelines and made them a minimum requirement by law in that state. Some states have done even better. If you have an old policy, it may fall below these minimum standards; check it out. One benefit of these minimums is that it makes it easier for buyers to compare any policy they are considering to determine whether—even in a state with lax requirements—they are getting at least minimum coverage.

Insurance companies sometimes make the best of these required minimums by presenting them in their literature as if they were especially generous benefits, with naturally not a word to the effect that these are the least the law allows them to offer. If you do not know, you might think the company was indeed going out of its way and that the policy was especially good. If, however, you compare it with any other policy sold within that state, you may soon see that the two policies are almost identical. This comparison is made especially easy for you by the states that require specific wording to be used and specify the size of type in which certain clauses are to be set and the placement—frequently on the first page of the outline of benefits—of limiting or restricting provisions.

These regulations create look-alike policies that even

the most poorly informed consumer can quickly recognize. In fact, a policy outline that looks quite different from others ought to be examined more carefully. One company, for example, in conforming to the requirement that certain limitations had to be set in 10-point type (which is fairly large), simply set the entire brochure in 10-point type, thus complying with the letter of the law but defeating its purpose. All the effort that is required on your part, in states with good laws, is to ask for an outline from two or three different insurance companies and then compare them with one another. (And buy only those policies approved for sale in the state.)

In addition to protective legislation, many states have gone to considerable trouble and expense to prepare booklets that are packed with a readable, easy-to-follow explanation of exactly what to look for in a Medicare supplement policy.

If you live in a state, such as Connecticut, that does not offer any helpful booklets, you may be able to obtain them from neighboring states or from a friend who lives in a neighboring state. If you are using material from another state, be sure to check with your own insurance commission to make sure the laws are the same.

In addition, Medicare itself puts out informative booklets on the subject. Just call your local Social Security office to obtain copies. Many organizations, such as the National Council of Senior Citizens (NCSC), also provide material. Most of this material is free for the asking. One exception is the rather expensive new book on Medicare from the American Association of Retired Persons (AARP).

Do your homework. In spite of government efforts on the consumers' behalf, it is still possible to be the victim of an unscrupulous salesperson selling a dishonest product. Also compare premiums when comparing benefits; some policies simply charge more than the additional benefits are worth. For instance, policies that pay the Day-1-to-Day-60 hospital benefit are usually much more expensive than those that do not. The reason, of course, is that even a short hospital stay incurs this expense. In New York State, 3 out of 10 beneficiaries spend a minimum of one day in the hospital annually. If you are willing to gamble that you will be among the 70 percent who do not—pretty good odds—you will not buy this coverage and will not feel badly if you have to pay it out of your own pocket on some occasions.

You might even prefer to take the savings you have just acquired and use it to buy prescription drug coverage, which you are much more liable to use.

KNOW YOUR MEDICARE COVERAGE

Unless you know what Medicare does and does not cover, you will not be able to judge how effectively a Medicare supplement policy picks up the uncovered costs. So the first step in buying a policy is to acquaint yourself with basic Medicare coverage.

There is a brochure called *Medicare Supplement Disclosure Form,* which state insurance commissions usually require be given to anyone eligible for coverage under a Medicare supplement plan. If the insurance agent doesn't give you one, ask for it. It contains only a summary of basic Medicare benefits; additional benefits, as well as limitations and exceptions, may not be shown. For a complete explanation of Medicare, read *The Medicare Answer Book,* also written by me and published by Harper & Row; it is the best source of complete information on Medicare and is recommended by Representative Claude Pepper, Senator Edward Kennedy, Senator Lawton Chiles, Maggie Kuhn, and the AARP, among others.

The free Medicare Supplement Disclosure Form you

THE PRUDENTIAL INSURANCE COMPANY OF AMERICA

This outline of coverage provides a very brief description of the important features of the group plan. This is not the group insurance contract, and only the actual group contract provisions will control. Your group plan contains benefits which are designed to supplement Medicare benefits. A detailed explanation of these benefits and the plan's cost can be found in the enclosed brochure. You may use this chart to compare this plan's benefits with any plan you currently have. Questions about coverage should be directed to the following address or phone number: The Prudential Insurance Company of America, Fort Washington, Pennsylvania 19034.   800-523-5800.

MEDICARE—HOSPITAL INSURANCE BENEFITS (PART A)*

FOR COVERED SERVICES—EACH BENEFIT PERIOD				PRIVATE INSURANCE CHECKLIST	
SERVICE	BENEFIT	MEDICARE PAYS	YOU PAY‡	WHAT YOUR CURRENT INSURANCE WILL PAY	WHAT PROPOSED INSURANCE WILL PAY
HOSPITALIZATION . . . . Semiprivate room and board, general nursing and miscellaneous hospital services and supplies.	First 60 days	All but $304	$304		
	61st to 90th day	All but $76 a day	$76 a day		
	91st to 150th day**	All but $152 a day	$152 a day		
	Beyond 150 days	Nothing	All costs		
Includes meals, special care units, drugs, lab tests, diagnostic X-rays, medical supplies, operating and recovery room, anesthesia and rehabilitation services.	A Benefit Period begins on the first day you receive services as an inpatient in a hospital and ends after you have been out of the hospital or skilled nursing facility for 60 days in a row.				
POSTHOSPITAL SKILLED NURSING FACILITY CARE . . . In a facility approved by Medicare. You must have been in a hospital for at least 3 days and enter the facility within a short time, generally 30 days after hospital discharge.	First 20 days	100% of allowable charge	Nothing		
	Additional 80 days	All but $38 a day	$38 a day		
	Beyond 100 days	Nothing	All costs		
	MEDICARE AND PRIVATE INSURANCE WILL NOT PAY FOR MOST NURSING HOME CARE. YOU PAY FOR CUSTODIAL CARE AND MOST CARE IN A NURSING HOME.				
HOME HEALTH CARE	Unlimited as medically necessary	100% of allowable charge	Nothing		
BLOOD	Blood	All but first 3 pints	For first 3 pints		

If you are considering buying insurance, use the chart on the left and this checklist to help you decide. If you are buying from an agent, ask him or her to help you complete this checklist.

* These figures are for 1983 and are subject to change each year.
** 60 Lifetime Reserve Days may be used only once; days used are not renewable.

MEDICARE—MEDICAL INSURANCE BENEFITS (PART B)

FOR COVERED SERVICES—EACH CALENDAR YEAR

SERVICE	BENEFIT	MEDICARE PAYS	YOU PAY‡
MEDICAL EXPENSE Physician's services, inpatient and outpatient medical services and supplies, physical and speech therapy, ambulance, etc.	Medicare pays for medical services in or out of the hospital. Some insurance policies pay less (or nothing) for hospital outpatient medical services or services in a doctor's office	80% of allowable charge (after $75 deductible)	$75 deductible* plus 20% of balance of allowable charge
HOME HEALTH CARE (Not covered under Part A)	Unlimited as medically necessary	100% of allowable charge	Nothing
OUTPATIENT HOSPITAL TREATMENT	Unlimited as medically necessary	80% of allowable charge (after $75 deductible)	Subject to deductible plus 20% of balance of allowable charge
BLOOD	Blood	80% of allowable charge (after first 3 pints)	For first 3 pints plus 20% of balance of allowable charge

* Once you have had $75 of expenses for covered services in a calendar year, the Part B deductible does not apply to any further covered services you receive in that year. The deductible amount is for 1983.

‡ **You pay** for charges higher than the amount approved by Medicare unless the doctor or supplier agrees to accept Medicare's allowable charges as the total charge for services rendered.

Are there any limitations on maximum dollar benefits? . . . NO.

Medicare deductibles and coinsurance (the portions you pay) change from time to time. Will this policy automatically increase your benefits to pay your increased costs? . . . YES.

Except for a general rate increase, does the cost change when you reach a certain age? . . . NO.

can get (see the illustration on pages 118–119) will show, in chart form, Medicare benefits, what Medicare pays, and what you pay. In addition, it contains blank columns, headed "Private Insurance Checklist," in which you can write what two supplemental policies cover for each uncovered area.

Notice the form has separate sections for Medicare Part A, Hospital Insurance, and Medicare Part B, Medical Insurance.

On the back of the form is helpful explanatory material, including definitions of some terms such as *skilled nursing facility care, home health care,* and *reasonable charge.* It is not helpful that what is called *allowable charges* on the chart side is called *reasonable charge* (with *allowable charge* in parentheses) in the explanation of this term, but that, unfortunately, is a problem you will run into in most explanations of Medicare. This is a useful form, however, if you depend on it primarily for a comparison of coverage and do not expect it to be a comprehensive explanation of Medicare itself.

If you are comparing more than two policies, simply cut up the additional copies of the free disclosure form (you should have gotten one from each company) and paste the blank columns together.

Always check the date the form was prepared; look on the back where it is noted. Medicare benefits, coinsurance, and deductibles now change frequently, and you need to know the current coverage, not last year's.

TYPES OF MEDICARE SUPPLEMENT INSURANCE

Private or Commercial Policies

These are Medicare supplement policies issued by for-profit insurance companies. Many but not all life insurance companies also offer accident and health, including Medicare supplement, policies. You should, of course, determine that the policy is licensed to be sold in your state. If your state does not mandate a loss ratio of 65 percent for individual policies and 70 percent for group policies, ask what the policy's loss ratio is. If the salesperson cannot or will not tell you, you might want to look at a policy that will. (If you still don't know what a loss ratio is, look on page 35.)

When a company or its salesperson tells you there is a Medicare supplement policy available, ask to see the outline of coverage. Since many companies offer more than one plan, with different coverage and premiums, ask whether there are other plans, and if there are, ask for outlines of all of them so that you can compare the coverage and see which one works best for you.

It is best not to attempt to compare various plans while the salesperson is sitting there hoping you will make up your mind and sign up for something. For one thing, you ought to be looking into other companies' offerings. For another, you can't possibly concentrate under those circumstances. Some salespeople are very pushy or persuasive, so make up your mind ahead of time that you will not arrive at a decision that day—no matter what the agent says—and you will find yourself pleasantly showing the agent to the door while he or she is still talking.

It is a good idea, however, to let the salesperson go over the outlines with you. Keep a sharp eye on the printed outline and ask immediately about any benefit he or she says the policy provides but that you don't see described in print. The agent may not be as organized as the policy, in which case he or she still will be able to find it and show you it in the printed material. If, however, the agent can't find it but assures you the policy does have that coverage, the agent either doesn't know the policy or is not being totally honest. Insurance companies do not pay claims based on their salespeople's promises but only on coverage spelled out in the policy.

All Medicare supplement policies use Medicare as their guideline. When, for instance, they say *nursing home,* they use the same definition as Medicare does for *skilled nursing facility*—the only kind of nursing home covered by Medicare. Usually they also require that it be a skilled nursing facility approved by Medicare; there are comparatively few SNFs, and by no means are all of them approved by Medicare. Fortunately, if you are buying your policy in a fairly strict state, the outline and the policy will be required by law to define terms like this and to use the same definition as Medicare. It's a good idea, however, to read the definitions over for yourself. It helps, of course, if you already know what these terms mean under Medicare.

No matter how good the policy sounds, it is only as good as the company issuing it. If the company is shaky financially and liable to go out of business, you could find yourself without supplemental health insurance at an awkward time. The financial stability of a company is easily checked out in *Best's Insurance Reports* (ask your reference librarian), which may save you an unpleasant surprise.

Usually a Medicare supplement policy accepts Medicare's definition of "reasonable or allowable charges."

Blue Cross/Blue Shield

The Blues are in a class by themselves. They are nonprofit and have very special contracts with hospitals by which they reimburse hospitals according to a special formula. Because they are nonprofit, they do not pay taxes and have certain other advantages that allow them to charge lower premiums and sometimes offer more coverage than commercial insurance companies. Their loss ratio is generally a whopping 90 percent or 95 percent. Their special status precludes most of them from offering other kinds of health insurance. Unfortunately for the consumer, they now would like to drop their nonprofit status and be able to sell all kinds of health insurance—which tells you something about the profit potential in other kinds of health insurance.

If you are familiar with the Blues, you may think you know all about their policies. That is unlikely both because they differ from state to state—sometimes even within a state—and because they change their policies and rates frequently. Some Blues Medicare supplement policies are excellent; some are not. Examine them just as critically as you would a commercial policy. When you are offered a choice of Blues supplement policies, don't assume the more expensive policy is the better one; often the additional coverage calls for too high a premium. For example, there is a Blues Medicare supplement policy that covers the Part B deductible, but the additional premium (compared to the policy that doesn't pay the deductible) costs almost as much more as the deductible itself. With this policy, any year in which you do not have to pay the Part B deductible (because you didn't incur medical expenses), you will pay that much out anyway in premiums for the unneeded coverage. You are better off paying the deductible yourself when you incur it and pocketing the savings when you don't. This is the way you have to examine even a good policy.

Unlike commercial insurance companies, the Blues generally do not sell their policies through salespeople or through direct mail or mail-order advertising. You may see a general informational advertisement, as when the Blues of New York recently advertised a "Wrap-Around" health insurance policy, but there is generally a free 800 number you can call if you want an outline-of-coverage brochure or have any questions. Lack of salespeople is not an inconvenience, since the 800 phone call doesn't cost you anything, and answers to any questions that may arise are as near as your phone. The people answering the phones are uniformly pleasant, though not always as forthcoming as you might wish. An area in which problems may arise is when you wish to transfer your coverage from one state to another. Although all the Blues are part of a national association, they operate quite independently and are, apparently, just as loath to lose customers to another state as any other insurance company would be to lose to a rival company. At any rate, they do not make changing easy and are at times almost obstructive. The machinery is there, however, and persistence on your part will get results.

Be sure to ask for the forms necessary to file claims when you take out your policy. Otherwise you will experience delay in receiving them. And ask for more as soon as you have used up your supply. (Always ask for several or they will send only one.)

Although Blues will pay claims in the long run, they sometimes exhibit what seem to be delaying tactics, such as sending out checked forms that ask for information you have already sent, though perhaps not exactly in the prescribed way. Patience and persistence will reward you; getting upset will not speed things up. Just remember it is not personal and that a loss ratio of over 90 percent is your assurance that you will get your money sooner or later.

HMOs

A health maintenance organization (HMO) is a prepaid medical plan that is now available to Medicare beneficiaries. Utilizing the services of a particular medical organization as you need them, you pay the HMO a hefty monthly fee (Medicare beneficiaries pay considerably less than other members) but pay nothing to Medicare, including no Part B premiums. In return the HMO theoretically provides both preventive and illness care. In practice HMOs usually now offer at least two plans for Medicare beneficiaries. The less expensive option covers only the same costs Medicare covers plus deductibles and co-insurance. The more expensive option offers that coverage plus some preventive medicine, such as regular physical checkups, flu shots, and so on. If you are lucky, you will also be covered for prescription drugs (for which you may pay a nominal fee, such as a dollar a prescription), and just possibly eyeglasses and examinations for eyeglasses, and various other health care services often not covered by health insurance.

A good HMO can be an excellent buy, if you can afford it and if you are temperamentally suited to this type of service, and if it is a good one. It is the closest we have to a national health plan and contains many of the same advantages and disadvantages. It takes a lot of the chores and decision making out of health care. There are no Medicare forms to fill out or claims to file, and no hassles as to what is covered and what is not. On the other hand, you must use that HMO's medical staff (unless you want to exercise the option you always have of paying a private physician yourself) and you must cope with the HMO bureaucracy, which can be just as difficult, unpleasant, and obstructive as any other bureaucracy. An HMO usually has an arrangement with a local hospital and will also refer you to (and pay for) a specialist outside the organization if it does not have one on its staff for your particular problem.

One of the biggest disadvantages of even the best HMOs is that you are poorly covered when traveling. If there is an HMO in the area in which you are taking your trip, it may have a reciprocal agreement with the one you belong to. It will, however, be difficult—even impossible—to get treatment (see p. 196).

There is also always the chance that the HMO in your travel area is an inferior one, with a medical staff that is not to your liking. There is no provision that takes care of this, as far as I know, but perhaps your own HMO, if it is a good one, will agree with your assessment and authorize your going to a local private physician.

If there is no HMO available in the area in which you are traveling, you will probably be covered for emergency care by any physician. There are, however, a number of minor illnesses that may arise when traveling, and you will have to assume the costs of care for these yourself.

If, however, you have a first-class HMO convenient to you and affordable, if you do not travel much, and if you like the convenience of having almost all your medical care in one building and appointments made for you more or less effortlessly by your attending physician picking up the phone and ringing the other doctor on another floor, you might want to try what many experts feel is the coming way of delivering health care.

The federal government looks kindly on HMOs, because they seem to cut down on hospital admissions and to be cost efficient. As a result, there are about nineteen

HMOs throughout the country, including the International Medical Centers in Florida, that offer free Medicare supplement policies. You read that right; they don't cost anything. These are so-called demonstration projects, so they may not be around very long. On the other hand, they may and are worth knowing about.

If there is such an HMO in your area, you have probably heard about it and wonder if it is any good. The answer is that the government thinks so and is backing up its opinion with money. If the plan works, both the HMO and the government will make money. The theory is partly that people who belong to an HMO take better care of themselves and are healthier because they do not put off going to the doctor until their condition has become serious and more expensive to treat. There is also not the same profit incentive to hospitalize patients that exists under regular Medicare coverage.

The number of HMOs has increased in the past few years, but since they require a large membership in order to work, they are to be found primarily in cities. It is not practical to get all your health care in one place if that place is an hour's drive from your home.

Although your family physician will not advise you as to what kind of Medicare supplement insurance to buy (he or she probably doesn't know anything about health insurance), you may find that your doctor has very strong adverse reactions if you mention HMOs. Some doctors feel threatened by HMOs because proliferation of them would cut down on the need for private physicians, so they are against them out of simple self-interest on the grounds of competition. Other, more public spirited physicians truly feel the level of care delivered by HMO medical staffs is inferior and would hate to see any of their patients in what they view as less-than-competent hands. Their attitude, if they are willing to talk about it, is generally that no doctor would work for an HMO who could make it in private practice. By extension, they therefore look upon all HMO doctors as incompetent failures who are working for the HMO as a last resort before becoming plumbers or backwoodsmen.

As with all judgments of this sort, there may be a certain element of truth in it. It is equally possible, however, that many HMO doctors simply do not like the hassle of private practice and prefer to be "organization men." They do not have to maintain an office, with all its expenses and problems, compete in the community for patients, hire staff, and pay for malpractice insurance. Their income may not be as high as that of some doctors in private practice, but in a thriving HMO, they may do very well indeed. And their work is less stressful. So their choosing to work for an HMO may be a matter of temperament rather than competence. Also, today's physician must be a businessperson as well as a healer. Not everyone in the medical profession likes business or is good at it. For that person, an HMO may be more congenial than private practice.

On an even more positive note, there is the possibility that the HMO physican is motivated by a desire for public service. Most HMO directors, for instance, have public service training and have always planned to pursue this as a career.

The fact is that incompetent doctors may be encountered in both private and public practice, in affluent communities as well as in rural areas. In this as in any aspect of the marketplace, consumers must be responsible for protecting themselves.

12

What To Expect from a
Medicare Supplement Policy

WHERE TO FIND A POLICY

When you are finally in the market for a Medicare supplement policy, you may find that the number of policies available is somewhat overwhelming. If you have group health insurance, check at the office. Also see Suppose You're Still Working, page 110. If for some reason you must go outside your job to buy an individual policy, your problem is more complicated. Many insurance agents do not know much about this type of policy. If the insurance companies whose policies they usually sell do not have them, you will draw a blank in asking for their advice. Your best bet is to ask friends or co-workers (if you are absolutely certain they are over 65 and admitting it); you can then also ask whether they have been satisfied with their coverage.

No matter what other sources you draw on, ask the 800 information phone operator for the number for the Blue Cross/Blue Shield office in your state; this should be the first place you look, because the Blues usually allow you to join only at certain specified times and you could easily miss out on an open enrollment period. If you are close to their deadline, you may want to come to a decision more quickly than if you have a couple of months to think about it.

If you have a job that includes group insurance with a conversion privilege as a fringe benefit, you now—having taken the advice in an earlier section—already know all the advantages of conversion, as well as when to apply for it. Your next step, therefore, is to examine the cards in your wallet to determine what groups you belong to other than your place of business. By now these may include the American Association of Retired Persons (AARP), which also includes the National Retired Teachers Association (in spite of its name, you don't have to be retired to join, just 55 or older), the National Council of Senior Citizens (NCSC), various church organizations, professional groups (Washington Independent Writers and The Authors Guild come naturally to my mind, but your frame of reference may be different), and even fraternal organizations. Just as employers with more than twenty-five employees can buy better policies, so can larger organizations. If you have a choice, go by the number of members.

Your state insurance commission is a good place to find the companies in your state that offer Medicare supplemental policies; usually it will send you a list, and you may find the number of choices confronting you a little disconcerting. For instance, the Florida Insurance Commission lists fifty-six companies!

Obviously it would be impossible to compare all the policies (many companies have more than one) offered by all fifty-six companies listed—though most of the time you will not be confronted by such a large list; New York State lists only thirteen companies. Friends and acquaintances will quickly help you eliminate many names by telling you about unsatisfactory experiences they have had with

one or another company. Your insurance broker, even if
he or she is not in this field, may have some scuttlebutt
from trade talk sessions and be willing to pass it on to
you. Even the insurance commission, if approached in a
very nonofficial and casual way, will sometimes drop hints
as to which companies to avoid. Sometimes the media—
a local newspaper, for instance—will publish helpful articles
or even detailed comparisons. If your local paper does not
do so, maybe the editors would welcome the suggestion
that they do. You have your work cut out for you, but it
is important work and you stand to gain a great deal from
taking the time to do it.

You will now have explored all areas except for
HMOs. If there is an HMO near where you live, look into
it. Some cities are fortunate enough to have more than
one HMO, in which case you should explore them all,
keeping in mind the convenience factor. In the suburbs
your community may fall in the middle between two
HMOs. In checking them out, look at the physical plant
as well as the outline of benefits, since it is within those
premises that you will receive most of your health care.

It is possible that you have never been aware that
there is an HMO in your area, so check it out even if you
think there is not. The local Social Services Director of
your community will have this information.

THE SHOPPING LIST

Looking for a good buy in Medicare supplemental policies
is not that different from looking for a good buy in making
any purchase; you need to know your requirements. It is
important to have a shopping list, so that you have thought
out what you need and do not fill your cart with sale or
impulse items for which you have no use, while overlooking

the staples that you cannot function without.

A shopping list not only keeps your mind on the ball, it also serves to intimidate insurance salespeople. They are primarily interested in making a sale; sometimes the poorer their product, the better their pitch. It is an unhappy fact that as you get older, you become more vulnerable to and malleable by people who are nice to you. Insurance salespeople can be very, very nice, but their personable appearance and manners can conceal some dubious intentions, as the next chapter will detail.

Your shopping list should include the following minimum items, which you should look for in your policy. Since many of them are required by some states before a policy sold in that state can be called a Medicare supplement policy, your first move should be to look at the policy outline (which you have, of course, already told the salesperson to bring). If it bears this designation and if you live in such a state, much of your work has already been done for you. This should not, however, put you off your guard. Check off all the items on your shopping list anyhow.

Minimum Necessities

A shopping list depends partly on your present circumstances. The state of your budget can be a limiting factor, in which case you will want to get only the absolute necessities. The following items come under this category.

1. *Coverage of Part A Medicare deductible and co-insurance for hospitalization from the first to the ninetieth day in any benefit period.* It is generally considered better to pay the first-day deductible yourself in return for a lower premium, but more and more policies do not offer this option. Short-term

stays are increasingly likely (they are promoted as a cost-cutting measure), but you may prefer the more complete coverage. The out-of-pocket cost to the consumer (with Medicare but without supplemental insurance) for 90 days of hospitalization (not including any other expenses) was over $3,000 in 1984 and will rise steeply in the future. Add surgery, therapy, and private nursing care, none of which Medicare covers half so well as hospital costs, and you see why a Medicare supplement policy is necessary.

2. *Coverage of Part A co-insurance for hospitalization during use of Medicare's lifetime hospital in-patient reserve days.* At $178 a day co-insurance (1984 rates), this period could cost you over $10,000 out-of-pocket just for the hospital. The odds are against your hospital stay lasting that long, but insurance is a what-if proposition; decide whether you prefer to gamble that you won't need it.

3. *Coverage of 90 percent of all Medicare Part A eligible expenses for hospitalization, not covered by Medicare, subject to a lifetime maximum benefit of an additional 365 days,* after all Medicare hospital inpatient coverage has been used up, including the lifetime reserve days. This sounds generous, but it is truly a minimum. It is important because you can use up all your Medicare hospital coverage after 150 days in the hospital. (Many beneficiaries do not realize this and think Medicare will always be there when they need it.) While it provides far from adequate health coverage, this benefit is a help. It is so necessary that many states stipulate it as minimum coverage in approved policies; you might be able to do even better—100 percent coverage or for a longer period. If the salesperson quotes statistics showing that only a small percentage of seniors spend anything like this long in the hospital,

argue that that is all the more reason why insurance coverage of this unlikely contingency should be available and inexpensive. If you are one of the few to whom it happens, the costs could bankrupt you.

4. *Coverage of the 20 percent co-insurance amount of Part B eligible expenses, regardless of hospital confinement,* subject to a maximum calendar year deductible of $300 of such expenses and to a maximum benefit of at least $5,000 per calendar year. (Since Part B is where doctor bills are covered, what this picks up is the 20 percent left of the bill of a doctor or other provider who "accepts the assignment.") Better but much more expensive policies will also pay part of the charges over Medicare's "allowed" or "reasonable" charge. This does not pick up the Part B deductible, which the beneficiary must pay before Medicare will pay its 80% and it imposes the additional cost of the $300 deductible. Also, it has the top limit of $5,000 for doctor bills, which may not go very far if you have major surgery, and may leave you holding a very empty bag if the surgeon and the anesthetist refuse to accept the assignment. However, since it pays on a yearly basis, you might be able to put off some of your doctor's services (and bills), including elective surgery, into the following year (always realizing that you will then have to pay again the Part B deductible).

5. *Coverage for pre-existing conditions may not be excluded for longer than six months* from the time the policy goes into effect. Before this time limitation was recommended by the federal government and mandated by many states, exclusions often lasted as long as two years. You still have to watch out for this in health insurance policies bought before age 65 in states that do not protect their citizens. At age 65

your pre-existing conditions, which may be arthritis, a heart condition, or hip implants, are just the conditions for which you are most liable to need coverage. Which is, of course, why insurance companies try to put off coverage for pre-existing conditions as long as possible.

TIPS FOR THE SMART SHOPPER

1. The insurance company should provide you with a simplified "Outline of Coverage," setting forth a summary of the benefits, limits, exclusions, deductibles, and premiums of the policy. It is a useful guide and will give you a quick way of comparing this policy with others. It should never take the place of a careful sit-down read-through of the actual policy once you have signed up for it. It will provide you with a reminder of Medicare coverage and show which gaps it covers (but not which it doesn't, so read between the lines).

   In addition, the company should give you some sort of general buyers' guide. The usual handout is a brochure called *Guide to Health Insurance for People with Medicare,* which has been prepared jointly by the Department of Health and Human Services and the National Association of Insurance Commissioners. Also call your state insurance commission on its 800 number and ask what booklets they will send you.

2. You should get a "free-look" period. This is time allowed, after you receive the actual policy, for you to decide you have made a dreadful mistake and want your money back. The federal government recommends ten to thirty days, but many states—New York, for one—require only ten. If you have only ten days, you should look at the policy as soon as you can after you receive it. If it seems to cover less than

you thought (use your shopping and checklist chart) or if any part of it isn't clear, ask your salesperson or the company. Do not, however, accept oral assurances that you have coverage; insist on being shown where in the policy this benefit is stated. If it isn't in the policy, you aren't covered, no matter what anyone says. If you want to cancel, do so in writing well within the time limit. Send your letter by certified mail, return receipt requested, so the company cannot claim it never received notification. If your money is not then refunded promptly, complain immediately to your state insurance department.

3. Ask what the loss ratio of the policy is. If the salesperson looks blank, pretends not to know what that is, or says he or she has never been asked that before, examine the policy extra carefully. It is possible the salesperson has never been asked that before, but if he or she is so lacking in the basics of health insurance as not to know what the term means, you can't have much confidence in the person's expertise in other health insurance areas. If the agent suddenly loses interest in selling you a policy and must leave quickly for another appointment, you ought to look into other policies with other companies.

In general a loss ratio of 60–65 percent is the least you should settle for. The Blues record of 90–100 percent (and even more in some instances, which is statistically confusing but possible) will not be equaled by any commercial company, which must show a profit to stay in business. Group policies are usually required to have a fair loss ratio. Many states specify a minimum loss ratio for Medicare supplemental policies. New York, for example, mandates a minimum loss ratio of 65%.

In the event that your salesperson seems reasonably trustworthy but gets back to you with the information that the company won't divulge what the loss ratio is, look at the policy extra carefully. And ask the state insurance commissioner to give you this information.

4. All health care costs should be covered the same way, regardless of whether they result from illness or accident.

Optional Shopping List

Choosing a basic policy is comparatively simple, but choosing more complete coverage is a balancing act. Since there is no policy that will cover all your health-care costs, you will have to decide which options are important to you. While more complete coverage is more expensive than basic coverage, the most expensive policy does not invariably provide the best benefits.

FOUR AARP POLICIES COMPARED

In order to compare the following policies, get out your Medicare Supplement Disclosure Form chart (see pages 118–119) and fill in a column for each option.

The American Association of Retired Persons (AARP), an association of more than 16 million people over age fifty-five, offers four Medicare supplement policies to people over sixty-five. In 1983 the monthly premium for the most expensive option was almost five times the premium for the least expensive. Let us see why the difference and what you get for your money.

Plan One pays in-hospital co-insurance for both the sixty-first-to-ninetieth-day period and the lifetime reserve days period. In addition, it pays 100 percent of Medicare eligible expenses for up to a lifetime maximum of 365 days, after you have used up your Medicare benefits.

It pays Part B co-insurance after a deductible (your regular Medicare Part B deductible counts toward the policy deductible). It pays co-insurance for days 21 to 100 in a skilled nursing facility (according to Medicare guidelines) and double that amount for days 101 through 365 (when Medicare pays nothing).

In addition, it pays up to $30 for a registered nurse ($25 for an LPN) for every eight-hour shift when you need a private-duty nurse in the hospital. (But no more than three shifts a day or sixty shifts per benefit period for either or both.) This is a particularly important benefit; almost all experts agree that given the present situations in hospitals, a seriously ill or postoperative patient really should have someone in the room to negotiate with the hospital staff and to keep an eye on things. At a time when surveys have disclosed that as many as one in six medications given in the hospital are subject to some kind of staff error, it is particularly comforting to have a check on whether the doctor's orders are being followed and that you have not been confused with some other patient. Reading such books as Dr. William A. Nolen's *Surgeon Under the Knife* should not be undertaken just prior to a hospital stay but is a good education for anyone who may someday be a patient.

Plan Two, called Medicare Supplement Plus, provides the same coverage as Plan One except that it also pays the initial hospital deductible, which is the hundreds of dollars that Medicare charges for even one day's hospitalization.

Plan Three has the same coverage as Plan Two plus paying the 20 percent of Part B charges that Medicare doesn't pay, after you have paid the annual Medicare deductible (but not imposing any deductible of its own) and paying 80 percent of the usual and prevailing expense for private-duty nursing care (the outline does not specify any limitation), and paying 50 percent of up to $500 a year of the usual and prevailing charges for out-of-hospital prescription drugs, after you pay an annual deductible. (The prescription drug coverage in the policy I am looking at whittles down a $500 prescription drug bill to $200 after you apply all the limitations. This is less than half the amount you might expect if you just took a quick look at this provision. On the other hand, Medicare pays nothing for out-of-hospital prescription drugs, so you have to think about this one.)

Plan Four, or Comprehensive Medicare Supplement, is the one that is five times as expensive as Plan One. For that extra money you get everything offered in Plan Three plus 100 percent of all the usual and prevailing Part B expenses not paid by Medicare after you have paid the annual Part B deductible. The outline states: "This plan pays benefits for charges even in excess of those allowed by Medicare," but do not assume it necessarily means it will pay 100 percent of all Part B bills. If it meant that it presumably would have said so; you need to look carefully at the definition on another page of the outline. What it says is: "Usual and Prevailing Charges are the normal charges made in your area by doctors, nurses, and druggists. Therefore, AARP's Comprehensive Medicare Supplement (Plan 4) when combined with your Medicare benefits, will cover 100% of your Part B medical care expenses unless the charges are exceptionally high for your area." How this works in practice only filing claims will tell.

(Note that the brochure in which these plans are described positions Plan Two first and Plan One second, both on the cover and in the text and chart. The rationale for doing it this way rather than in the usual order of least comprehensive (and least expensive) to most comprehensive (and most expensive) may be that in AARP's judgment, Plan Two is the one most people will want, or the one they have found to be the most popular, or that AARP considers the best buy. Whatever the reason, it adds confusion to an already confusing subject, does nothing to help the already muddled senior, and is irritating to someone really trying to compare all four options. Even from a marketing standpoint, there are better ways of highlighting a particular policy within the brochure.)

The cost for these AARP policies is the same for all members, regardless of age. Some policies increase their premiums by age so that sixty-five- to seventy-two-year-olds pay less than seventy-three- to seventy-seven-year-olds, seventy-eight- to eighty-two-year-olds pay more than the latter group, and eighty-three-year-olds and over pay a still-higher amount (in policies of this type premiums may change yearly or only as you move from one group to another). Always check policies to see whether the premiums will change with age, and be sure to compare policies in this regard.

AARP plans One and Two are not approved for sale in Connecticut, and you may wonder why. The insurance commission there told me it is because the commission has found that seniors are confused by deductibles and co-insurance. Both these plans have a $200 deductible feature, and the commission felt that compounded Medicare's already confusing features. You may not feel that is a serious flaw in these policies, and if you do not live in Connecticut, you may feel comfortable buying one of them if it otherwise meets your requirements. It does show, however, the extent to which state insurance commissions will go in an effort to help the consumer.

BLUE CROSS/BLUE SHIELD POLICIES

Since everyone recommends that you at least look at the Blues policies when you are shopping for Medicare supplemental insurance, let us see what happens when you try to compare the Blues with the AARP policies we have just looked at.

The first problem is that you cannot simply compare premiums, because the policies themselves are not comparable. Although both offer more than one option, none of the policies is identical with any of the other company's offerings. To confuse matters even further, Blues policies and premiums vary from state to state; there is no one standard Blues Medicare supplemental policy. You will find considerable differences, for example, between New York and Connecticut Blues, both in coverage and in premiums. (In the following discussion I have used a Connecticut Blues plan as the model.) This lack of uniformity creates a difficult situation for the consumer. You have to look at the specific benefits of each specific policy available to you and determine as best you can which is better for your situation. AARP's plans One and Two, for example, have no prescription drug coverage. The Blues policies have limited coverage and require prior hospitalization. The Blues premium is higher than AARP Plan One but less than Plan Two. It is almost half of Plan Four.

The Blues pay for the day 1 hospital deductible; AARP plans Two, Three, and Four do, but not Plan One. On the other hand, all AARP policies pay for an additional period from day 101 to day 365 in a nursing home, when Medicare benefits are exhausted; the Blues do not pay anything for this period. Only 5 percent of the over-sixty-five group is in nursing homes, so you may decide to take your chances on this coverage. Both provide a 365-day lifetime hospital coverage after Medicare-covered benefits are exhausted. The average stay of a sixty-five-or-over patient in the hospital is about eleven days—but you might not be average. The average stay in a nursing home is two-and-a-half years—but that's in all types of nursing homes, not only skilled nursing facilities (and both Medicare and Medicare supplement cover only SNFs); there were no figures available for just SNFs. It would appear, therefore, that it is unlikely you will benefit from the coverage in either case. It may be argued, however, that it is just this unlikely contingency that you need insurance for, since even though a long stay is unlikely, there is no doubt that anyone unfortunate enough to need it would go broke trying to pay for it. The small chance of the insurance company having to pay off on this benefit should mean a low premium for this additional coverage. (But the insurance company could argue that the odds against having to pay are more than offset by the enormous sums that could be involved in such extended care. And you could reply that extended care usually means custodial care, which insurance doesn't pay for.)

When you are examining nursing home coverage, be sure to take into account the fact that Medicare pays only for admission to a skilled nursing facility after a minimum of three days of hospitalization. There may not even be any skilled nursing facilities in your area (check with the Medicare office in your state). And if there is, there may be a long waiting list. Even in an SNF, you will not be covered by Medicare or most insurance policies if all you require is custodial care. There aren't too many illnesses that will last for a really extended period without going from the acute illness to the custodial care level. Medicare's rule of thumb is that unless medical treatment is improving your condition, it is custodial care. I emphasize Medicare's position because most of the health insurance policies you can buy use Medicare's definitions. By definition, therefore, they eliminate custodial care, and you could find yourself up a creek without a paddle, not covered equally by Medicare and your expensive private insurance, just when you need help most.

When you bring up some of these questions, do not accept oral assurances that all is taken care of; request that areas you find ambiguous or unclear be spelled out in writing from the company.

It may be that the major medical insurance you have been able to convert from your on-the-job insurance will cover the area of extended illnesses. Before paying for a Medicare supplement policy that is expensive just because it offers this particular benefit, make sure you aren't duplicating coverage you already have. If you don't have major medical before you reach sixty-five, you will have trouble getting it.

COVERAGE ABROAD

One benefit provided by the Blues but not by AARP is coverage outside the United States. Seniors who travel fairly often would probably want this benefit. AARP coverage abroad is based on Medicare coverage in the United States. Medicare coverage abroad, except in a few special situations, is nonexistent.

The fact that Blues policies are generally highly recommended should not lull you into a false sense of security; some are good and some are not so good. New York City Blues used to have one of the best Medicare supplement policies, as Connecticut Blues freely admitted. At the time of writing, individual New York Blue Shield does not cover doctor office visits; the only coverage is for hospital-related doctor bills. This is a very big unfilled gap, and Connecticut Blues now offer much better all-around coverage. Policies are changed so often, however, that you cannot take it for granted this will be true months from now. The only sensible way to buy a policy is to compare it with other policies when you are ready to buy.

13

Medicare Scams and
How to Spot Them

It seems like adding insult to injury when something as difficult as buying health insurance is made even more so by dishonest practices. Unfortunately, however, there is no doubt that scams exist in the marketing of health insurance, especially health insurance targeted for the elderly.

In 1978 Senator Lawton Chiles, conducting a hearing before the Special Committee on Aging to look into abuses connected with Medigap policies, said, "I was distressed to hear from consumers and state insurance commissioners that many older Americans were clearly being taken advantage of by unscrupulous insurance agents eager to make high commissions.

"We were also distressed to hear that in some cases insurance company policies encourage oversale and misrepresentation of health insurance policies to the elderly—while the insurance company at the same time does not take the responsibility for its own agents. . . ."

In the House of Representatives, the House Select Committee on Aging described the same situation (also in 1978) as "a colossal racket." Representative Claude Pepper of Florida, known for his lifelong work for the elderly, said, "We have found that many unscrupulous insurance agents have been preying on the fears of the elderly and selling them three, four, five and sometimes as many as thirty different policies." These scams were not perpetrated only on the poor and illiterate; the thirty policies were found to have been sold to the mother of a judge. According to the House committee, more than half of the commercial Medicare supplement policies had a loss ratio of less than 50 percent.

Today, in spite of federal and state legislation that protects the consumer of Medigap policies, scams still exist. The buyer must be careful not to be tricked into falling for them.

THE AARP SCAM

A recent item in the AARP *Bulletin* is headlined: "Members Urged to Shun, Report, Insurance Scams." The item continues, "The Association has been receiving an increasing number of complaints about insurance agents who claim to represent the AARP Group Health Insurance Program, particularly in such areas as Florida, Texas, Oklahoma, Utah and Washington State."

Since AARP policies are offered by mail and never through agents, members can easily identify fraudulent claims by those who say they are agents. The problem is that not everyone realizes this, and many are favorably impressed by claims of an AARP connection. This particular scam is usually initiated by a phone call from someone purporting to be an authorized agent selling policies on behalf of the AARP Group Health Insurance Program. The sales approach is usually high pressure, and the salesperson is charismatic and convincing. Once you know there is no such animal as an AARP insurance salesperson, you cannot be conned.

A variation on this scam is the agent who claims to be from the federal government; some have even claimed to be from Medicare itself. Naturally if you believe this you are sure that any policy sold by such a person would have to be a good deal. Of course, the truth is that neither the federal government nor any part of it has insurance policies for sale. The closest thing to it is Medicare, and only your local Social Security office and your state Medicare offices have anything to do with it. You can be sure they will not be knocking on your door trying to sell you insurance.

THE FAKE MEDIGAP POLICY SCAM

Now that most states (Rhode Island is an exception) have passed at least some consumer-protection laws regulating Medicare supplement policies, a policy that clearly identifies itself as a Medicare supplement policy is probably going to be all right. (It may not be your best buy, but at least it will be in the ballpark.) If it calls itself something else but is being sold to you as this kind of policy, it may or may not be all right. For instance, Blue Cross of California has one it calls Senior Care, and National Home Life Assurance Co. has one called Secure Care Plus. These are perfectly bona fide policies, and the catchy names are probably just an attempt to stand out from the crowd; they are not intended to deceive and are completely trustworthy. But not all companies are that careful, and salespeople are even more liable to push a policy as a Medicare supplement policy when it falls far short of that type of policy. Be wary of policies with cute names and take two precautions if you have any doubts: (1) Check to make sure the policies are approved for sale in your state, and (2) see if the policies are being sold by a company you know and if the state has had any complaints about the company or the policies.

THE SCARE TACTIC SCAM

Scaring people seems to be a very successful way of selling health insurance. It is especially effective with elderly people who worry not only about the financial costs of a serious illness but also about becoming a burden to their children. The elderly person often doesn't tell the children what he or she is doing, and the salesperson worms in and proceeds to sell innumerable unneeded policies, duplicating coverage the person already has (a practice called loading up). One such agent was found to have sold a sixty-seven-year-old woman seventeen different insurance policies over a two-year period; 68 percent of her entire annual income was being used to pay premiums on these worthless policies. Since insurance companies will not pay benefits that are covered by another policy you already have, there is no way you can benefit by falling for this scam.

So-called dread-disease policies, though sometimes sold by legitimate companies, are looked upon by many consumer activists as falling into the scare-tactic category. The consumer should know better than to buy such limited protection, but some words, like *cancer,* scare people so much they rush to buy insurance that will cover such a terrible contingency. The fault with these policies lies not in any hidden trickery but in the fact that the coverage provided is extremely limited (to one disease); usually much broader protection (for many diseases) can be acquired for the same or practically the same premium. Accident policies sold at airports fall into the same category, in that they are overpriced compared to a regular accident policy and their payoff is poor compared to regular policies.

They are sold as impulse purchases to people who are perhaps afraid of flying and are usually bought just before boarding a plane. If you find yourself tempted by these policies, talk to your agent about a full-fledged accident policy that will cover you for all flights—not just one— and for other transportation as well.

THE CLEAN-SHEETING SCAM

Now that most Medicare supplement policies must limit preexisting exclusions to a six-month period, the consumer stands a better chance of being covered for the illnesses most liable to occur. There is one loophole, however, that the company can still use to avoid paying claims, and that is an accusation that you have been less than forthcoming (or even downright dishonest) about your medical record. The basis for this is what you put down on your application. Without detailing every sniffle, it is advisable to be fairly accurate. Insurance companies have an excellent health record data base and a central data bank that they share. If you have been hospitalized or have had various other kinds of treatment, it may already be a matter of record. As long as you have had no medical treatment (including filling a prescription at the drugstore) for the six months, you should then be covered. But if you have not disclosed an illness, the whole policy could be voided.

Most people hate to fill out forms, and the nice young person who is the agent may offer to fill out the application for you ("And all you'll have to do is sign it"). The problem arises when you are honest but the agent is not. He may know that certain illnesses may mean you will not be eligible for the policy or will result in permanent exclusions that will not be acceptable to you. In order to make the sale, he may deliberately leave these illnesses out of the application, thus giving you a "clean sheet." If you don't check the application carefully, you may sign it without realizing it is inaccurate. When you file a claim and the company finds out your application was incomplete, you will lose the policy.

Some companies check the application when it comes in, but some wait until you file a claim. In the latter case you may go along for years thinking you have coverage you really don't have.

If, when you check the filled-out form, you notice a discrepancy in the way the application has been filled out, insist it be corrected no matter how much the agent says no one will know and it's just between the two of you.

Don't let him fill it out in pencil.

Ideally, ask to keep it for a couple of days and meanwhile make a copy for your files (complete with your signature and the date). Put a line across any blank spaces. You will then have a record in case changes are made in the application after it leaves your hands.

THE "BETTER" POLICY SCAM

Policies change so often these days that it is possible yours is out of date and could be better. You should look over all your policies every so often and listen if your regular agent suggests you might want to make a change.

Be careful, however, to change for a good reason and to know the disadvantages. Some agents make a good business out of getting their customers to switch policies every time the six-month pre-existing clause is used up. In other words, just when the customer would begin to be covered for the pre-existing condition, the agent switches the buyer to a new policy and the six months begin all over again. Some companies love this because it increases the odds that they will never have to pay a claim for the illnesses you are most liable to get.

How to Size Up an Insurance Agent

There are some ways to help you decide whether an agent who comes to sell you a policy is bona fide.

1. *Ask for the agent's business card.* It should have the company's name, address, and phone number and the agent's name. It may also have a local number where you can reach the salesperson out of office hours. If the information on the card is sketchy, ask for more and write it down. If you have any reason to be suspicious, phone the company number when the agent leaves. (This won't protect you completely; there are dishonest companies as well as dishonest salespeople, but there are not so many of them.)

2. *Ask for proof of licensing by your state.* If the agent puts you off, saying he or she forgot to bring it or lost it or some such excuse, you can later check out both the salesperson and the company with the state insurance commission.

3. *Ask the agent to come when you can have a friend present.* If the salesperson prefers to see you alone, don't waste your time.

Good agents are a little like doctors; they are reluctant to bad-mouth other companies. Sometimes, however, they will drop hints, and you may be able to avoid a bad mistake if you can get one to tell you what companies to avoid altogether.

4. *Always pay with a check made out to the company.* Never pay in cash or make out the check to an individual. This is not common trade practice and is one of the surest indications that something is wrong.
5. *Tell the salesperson you want to talk to other agents,* or you at least want to think about it. Most insurance agents are pretty hard sell; it's a tough business. But there is a limit, and there is a difference between urging you and trying to bully you. What you are looking for is a truly helpful agent, not one who just wants to make the sale whether or not the policy is right for you. You may be sympathetic to an enthusiastic salesperson who seems to truly believe in what he or she is selling, but most agents don't really know about other companies' policies and aren't really in a position to compare what they are selling with what else is out there. You will have to find out for yourself.

V

THE UBIQUITOUS
BLUES—
BLUE CROSS/BLUE SHIELD

14

Looking Behind the Blue Label

Most people are surprised to learn that Blue Cross/Blue Shield is not a single company but rather a kind of trade association to which a number of autonomous companies belong. On discovering this the consumer might then assume that the Blues are a kind of franchise operation, each individually owned but with the right to use a common name and trademark, with rules and regulations formulated by a parent company and with a strictly predetermined uniformity. The consumer is used to Holiday Inns and McDonald's operations, where "no surprises" is the norm and the menu and ambiance will be the same in Los Angeles as in Podunk. No matter where a Howard Johnson restaurant is located, for example, the experienced traveler can always head directly for the rest rooms. As soon as you come in the door, you recognize the layout as one of several standard floor plans and know, therefore, where the rest rooms are located. This engenders a sense of security, and the lack of excitement and novelty are more than made up for by the assurance of knowing exactly what will be found inside. McDonald's may not offer haute cuisine, but wherever the McDonald's arch rises, the consumer can look forward to the familiar french

155

fries and other specialties associated with that name.

Imagine, however, that McDonald's suddenly changed its way of operating so that you might unwittingly walk into one that offered only Mexican dishes, while another specialized in Italian and a third served the traditional hamburgers. The name and the physical restaurant might look the same, but they would not be a guarantee of what you might find within. This is closer to the situation of the consumer trying to buy insurance under the Blue Cross/Blue Shield label.

Blue Cross/Blue Shield is one of the largest and best-known purveyors of health insurance in the United States; its policies can be bought and used nationwide. But it consists of not one but ninety-eight locally governed, autonomous corporations held together loosely in a nationwide federation but operating independently of one another. In spite of their independent operation, until recently all Blues have had certain characteristics in common, such as nonprofit status, and are generally given the same privileges by all the states. It used to be that Blue Cross/Blue Shield was always a nonprofit organization, but even that is changing; today more and more Blues are turning themselves into for-profit companies.

At the heart of the Blues' system is their relationship with hospitals. All the Blues function primarily by establishing contracts with "participating" hospitals, under which they pay negotiated fixed fees for services rendered to subscribers. A subscriber's Blue Cross premium means that almost all hospital costs are covered; there are no out-of-pocket payments for covered services. It is this arrangement that qualifies the Blues to be called *prepaid* health care providers. Through this arrangement they are able to provide broad hospital coverage, usually at a lower cost than commercial insurers. They are different, however, from health maintenance organizations, which also offer prepaid health care (although this difference is being blurred by the fact that some Blues now have a relationship with HMOs).

True Blues

In addition to their contracts with hospitals, the Blues have attempted—not nearly so successfully—to establish contracts with area physicians and other health care providers. Their unique relationship with hospitals remains their unusual feature, but they have recently stepped up efforts to enlist the medical profession.

It is interesting to note the extent to which the Blues have successfully carved out a very special niche for themselves in the highly competitive insurance field. The foundation of their success is still their unique relationship with the hospitals, which may not survive some of the present trends toward hospital cost-containment legislation. Meanwhile, however, the industry is still strongly battling the Blues.

The New England Insurance Times, on March 27, 1984, ran an item under the heading "True Blues" that illustrates the problems commercial insurers have with the favored status of the Blues. It began, "In a move which has commercial health insurers up in arms and concerned over their own survival and that of the state's cost containment law, Blue Cross of Massachusetts is seeking a 23 percent discount on the charges it must pay for hospital services. Blue Cross says it is entitled to the sizable break because it saves hospitals money and spares them from a lot of bad debt."

Pointing out that Blue Cross currently controls about 60 percent of the market, it goes on: "If the discount is allowed, Blue Cross will be handed an even greater monopoly in the marketplace and others will have to pick up the costs left behind." The reference to "others" refers to the possibility that hospitals will tack on what they lose in the discounted charges to patients not covered by Blue Cross and therefore subject to higher prices. Since hospitals routinely add charges for unused hospital beds to their bills, this kind of bookkeeping is entirely possible. The article claims that approval of the requested differential would have "the effect of maintaining the unjustified historical cost-shifting to commercial insurers and self-paying patients," and would increase the cost to these patients by 15 to 20 percent.

Elizabeth J. Connell, president of Life Insurance Association of Massachusetts, which represents the state's fourteen domestic insurers, stated, "We believe it runs counter to responsible public policy to grant a billion-dollar tax-exempt enterprise, already controlling three-quarters of the private health insurance business in Massachusetts, a monopoly."

Part of the reason the timing is right for this move is the increasing feeling among legislators and consumers that health care costs must be prevented from further escalation. More and more doctors are coming to realize that they are being targeted as one of the key factors in rising costs; both hospitals and doctors are under fire, and hospitals are already being subjected to cost containment in many areas.

In 1984 Blue Cross/Blue Shield of Connecticut published a 136-page book, distributed free to its subscribers, called *Directory of Participating Physicians and Providers*. An accompanying letter states, "The directory lists over 5,000 health care providers, dentists, pharmacists, physical therapists, optometrists and hospitals. What makes these providers unique is that they have agreed to accept Blue Cross and Blue Shield payment as full reimbursement for covered services for members enrolled in contracts such as the 'Century' medical/surgical contract, 'Semi-private' hospitalization plan, 'Full Service' prescription drug program, and 'Full Service' dental plan. This means millions of dollars of savings for our 1.5 million members across the state."

While this may be viewed as a step toward savings, it is hardly a giant step. For one thing, the directory isn't much use to the individual subscriber. I called the Blues and asked if the plans mentioned were all group plans.

"Oh no," the pleasant person on the other end assured me. "Not at all." I said I had a Comprehensive 20 policy; was that covered?

"Well, no."

"Well, then, maybe I should switch to one of the policies that is?"

There was a short silence. "I wouldn't recommend it. The Comp 20 policy pays 80 percent of reasonable and customary charges."

"How do those charges compare with the fee schedule the *Directory* doctors have agreed to?"

"It's higher."

I thought a minute. "What about the Century contract?"

"That doesn't offer hospital coverage, so we wouldn't recommend it to someone who had no other coverage."

"And the other policies?"

"Well, the Semi-Private hospitalization plan is available only to someone converting from a group policy. And the Full Service prescription drug program is only for groups."

"What about the dental plan?"

"That's only for groups too."

So in spite of assurances to the contrary, except for one plan "not recommended," all the other policies were group or group-related. This is typical of what is happening to nongroup individuals in search of good, affordable coverage.

The directory lists physicians by specialty and by geographical location as well as alphabetically. Not surprisingly, affluent Fairfield County, especially towns like Westport, tended to have the fewest participating physicians, in spite of the fact that it has a high physician-to-patient ratio. Not a single Fairfield County anesthesiologist chose to participate.

In contrast, the directory also lists participating general hospitals, alcohol treatment facilities, rehabilitation centers, home health agencies, and similar facilities; all the major ones are participating.

How long this directory will be in effect is also a question. In March, three months after the issuing date of the Connecticut directory, a U.S. District Court ruled that Massachusetts Blue Shield's practice of prohibiting doctors from billing patients for charges in excess of what Blue Shield pays them is an antitrust violation and "must be halted." According to *The New England Insurance Times* (March 27, 1984), "The court said the practice has prevented doctors from competing on prices . . . [and] the insurer's position in the marketplace places heavy pressure on doctors to participate and accept Blue Shield's lower prices."

The *Times* article states that Blue Shield pays about 30 percent less than doctors actually charge and that this "balance billing" requires doctors to accept the Blue Shield payments as payment in full. If Blue Shield loses this round, it has threatened to take the matter to the Supreme Court. While a decision against Blue Cross would undoubtedly raise subscriber rates, it would have an even greater effect on Medicare beneficiaries in those New England states where Blue Cross is strongest. At present those states are among the highest in percentage of doctors who accept the Medicare "assignment," and this is widely viewed as the result of the pressure that Blue Shield can bring to bear. If this power is weakened, it is possible that the assignment rate—as high as 90 percent (percent of doctors' accepting assignment) in some states—may drop to less than the 50 percent that is presently the nationwide average.

From the health care consumer's point of view, a favorable aspect of the Blues is their excellent loss ratio; they pay an average of 92 cents in benefits for every premium dollar—a 92 percent loss ratio. No insurance company can match that, and even states that have minimum standards usually require no more than 65 percent or 70 percent.

The reason that is given for the Blues' loss ratio being so much higher than that of other health insurance companies is their unique position under the law. Since 1934, when a special enabling act was passed in New York State, the Blues have been granted nonprofit status, which exempts them from state and federal income taxes and grants them various other privileges and exemptions, such as exemption from the need to maintain policy reserves.

In spite of this advantageous situation, there is some indication that the Blues organizations would prefer for-profit status. A move has been under way in Detroit, for example, to get the state's permission for such a change. Among the reasons cited is the fact that the Blues are limited, under their present status, in the types of insurance they may offer. They say they would like to be free to go into other types of policies and clearly feel that the resultant profits would more than offset the taxes that would then have to be paid. Presently seven or eight of the Blues corporations are allowed to sell life insurance policies. At this time a bill has been approved in the Connecticut legislature's Income and Real Estate Committee that would permit the Connecticut Blues to become a mutual insurance company. Under the provisions of this bill, Blue Cross will split into two companies: Blue Cross Mutual Insurance Company, to sell accident and health policies, and Constitution Mutual Life Insurance Company, to sell life insurance. To reduce resistance from commercial insurers, Blue Cross Mutual will relinquish its negotiated hospital discounts. This have-its-cake-and-eat-it-too goal would require Blue Cross Mutual to pay all state taxes but would still allow it to be exempt from federal taxes. (This is similar to what has already been agreed to in the seven other instances where Blue Cross companies have converted to mutual companies.) Constitution Life would pay both state and federal taxes. The only limitation on the new companies is that they would not be permitted to sell property-casualty or workers' compensation policies.

The difficulty up to now has been that commercial insurance companies resent this attempt by the Blues to muscle in on their business and—just as savings banks and commercial banks both want it all—each is fighting attempted expansion by the other. The situation is further complicated because the Blues are working hard to retain some of their favored status and still be allowed greater freedom.

There are signs, however, that the commercial insurers are learning to live with the idea of being joined by Blues companies. Michael Menotti, counsel for the Insurance Association of Connecticut, was quoted in the *New England*

Insurance News as saying the Connecticut bill will make the health insurance industry "more competitive." Agents, who have been selling about half the Blue Cross group health policies without receiving commissions, would benefit from the change (although they worry that they might lose on the life insurance side of the market). The consumer would, as usual, be the real loser, since premiums undoubtedly would be higher under the new system. If you keep an eye on the bills in legislation in your state, you will at least be aware of developments that may affect your health care coverage and your pocketbook.

HOW DO THE BLUES WORK?

As with all insurance, the basis of the Blues premiums and coverage is statistical. With health care statistics, it is possible to predict very closely how many cases of any given illness or injury will occur per thousand families. If the statistics are accurate—and they have proved to be over many years—the premiums paid by a large number of subscribers will be more than sufficient to cover all claims, even very large ones such as the expenses associated with bypass surgery. In all insurance, the many healthy subscribers help pay for the coverage of the comparatively few ill ones. Since there is no way of knowing in which group you or your family will fall, this is fair and equitable; at the very least it means peace of mind.

There exists, however, a strong feeling in some areas that the exorbitant costs of hospitalization are due in part to the symbiotic relationship between Blue Cross and the hospitals. Instead of using its influence to contain these costs, it has been charged that Blue Cross has been in effect giving the hospitals a blank check. Although the states could theoretically oversee this area on behalf of their citizens, this has seldom been attempted. When Blue

Unfair Play

In May 1983 the New York State Insurance Commission approved a rate increase in monthly Blue Cross premiums of 16.5 to 21.8 percent. This affected more than 4 million individual and small-group subscribers of Blue Cross and Blue Shield of Greater New York and 730,000 Medicare beneficiaries. Notably unaffected by this rate increase were the large group subscribers, all 5.5 million workers covered by health-benefit plans in large companies.

Blue Cross justified this increase by citing a recent 3 percent surcharge, which had been imposed on it and other health insurers, to help pay for care for the uninsured poor. (Not being an accountant, I am somewhat puzzled as to how a 3 percent surcharge can be a "major factor" in a 21 percent increase, but maybe some of my more knowledgeable readers can figure it out.)

In a *New York Times* news item on the subject, John Burns of Blue Cross is quoted as saying, "The increase we have been given is an unfortunate outcome

Cross asks for permission for a rate increase, it has more often than not been granted without detailed scrutiny of the rationale that justifies it. In 1969, for example, when subscribers in New York State went to court to protest increases in premiums averaging 33 percent, the court affirmed the rate increase, citing the financial needs of Blue Cross, but castigated the insurance commissioner (whose job it was to ascertain the accuracy of the figures on which the request was based), saying, "Both Blue Cross and the Superintendent seem intent on adopting the notion that no matter how costly operations become, for whatever reasons, eventually and inevitably [Blue Cross] subscribers of that program, and we are compelled to pass it on to our subscribers. We are being asked to help subsidize the burden of caring for the poor." No word as to who was "compelling" Blue Cross or that many of those being asked to shoulder this burden were almost poor themselves (the elderly on fixed incomes and the individual subscriber who is generally in poorer circumstances than the salaried worker with the security of large-group insurance through on-the-job coverage). And, although he said *we,* the insurance companies were, in fact, not taking on any part of the "burden." It is unlikely that soaking the near-poor was the original intent of the legislation to aid the poor, but nevertheless that is how it was implemented.

This increase of costs for the individual subscriber was by no means a first. In 1980 the state granted an approximately 18 percent increase, and in 1982 an additional 19.5 percent was imposed on the beleaguered subscriber.

will shoulder the load. Small wonder that subscriber rates have increased 124% in the past five years."

The relationship between the Blues and the hospitals is more easily understood if one knows the history of the Blues.

During 1929 and 1930, the Depression hit hospitals with falling receipts—from $236.12 per patient to $59.26. At the same time more and more patients were unable to pay even these smaller bills. The American Hospital Association (AHA) realized that some mechanism was needed to enable the consumer to meet the costs of hospital care and to assure the hospitals that they would receive payment for services rendered. Health insurance did not exist, and the United States then, as now, had no national health plan. In 1929, however, Dr. Justin Ford Kimball, who was executive vice-president of Baylor University in Dallas, Texas, discovered that the university's medical facilities were carrying unpaid bills incurred by local schoolteachers. He conceived the idea of reducing his accounts receivables and ensuring that this situation would not arise in the future by getting 1,250 of the teachers to join a program of prepaid health care. Under this plan, each teacher would pay 50¢ a month. In return they would be insured for twenty-one days of hospitalization in a semiprivate room at the Baylor University Hospital. This $6 annual premium was good for care only at the one hospital. The idea caught on, however, and soon groups throughout the nation were being formed along the same lines, with the blessings of the American Hospital Association, which in 1933 entered the picture to resolve a legal tangle that had arisen in connection with the applicability of insurance laws to this new type of plan. By 1936 the AHA had obtained money from the Rosenwald Fund to finance a Committee on Hospital Service, charged with establishing standards for nonprofit hospital care plans. Dr. C. Rufus Rorem, associate director of the Julius Rosenwald Fund, became the committee's first executive director; under his guidance fourteen standards were established in 1938. One of the standards was the requirement that any such plan had to have the approval of the AHA.

The AHA and the committee, with the support of the New York United Hospital Fund, with its influential civic leaders and other key citizens, succeeded in getting the first hospital service plan enabling act through the New York State Legislature. This act established the favored status under which the Blues function today.

As similar plans arose throughout the nation, certain changes occurred; coverage was no longer limited to a single hospital, and the AHA gave the plan permission to use the association symbol, the blue cross, in 1939, just ten years after the idea was first conceived.

Blue Shield, on the other hand, grew from pioneer programs of county medical prepayment bureaus, which arose shortly before the turn of the century in the Northwest. The first actual Blue Shield–type plan was called California Physicians Service and was founded in 1939.

Historically, therefore, Blue Cross primarily covered hospital expenses; Blue Shield mostly covered physicians' services. They are still separate organizations, although they operate in different ways in different states. In some states, for instance, they are two corporations under a single management. In others they are joint corporations, or they may simply share office space and conduct joint enrollment and billing. Sometimes, as separate organizations, they may actually compete with each other in overlapping benefits. Fortunately, the Blue Cross and Blue Shield Association, a national organization, exists as a coordinating agency that works with both plans.

Blue Cross has always maintained its close ties with the American Hospital Association and has operated with the support and trust of the hospitals. Blue Cross negotiates with participating hospitals so that it pays discounted prices for hospital services, which makes it theoretically possible for the Blues to charge less for better coverage. This puts commercial companies that pay the undiscounted charges at a disadvantage. Recently, however, commercial companies have been trying to negotiate discounts for their own policies, and it seems likely that something along those lines will be worked out. So far Blue Cross, which insures about 60 percent of the insured population of the United States, has been successful in maintaining its favored status. Now, as we have seen earlier, the Blues themselves are looking for a change, so the whole structure of health insurance in the United States will undoubtedly be quite different within the next decade.

Under the circumstances, it is not surprising that Blue Cross seems to have played a minor role in health care cost containment, although in recent years it has instituted studies of coverage of second opinions and similar ideas in an effort to reduce hospital utilization and increase efficiency. Unfortunately, the Blues, along with all health insurance, encourage an escalation of costs by their ability to pay charges that would be beyond the means of the individual. Through the enrollment of millions of healthy Americans in these programs, the many not only contribute to the health care of the few, but they do it on a scale that none of them could afford singly. And, unlike a national health care plan, this is done with very little control over profits, waste, and inefficiency. As costs escalate, they are passed on to the health care consumer in more and more frequent rate increases.

THE BLUE CROSS/BLUE SHIELD ASSOCIATION

The association is the Blues' spokesman on matters of national concern. Like any association, it initiates and coordinates programs of public education and professional relations. It works with the Blues on cost containment, and it collects and provides research, statistical, actuarial, marketing, and other information. In addition, it maintains a computerized telecommunication system that links all the state organizations.

One of the most important functions the association performs is in the area of group health insurance. Employers who have plans and offices in more than one state would not be able to offer their employees standard health insurance coverage if they had to take into account the differences among the policies of the various Blues. To reach this lucrative market, the Blues nationwide work with the association to coordinate health policies, so that all the various independent corporations will agree on the premiums and coverage for a given group policy. This complicated negotiation must take place every time a union changes its health care coverage requirements.

The ability to design a health care policy that all the many independent corporations will agree to has led to an enormous expansion of the Blues' influence. Presently, for example, the association is the prime contractor for the Blue Cross organization's administration of Medicare's Part A or hospital insurance. It also coordinates other federal and state health programs. No Medicare beneficiary can be unaware of Blue Cross/Blue Shield, and this has made it highly visible in an area in which there are over one thousand commercial companies competing for the health insurance market. In Oklahoma alone, over 600 companies are licensed to sell health insurance; many of the names are far from memorable, and the Blues have a decided edge.

BLUES PLANS VS. THOSE OF FOR-PROFIT COMPANIES

If you travel out of the country at all, you will immediately notice that the Blues' coverage operates even when you are abroad. It has affiliated plans in Canada, Jamaica, and England, but regardless of where you have bought your plan, you are covered anywhere on the globe. This is very unusual and means that the elderly or someone not in the best of health can travel with a degree of security not otherwise possible. I recently checked to make sure that this coverage was really available, using a trip to Mexico for my query. I was told that coverage was universal but that in a non–English-speaking country, it would be helpful if I got the bills translated before I returned to the United States.

With a Blues policy, your hospitalization will probably be covered in full for approved services, from the day you enter until the day you are discharged, providing you have not used up your coverage or your maximum. The relaxed attitude of the hospital's business office when you are admitted with Blue Cross coverage is proof of the good relationship this organization has with hospitals. Blues never pay cash to you for any covered hospital services; payment is always made directly to the hospital, according to the contract the organization has with that particular hospital. If you should be so conscientious as to check the itemization of your hospital bill and to report an overcharge or charges for services you did not receive, you may find— as I did—that Blue Cross will not even respond to your letter of notification. If you wonder what difference it makes as long as Blue Cross takes care of the bill and asks no payment from you, think back to this incident the next time your premium rises.

Payment for physicians' services is supposed to work the same way, but doctors are less likely to agree to a prepaid arrangement and discounted fees. In that event your Blue Shield policy will pay the approved charge directly to you, and you will have to work it out with your doctor. Some doctors will not accept payments from any insurance company because they do not want to be held to the schedule of charges those companies pay. This makes matters difficult for the careful health care shopper, since it is often impossible to get a copy of the fee schedule from the insurance company so you have no way of knowing how big the gap is between what the insurance pays and what the doctor charges before you are hit with a bill.

Although not all hospitals have a contract arrangement with the Blues, you are usually free to choose any approved hospital you wish, even if it is not a participating hospital.

Another difference between the Blues and other policies is that they are widely available, regardless of age or health. They will accept the "poor risks" that other companies would turn down, and they do not cancel coverage when you become seriously ill or if you file a large number of claims.

Like other insurance companies, the Blues offer both group and individual policies (as usual, the individual subscriber pays more for less coverage) and allow conversion from group to individual policies if you change or lose your job. When you reach age sixty-five, the Blues have Medicare supplemental policies, usually with a high and low option to choose from.

Blues policies always provide for "coordination of benefits." This clause in your policy means that you will not be paid by two companies for the same charge; they will work out which one pays but only one will pay. If, therefore, you have overlapping benefits in two policies, you are paying for coverage on which you cannot collect.

Commercial companies, on the other hand, often omit this clause from their Medicare supplement policies. In this event, you can collect from both policies for the same charge. If, for instance, you have a doctor bill for $100 and file it with both companies and both policies pay, you may pay the doctor and keep the second $100 for yourself. This kind of double dipping is prohibited in group policies but is perfectly legal in individual Medicare supplement policies that do not prohibit it. Do not assume that this is a great way to augment your income, because you will have to pay a hefty annual sum in premiums, all on the gamble that you will collect enough in claims to make it worthwhile. That is betting against yourself, since it is to your interest not to get ill and not to have claims to collect on. If, however, you decide that you need two policies that have some overlapping benefits in order to get the coverage you want, the possibility of collecting twice may take some of the sting out of paying two premiums.

HOW DO THE BLUES POLICIES DIFFER?

The only answer to that is, greatly. For example, in New York City there is a group policy that actually has made contractual arrangements with a number of physicians who have agreed to participate. On the other hand, in New York State the Blues Medicare supplement policy available to individuals covers hospital bills but not bills for physicians' office visits. Connecticut's Blues Medicare supplement policy does cover physicians' office visits.

Not only do Blues policies vary from state to state, they also vary within the states and within each company through the various policies that are offered. When Consumers' Union did an article on Medicare supplement policies in June 1984, they compared thirty-two policies in detail; eighteen of them were either Blue Cross or Blue Cross/Blue Shield. They included two Blue Cross/Blue Shield policies from Massachusetts, five Blue Cross policies from California, one Blue Cross policy from western Pennsylvania, one from southwest Ohio, one from Greater Philadelphia, two from Maryland, one Blue Cross/Blue Shield from Greater New York, one from Florida, two from Illinois, and two from New Jersey.

Since there are ninety-eight Blue Cross/Blue Shield corporations in the United States, there are obviously an incredible number of permutations and variations of policies, premiums, options, benefits, and limitations. You are theoretically eligible only for the policies offered in the state in which you reside. In practice, however, you may have group Blues coverage at your job, which may be in a different state (as when a Connecticut resident works in New York or Massachusetts). If you change jobs, you may be able to convert your policy to an individual policy in the state in which you work rather than where you live. If this is allowed, check out both states and see which offers the better coverage (be sure to compare premiums, too). If you decide to switch to your home state, this can be done without a waiting period and without any gap in coverage during the changeover.

It is necessary, however, to know the ropes. A Connecticut resident who wished to switch a Medicare supplement policy from New York called the New York office to find out what the procedure was. He was told that he could switch but that he would have to wait three months before he could change over. He had just paid his advance quarterly payment but the new quarter had not begun. Upon protesting that he wanted to change right away because he had just found out the New York policy didn't cover physician office visits, he was told it wasn't possible for him to change until the next quarter. He continued to argue that he was being held captive for an additional three months and that he would complain to the New York State Insurance Commission, whereupon the telephone person said that if he really wanted to change immediately (as he had been insisting for the past fifteen minutes), he would in that case have to request the change in writing. And if he did so, it was essential that he actually state he wished the change to be effective immediately. Without the key word *immediately,* the change would be made at the end of the next quarterly period. Needless to say, the required letter went out, along with a complaint to the commissioner, and the matter took only thirty days instead of three months. (See following information on The Captive Subscriber.)

The Captive Subscriber

Following the conversation described in the text concerning switching from New York to Connecticut Blues, and subsequent to a written complaint to the New York State Insurance Commission, the subscriber received the following letter:

Dear Mr. [X]:

We were contacted by the State of New York Insurance Department concerning your coverage with us.

May we begin by explaining that each Blue Cross and Blue Shield Plan is a separate, financially independent corporation. However, we do maintain an Inter-Plan Agreement whereby subscribers may transfer to their local Plan if their subscription charges are paid in advance. [Mr. X: Why do I have to pay in advance for a policy I am cancelling?]

When you called us about transferring your Medicare Plus coverage to Blue Cross and Blue Shield of Connecticut, your charges were not paid sufficiently in advance for transfer in accordance with the Inter-Plan Agreement. [Mr. X: What do they mean by "sufficiently"? My next quarterly payment wasn't even due yet. Also, how come they never say specifically how much advance notice they require?] Therefore, we could only advise you to remit your next quarterly payment if you wished to transfer. [Mr. X: Blackmail?] Your remittance has been applied to your coverage from November

1, 1983, to February 1, 1984. [Mr. X: Aha! This is a cute way of getting three-months' premium out of me; my request was made in October and I wanted to transfer to Connecticut in October, not in February. Suppose I incurred doctor bills—not covered by New York Blues—in the meantime?]

Since you have requested immediate transfer, we are sending information to the Connecticut Plan for the transfer of your coverage as of December 1, 1983. [Mr. X: Okay, they dragged their heels so I lost November, but at least I gained two months by latching on to the magic word *immediate*.] A refund of the subscription charges you remitted for coverage from December 1, 1983, to February 1, 1984, will be sent as soon as our records can be adjusted.

It's true that when a subscriber who is paid in advance requests transfer, he will be transferred as of his paid-to date unless there is a specific request for immediate transfer. [Mr. X: Not true except technically. I said I wanted to be transferred right away and that certainly is equivalent to *immediately* in anyone's lexicon—except apparently the New York Blues'.] Please be assured that we do not "obstruct transfers to any other states" or "subvert the best interests of the consumer," as you state. Rather, our procedures are in accordance with the Inter-Plan Agreement [Mr. X: I'd like to see that sometime] and allow the time necessary for the processing of the transfer by both the Plans involved. [Mr. X: Connecticut had no problem with taking the transfer right away; they said New York was making problems unnecessarily so "both the Plans involved" would not appear to be accurate.]

We hope this clarifies our position. [Mr. X: Not really.]

Sincerely, etc.

The moral is, always find the magic words. Like *immediately*. (My comment: And I always thought they were *please* and *thank you*.)

15

A Comparison of Two Blues Policies

The policies that are offered and the benefits they cover change as often as the weather, so neither of these two examples may be exactly what is offered when you read this book. They will serve to indicate, however, how little the appellation *Blue Cross/Blue Shield* on the cover of the good-looking blue-and-white leaflet tells you about what is inside.

What I am looking at is Medicare Plus, the only Medicare supplement policy offered at this moment by the Blues in New York City and one of two policies offered at this moment by the Connecticut Blues association.

1. *Premium.* Connecticut says apologetically that its policy costs a little more than New York City's $401 (1984 premium). The additional cost is about $25; let us see if it is worth it.
2. *Hospital benefits.* This category deals with Medicare Part A benefits. Both policies pay the hospital deductible and co-insurance from day 1 of hospitalization through day 150 (at which point you will have used up all your Medicare hospital coverage for that benefit period, as well as all your lifetime reserve days).

Once you have used up all your lifetime reserve days, both policies will pay 100 percent of the covered hospital charges for an additional 365 days, to a total of 455 days of hospital coverage.

If you go abroad, Medicare coverage ceases, but both these policies provide some coverage, which is typical of Blue Cross policies. The New York City policy will pay for 90 days of hospitalization abroad; Connecticut will pay for only 30 days.

Coverage of skilled nursing facilities is identical; both cover the co-insurance for days 21 through 100.

It is in the out-of-hospital coverage that important differences arise. The Connecticut policy pays the "approved but not covered" physician and other Part B charges, including office visits. This means, basically, the co-insurance. Unlike some commercial policies, it pays nothing above Medicare's approved charges. There are two Connecticut policies (at this moment) with this coverage; one also pays the Part B deductible, one does not. Since the premium on the one that pays it is higher by just about the amount of the deductible, it doesn't make much sense to buy this coverage. Any year you don't have doctor expenses, you save the cost of the extra premium. When you do have those expenses, the cost is no greater with or without the more expensive policy.

The New York City policy, on the other hand, does not pay anything for doctors' office visits. The only coverage in this area is 20 percent of the bill for surgery and dialysis, in or out of the hospital. Most Medicare beneficiaries are very concerned about coverage of doctor bills, and many of them, on reading the benefits of this policy, did not realize it would not pay such bills.

Another area in which there is less than satisfactory coverage is outpatient and emergency room benefits. Here the coverage is only for the first visit, if no later than 72 hours after accidental injury. This goes against our guidelines for recommended coverage, which say that there should be no differentiation between illness and accident. If one needs emergency room coverage because one is having an asthmatic attack or a heart attack, it apparently would not be covered under this definition, or at least not until you had been admitted on an inpatient basis.

A further difference, also in an area of importance to the elderly, is coverage for prescription drugs. This New York policy has no coverage for prescription drugs. The Connecticut policy, while not outstandingly generous, at least covers up to $500 for 150 days following a hospital admission, not less than 120 days following discharge. Also, each time you start a new benefit period, this coverage again becomes effective. From the beneficiary's standpoint, it would be much better if hospitalization were not necessary to receive this benefit, but it is certainly better this way than not at all.

It becomes clear upon comparison of benefits of the two policies that the Connecticut policy is not really more expensive when what your premium dollar buys is figured into the equation.

It is only fair to mention, on the other side, that this has not always been the case. In the past the Connecticut Blues policies have often been inferior to the New York City Blues, and this may happen again in the future. The point I would like to make is that you cannot buy blindly; only a comparison of costs and benefits will show where your insurance dollar is best spent. It may even be, for instance, that a commercial policy might be better at the time you are ready to make a purchase, or that you might buy two cheaper policies that supplement one another as well as Medicare, rather than one more expensive policy (though generally speaking, one good policy should be enough). There is no way to avoid the chore of filling out checklists and making the comparison.

HOW TO BUY A BLUES POLICY

Buying a Blues policy is no easier—or harder—than buying any other health insurance. All the same rules—open enrollment, for example—apply. If you are eligible for a group policy, first read Part Two on Group Insurance. If you are so unfortunate as to be limited to an individual policy, read the advice in the part of this book devoted to that discussion. Then read the policies offered you, make your chart, add a couple of commercial policies for comparison, and pick your best deal. And if you cannot find an 800 phone number for Blue Cross/Blue Shield in your state, check with your insurance commission; maybe it has switched to for-profit status and is now Mutual something-or-other instead of Blue.

VI

HEALTH MAINTENANCE ORGANIZATIONS— AN ALTERNATIVE

16

The HMO—Theory and Practice

WHAT IS AN HMO?

HMO stands for "health maintenance organization," a form of prepaid health insurance. Prepaid health insurance is entirely different from any other kind of health insurance with which you may be familiar, and you may or may not find it suitable to your situation. Although the concept is not new, it is only in the past decade, with encouragement from the federal government, that it has become more widely available. According to the Health Insurance Association of America (HIAA), the number of HMOs increased from 39 in 1972 to 277 in 1982, and the number of subscribers for the same period increased from 3.5 million to 10.8 million. Obviously, however, 277 HMOs nationwide leaves many areas without access to this kind of health insurance.

HOW DOES AN HMO WORK?

The most obvious difference between an HMO and any other form of health insurance is that with an HMO you pay your health care costs before you incur them, hence *prepaid* insurance. A monthly premium gives you comprehensive coverage of hospital, medical, and prescription drug costs, with little or no additional charges incurred no matter how much you use these services. Say, for example, a man needs a flu shot, his wife has several office visits in connection with a back problem, and one of his children breaks an ankle—all in one month. In many HMOs, his monthly premium will fully cover all these services. In others, he might have to pay a nominal amount—perhaps $1 for an office visit and for each prescription drug filled at the HMO pharmacy. (Since each HMO is different, this is only an example, but all of them operate along the same basic lines.)

TYPES OF HMOs

Although the type of HMO we will be discussing is the so-called staff HMO, there are variations you may encounter. Here is a quick rundown of the differences among them.

A *staff HMO* is the most complete kind, consisting as it does of both physicians in general practice and specialists, and health professionals, such as registered nurses, therapists, social workers, pharmacists, and radiologists; usually with its own building and with a contractual agreement with a local hospital.

An *IPA,* or *individual practice association,* is the medical profession's answer to the threat that some private physicians perceive in the HMO mode. Under this plan, a group of doctors get together and form a loose group that establishes uniform premiums and, to some extent, shares costs. With this system each doctor still maintains and works in an individual office setup, just as with his or her private patients (whom the doctor does not give up). Member patients pay the premium to the HMO, and the individual doctor is compensated on a fee-for-service arrangement. For instance, the physician may set up a fee schedule with the plan and bill the HMO for each visit at the agreed-upon fee. The plan would then pay 80 percent of the fee to the doctor and retain 20 percent as a reserve for administrative and other costs.

With this type, as with staff HMOs, physicians gain financially if they can keep down costs. If the reserve is insufficient to meet costs, participating physicians are assessed an amount to cover them. If the costs are lower than the reserve, the surplus (profit) is distributed among the physicians.

The only advantage this type of plan has over the staff plan is that doctors join it more readily and you are therefore more likely to find your family physician belonging. On the other hand, there is always the danger that a doctor may keep down the amount of service given to HMO patients because he or she knows giving them "excessive" time and treatments will materially affect his or her income. In a profession the practitioners of which are increasingly vocal about medicine being an art, not a science, there is a great deal of leeway in deciding when to provide and when to withhold treatment. A patient would not like to think that economics was influencing the decision.

Although it is not technically an HMO, there is a new wrinkle to group Blue Shield organizations in some communities, New York City among them. With this type of plan, which New York Blue Shield calls *Wrap-Around,* doctors agree to participate in the Blue Shield plan and to hold their fees to members to a negotiated schedule. This arrangement is similar to the one Blue Cross has traditionally had with hospitals and it is apparently working well, since private insurance companies are now moving in the same direction.

It is also possible to come upon local variations of

HMOs. In Washington, D.C., one such plan is called CHOICE. As its name implies, the consumer can choose any physician as the primary care provider. A consumer who requires hospitalization, however, must then become the patient of a "participating" specialist; his or her own doctor cannot admit him. While in the hospital, the patient will be under the care of the specialist (who will write all the orders) and not of the family doctor.

The best HMO from the consumer's standpoint is probably the staff HMO (called by various names, including PPGP, or prepaid group plan), but any type of HMO is worth investigating as a cost-saving way of obtaining health care. An HMO should, at the minimum, cover preventive medicine as well as illness, so that is the first item to check in considering your local option.

Remember that from now on we are discussing only staff HMOs.

COSTS OF HMOs

Costs vary considerably from one section of the country to another, even for the same HMOs. The following examples were compiled for government employees and are based on 1983 figures. It is interesting to note that retirees' premiums are higher than the figures shown; post office employees' premiums are lower.

HMO	CITY	ANNUAL INDIVIDUAL PREMIUM	ANNUAL FAMILY PREMIUM
Kaiser	Dallas	$440	$1,320
Kaiser	Washington, D.C.	590	1,530
PruCare	Nashville	500	1,840
PruCare	Richmond, Va.	660	1,870
PruCare	Chicago	910	1,930

HOW HMOs PROVIDE COMPREHENSIVE SERVICE

Unlike health insurance policies, which pay after the fact on a fee-for-service basis, HMOs pay their health care personnel—physicians, surgeons, nurses, therapists—a regular salary plus adjustments according to a capitation formula (based on year-end profit/loss). It makes no difference how many patients the doctor sees in a day or how long an office visit takes (within reason); the physician's income depends on the overall profitability of the group, not on individual efforts. The HMO knows its approximate income before the fact, because it knows how many members it has (paying the monthly fee) and what its operating costs are. It usually has its own building and a contract with an area hospital to which it sends all its members. The more efficient the HMO is, the more money it and its staff make. Since profits are disbursed on a capitation basis among its staff, everyone works to keep costs down. Theoretically, this operates to the patients' benefit; no unnecessary tests, fewer hospitalizations, no proliferation of unnecessary doctor visits, and greater emphasis on preventive medicine.

A recent study indicates just how much HMO membership may cut down hospital admissions. Done in the Washington, D.C., area, it compared hospitalization of the patients of fee-for-service physicians and patients of Group Health (one of the area's HMOs). The former group had 793 hospital days per thousand (adjusted for age and sex), as against 459 days per thousand for the HMO. (The fee-for-service group were Blue Cross/Blue Shield enrollees.) In addition, the HMO patients were admitted 37 percent less frequently for appendectomies than comparable Blues enrollees, but there was no indication that their health was in any way impaired by the fewer operations.

Other studies have shown hospital utilization by HMO members to be half the rate for persons covered by conventional insurance. In *Never Too Old* (Times Books), the authors (Geri Harrington and Ty Harrington) partly ascribe this to "the detection of illnesses before they become serious enough to require hospitalization. Furthermore, conventional insurance plans often will not pay for diagnostic tests unless they are performed in the hospital, whereas HMOs try to provide as much medical care as possible out of the hospital."

WHO CAN JOIN?

Theoretically, anyone of any age or state of health can join. An HMO is supposed to be open to everyone and not to turn away a person because of poor health. This has not always been the case. In December 1980 a packet from the Connecticut Health Plan included a sheet headed "HEALTH STANDARDS FOR INDIVIDUAL ENROLLMENT." The sheet said:

Eligibility for individual (direct) membership in Connecticut Health Plan (CHP) is open to applicants who:

1. Do not have conditions requiring hospitalization, for example, pregnancy.
2. Do not have conditions requiring surgery, for example, gallstones.
3. Do not have conditions requiring frequent medical attention, for example diabetes, arthritis, heart disease and frequent hospitalizations.
4. Do not have health factors associated with increased risk for disease, for example, obesity, excessive alcohol, tobacco or drug abuse.
5. Are not home-bound.

Individuals with chronic illnesses or conditions that

are in good control and do not require excessive medical attention (3–4 visits per year) may be accepted. Applicants who are ineligible because of conditions or risk factors which are correctable or changeable (for example, obesity, pregnancy, gall bladder surgery) can be reconsidered once these conditions or risk factors have been removed.

In contrast, an HMO in a neighboring Connecticut city said they would accept anyone, even people so ill they had to crawl in over the threshold.

Because they seem to deliver health care more efficiently, the federal government gave health maintenance organizations its blessing in 1973, when Congress passed the Health Maintenance Organization Act. By 1977 approximately $132 million had been awarded in federal grants, loans, and loan guarantees to encourage the development of new HMOs. Unions, such as the United Automobile Workers, have organized their own plans, such as the Metropolitan Health Plan in Detroit, which covers about 75,000 workers, and have been more than satisfied with their experience with this form of health insurance. HMOs are protected in the marketplace, because the federal government requires any employer with twenty or more employees who offers health insurance as a fringe benefit to include an HMO among its options, if there is one in the area.

In addition, Medicare has worked out a special arrangement whereby anyone on Medicare can join an HMO and receive covered health care through that organization.

HMO LIMITATIONS

Comparatively few exist. There may not be one in your area. HMOs are mostly geographically local organizations (except for the giants like Kaiser-Permanente, the largest in the country), and they do not exist in all areas. If you live in a big city or a heavy industrial area, there is probably one or more. If you live in a rural area, you may be out of luck.

Limited local eligibility. You may not be eligible for the HMO you think is in your area. All HMOs limit their membership geographically to an arbitrary selection of towns surrounding the town in which the HMO is located. If you live just over the border of this geographical limitation—even if it is just across the street—you cannot join.

Limited size. The HMO in your area may be full. Since the HMO is using its own facilities and staff, it cannot function with too large a membership. All HMOs, when they are first setting up, determine the ideal number of members they can most efficiently serve. In the beginning they operate at a loss, trying to build up membership. Once they have filled their quota, however, there is no way to increase the size of their plant, and an overlarge membership puts a strain on the whole operation. As a result, an HMO that has filled its quota will not take on new members until openings occur. This is another situation in which the direct-pay individual is at a disadvantage. Medicare beneficiaries and employee groups will be accommodated first, and it will take time for the HMO to expand sufficiently (if at all) to open membership to individuals. If your area HMO says it is full and will have no openings in the foreseeable future, you had better make other arrangements; it is possible you will never be able to get in.

There is always the chance, however, that a rival HMO will start up in what is obviously a good area for this kind of health care. Read the local papers and check occasionally with the Social Services office in your community.

ADVANTAGES OF AN HMO

If you have a chance to join an HMO, why would you want to? If it is a good one, there are several theoretical advantages.

Preventive medicine. Most health insurance specifically excludes the procedures that help you keep tabs on your health and become aware of serious illnesses while they are easily treatable. Chances are your regular policy will not pay for routine physicals; even Medicare won't. An HMO, on the other hand, is committed to the proposition that it is important to maintain good health, not just to treat illness; after all, it is called a health *maintenance* organization. It will cheerfully provide well-baby care and various other health maintenance services for no extra charge.

Studies here and abroad have shown conclusively that health maintenance results in a higher level of health, reduced incidence of serious illness, and lower health care costs. With membership in an HMO, you will benefit from these statistics because you will feel free to take care of yourself. Without an HMO, a once-a-year checkup for you and your family, including charges for laboratory tests and X-rays, might easily cost almost $1,000. Faced with this kind of out-of-pocket expense, you might decide to let it go longer than you should.

Lower health care costs. As we have seen, preventive medicine, instead of being an out-of-pocket expense, is a covered service. So are prescription drugs (with maybe a nominal fee for each prescription) and all the usual procedures, such as X-rays, EKGs, and both physical and mental therapy. Your monthly fee may seem large compared to a regular policy's premium, but to arrive at a fair comparison, you have to combine the premium, deductibles, and co-insurance of a private or Blues policy with out-of-pocket costs. A Stanford University study (HMOs are very big in California) found that HMOs cost 10 percent to 40 percent less than private insurance policies, when both premiums and out-of-pocket costs were figured into the equation.

One-stop shopping. It can be a great convenience to have all your medical care providers under one roof. Suppose, for example, you have some vague symptoms you want to check out. Your primary doctor may decide he wants you to see a dermatologist and a neurologist, and maybe an ophthalmologist. If you have gone to a private primary care doctor, you will now have to call around to make appointments and then trot from one doctor's office to another, maybe taking time out from work to do so. With an HMO, going from one doctor's office to another means—at the most—going to another floor in the same building.

If someone else in your family is sick at the same time, ordinary running-around time can double or even triple, especially if you have to add pediatricians to all the other doctors you have to see. And you don't have to be a sickly family for the events of this scenario to occur; an ordinary healthy family can have the flu go right through all its members in a short space of time.

If you belong to an HMO, on the other hand, you could conceivably simply bundle everyone into the car and go to one building, where all the doctors and specialists have their offices and where your primary care physician sets up the appointments for you merely by picking up the phone. While you may not be able to get all the appointments in on the same day, you certainly will if it is any kind of an emergency. And if not, the staff will probably work with you to reduce the number of trips you have to make.

Availability of records. Your medical records at an HMO are kept in a central file and are quickly available to any staff member. A specialist may want to know your medical history and look at your X-rays and other workup material. Your private primary care doctor's original notes may be practically indecipherable to anyone else (think of the writing on prescriptions), and she or he may have to find time to rewrite your file and have it typed for the specialist. All this means delay, which may be detrimental to your health. In an HMO the file is more carefully written up in the first place, because each doctor knows it may be reviewed by another doctor at any time. It will always be as complete as possible, and all the details will be there. With your file so readily available, the consulting doctor is more likely to refer to it rather than settle for asking questions you may or may not be able to answer accurately.

The same applies to EKGs, other test results, and any other procedures you may have undergone; all will be readily available for consultation.

No claim forms. The HMO providers keep all the records for you. Since there are no bills to send or pay, you are not involved in the process. Paying the premium and the occasional nominal fees are your only responsibility. Medicare beneficiaries in particular appreciate this feature.

Access to health care. Most staff HMOs are open twenty-four hours a day, seven days a week. In an emergency your usual doctor may not be available but some doctor will, who will have immediate access to all your records. If you didn't belong to an HMO, you might go to the emergency room of the nearest hospital, which would be unfamiliar to you and would not have your records on hand; the HMO setup is much more satisfactory and more likely to result in correct treatment.

Access to other medical personnel. Sometimes you have a question but feel it is not important enough to bother your doctor with. HMOs often rely on nurse-practitioners to advise you in such a situation. They are usually very pleasant to deal with, not at all intimidating (as some doctors can be), and extremely knowledgeable. Also—a big plus—they never seem in a hurry and you don't feel guilty about taking up their time with a detailed description of your problem. You can also trust them to refer you to a doctor if your question is beyond their level of expertise.

Peer review. It is considered a plus that HMO doctors work in a goldfish bowl. Unlike private physicians, whose work is their own business (most of the time), HMO doctors are subject to peer review and are always working with other physicians. This is thought to be a form of quality control, but should not be taken without a grain of salt. Most health care consumers are only too well aware of the extent to which the medical profession refuses to be its own watchdog. Popular TV shows are always writing in an elderly or alcoholic or simply incompetent surgeon whose incapacities are known to the whole hospital staff but who is nevertheless protected from exposure by the entire medical establishment. And many people know firsthand of real cases of cover-ups. An HMO cannot automatically be presumed to be any different from any other medical establishment in this respect. Some doctors may be personally intimidated by the thought that all their decisions are open to review and this may make them more cautious, if not more conscientious, in their work. Peer review works, however, only if the peers are willing to take strong measures to protect the patients, even if this means terminating the career of a friend and colleague. In addition, much depends on the individual physician's own conscience, thoroughness, and skill; even good peer review can only weed out the obviously incompetent, and then only after a number of mistakes have been made.

DISADVANTAGES OF AN HMO

The nonmedical staff. Most discussions of HMOs never refer to the bureaucracy, but anyone who has had actual experience with an HMO will understand why it might be listed first among the disadvantages. From the director on down, the organizational structure depends heavily on nonmedical, administrative staffers. The director is usually a trained public health administrator who is first and last an organization person, trying to keep the company running smoothly, sometimes regardless of the cost to the individual consumers who make up the membership.

The nonmedical staff is the same mix to be found in any bureaucracy, so you may run afoul of a petty bureaucrat throwing weight around in a sheer exercise of power. Do not expect fairness in this situation; you will disappear under the wheels of a juggernaut. The director may perhaps feel that the end (protecting the HMO so it can continue serving its other members) justifies the means (dealing with one patient unfairly when an HMO staffer is clearly in the wrong). Faced with this situation, the patient may end up totally frustrated and, what is even more serious, without access to treatment to which he or she is entitled.

If this should happen, your only recourse is to go outside the organization. Your first complaint should be to the local medical society. This will not be effective if the head of the HMO is on the board or otherwise influential. The next step is the state medical society and all the consumer protection agencies, state and federal, you can think of. You can also make use of local broadcast and network TV stations, which frequently have consumer advocate reporters, and local radio. It all depends on how angry you are. Unfortunately, it is hard to sustain the energy needed to pursue all these avenues when you are sick (which is presumably why you went to the HMO in the first place).

Fortunately, you are least liable to have this particular problem with your own HMO, but you may run into it when you are traveling and have to use a "cooperating" one. Which brings us to our next disadvantage.

Getting sick away from home. It is never pleasant to get sick while traveling; if you belong to an HMO, the experience could be traumatic.

As we have seen, HMOs are very local. If you travel away from your HMO's geographical area, your coverage is limited to emergency care only. And even that depends on the presence of an HMO where you become ill as well as whether that HMO is willing to work long distance with the one to which you belong. I know of an instance in which eight long-distance phone calls back home were necessary to establish which HMO could be used in another state. The patient then phoned the "cooperating" HMO to make sure he would be accepted. He was told everything was in order. But when he turned up and was in the middle of an office visit—the doctor had just declared his situation an emergency—he was summarily and physically ejected by a staffer who burst into the doctor's office and said the patient was not eligible for care at that HMO. The staffer who had made the original arrangements was out that day. It was never explained why the intruding staffer had the authority to act as she did, especially in view of the doctor's diagnosis of the patient's need for emergency medical care and in spite of careful preparation on the part of the patient to assure that he was going through proper channels. This nightmare situation was finally resolved—most unsatisfactorily—by the patient going to a private physician and paying the costs out of his own pocket. The offending HMO might just as well have been in the business of selling popsicles for all the interest it took in the welfare of the patient.

Keep a sharp eye out for this kind of attitude among the HMOs with which you come in contact. To avoid joining one of this ilk, talk to members and see what experiences they have had and whether they are satisfied with both the medical and the nonmedical staff. If you sense any of this kind of staffing, avoid that organization; one petty bureaucrat between you and medical care can create a serious health hazard.

When you are traveling, be prepared to pay out of your own pocket unless you are going to be in large cities and unless it is an emergency (which may or may not help).

Limited choice of doctors. HMO members may choose among the doctors on the staff but will not be covered for visits to a nonstaff doctor unless that specialty is not available within the HMO. If you are sent to an outside doctor by the HMO, the costs will be covered, but this won't happen very often.

The question then arises, how good is the medical staff from which you must choose? And aside from competence, can you find a doctor whom you like? The doctor-patient relationship is important to health maintenance; you will get better faster if you have confidence in your doctor. If you don't have a good relationship, it may adversely affect your health.

The question of competence is not easily resolved. If the HMO is large, you can choose your primary physician from among a number of staff doctors. But even in that case the number of specialists will be limited. Anyone who has had skin problems, for example, knows how difficult it is to find a satisfactory and effective dermatologist; with perhaps only one on the HMO staff, your options are severely limited.

If you have a friend who is a private physician (but who is not your doctor), you might solicit his or her opinion in deciding whether to join an HMO. It will soon become clear that you will have to make your decision without the physician's support. It appears that many physicians in private practice do not have a high opinion of HMO physicians, and this seems to stem from more than the element of competition. When I asked private physicians what they thought of HMO medical care, the most common response was, "If they could make it in private practice, they wouldn't be working for an HMO." This isn't entirely fair; a physician may not be competitive enough for private practice but may still be a good doctor. A doctor may not have the financial resources to furnish a modern office and carry the overhead until the practice becomes profitable. Or a doctor may be the kind of person who prefers the security of a steady salary to the hassles of running a private practice, even with its greater financial rewards. There are good and bad physicians both in HMOs and in private practice; as in every other marketplace, it is up to consumers to buy health care with their eyes open and to change providers if they are not acting in their best interests.

Clinic atmosphere. Although HMOs insist they take emergency cases promptly, there can be a long wait in scheduling an appointment and in getting into the doctor's office once you are in the building. Some very efficient HMOs have guidelines, and their doctors who keep patients waiting too long are usually helped to develop a more efficient schedule. Others seem unable to control this problem. When you look over an HMO, ask people if they have had to wait a long time. If they say no, ask them what they consider a reasonable time to wait; you may not agree. (You might also ask them how long they have been waiting this time.)

Hidden limitations. Because of the way an HMO is structured, you may run into problems without knowing the reason. For instance, if you have a chronic condition that requires regular prescription medication, you will save a lot of money filling that prescription at the HMO pharmacy. (In fact, you may not be able to fill it anywhere else.) Since the HMO is unlikely to be as handy as your neighborhood pharmacy, this may mean making a special trip each time you need a refill. After a couple of months of this, you will probably ask your doctor to give you a prescription that will last longer—at least a month or more. The doctor may simply refuse or may even say the distance you have to travel is not his concern. What he is not telling you is that he can't give you the kind of prescription you require. Because of the nature of an HMO pharmacy, doctors are limited in the number of pills they can include in a single prescription. Your tradeoff is the money you save on prescription drugs against the inconvenience of unnecessarily frequent refills. If, in addition, you have to take a taxi to and from the HMO, you may have the inconvenience without the saving.

Possible bankruptcy. An HMO's financial health depends not only on good, experienced management; it also depends on numbers. A successful HMO must have all the members it can handle or its overhead will be greater than its income. The federal government helps HMOs that are just starting up and, by requiring HMO membership to be an employer-offered health-insurance-benefit option, increases the likelihood that an HMO in an industrial area will be adequately supplied with members. There is still a chance, as with all new enterprises, that you may join an HMO that goes out of business. Try to avoid this by checking before you join to see what the community thinks of the HMO and how long it has been in business. Of course, if it is part of a large chain, you probably don't have to worry.

False sense of security. In the beginning the HMO seems to cover so many bases that you may begin to have the feeling there is no medical problem for which you will not have coverage. This is not quite the case.

As usual, mental health coverage leaves much to be desired. By setting comparatively low caps on how much it will cover, an HMO restricts coverage to short-term treatments. Some plans do not specify a cap; in fact, they make a point that their coverage is "unlimited." The catch here is that their coverage still applies only to short-term treatment and that, further, you have access to mental health services, such as psychiatric, only if the plan doctors agree it will improve your condition. (Maintenance never seems to apply to mental health.) The fact that you might want to give the service a try and see if it will help will not carry any weight. In private practice, in which you are paying for each treatment, you can sometimes persuade a doctor to try something with the argument that it won't do any harm; but with the HMO, you would be asking them to spend their money against their professional opinion that it was worthwhile.

Generally speaking, HMOs will not pay for routine dental care, removal of impacted wisdom teeth, and other similar services. Since more and more private insurance policies do cover some of these areas, be sure to compare coverage for dental bills. Charges from chiropractors, Christian Science practitioners, acupuncturists, and similar nontraditional medical professionals are not covered by HMOs any more than they are by most other forms of health insurance. (Medicare does have some limited coverage for some of these.)

When you are looking at HMOs, ask about home health care. You don't tend to think about this until you need it, so make a special note; it is another way of cutting down on hospitalization, so HMOs should be in favor of it. It is also cheaper and pleasanter for the patient to be taken care of at home.

GROUP MEMBERSHIP

As with any other kind of health insurance, group HMO membership is the cheapest and best. You will also have more clout than if you join as an individual. Individual HMO membership will probably cost more than the other health insurance plans your employer offers, however.

If the premiums are higher and your employer pays all or part of them, what your employer may do is charge you whatever the HMO costs over other plans. The HMO may be a better deal for you nevertheless; even with the excess charge, your total cost may still be less than with more traditional forms of health insurance. On the one hand, if you are single, healthy, and not given to frequent consultation with doctors, an HMO plan may not be your best buy. But if you are married, especially with children, it may be. Also, if you believe in preventive medicine and like the security of having regular physicals, be sure to include that as an out-of-pocket cost, since most insurance policies won't cover preventive medicine.

It comes down to a question of your life-style and personal situation, and what is best must be determined on an individual basis.

INDIVIDUAL MEMBERSHIP

If an HMO in your area has an opening, the premiums will be much higher for an individual than for a comparable group membership. To be sure, the coverage will be more comprehensive than any other individual health insurance you can buy, but maybe you don't need that much coverage. Look at your health care costs for the past few years, including insurance premiums. Compare that total to the annual cost of HMO premiums, plus whatever nominal fees you would have incurred. It should be easy to determine which decision is financially advantageous. Of course, like all projections, projecting your health care costs in the coming year is subject to error; an unexpected illness may throw all your calculations out the window. But all insurance is a gamble anyway. If you decide against the HMO, hedge your bets by choosing a health insurance policy that will protect you against the big bills.

FOR THE MEDICARE BENEFICIARY

If you are a Medicare beneficiary and are temperamentally disposed to an HMO, it has certain specific advantages. Because they have won the favor of the federal government, HMOs are allowed to participate fully in the Medicare program and to file claim forms directly with Medicare. This means an HMO member who is a Medicare beneficiary is freed of the necessity of asking the doctor or health care provider to accept the assignment and of filing any claim forms. All that is taken care of automatically.

The HMO monthly premium is much lower for a Medicare beneficiary than for an under-sixty-five individual. It may be, however, that you will be offered a choice of plans, high- vs. low-option. The high-option plan will be the more expensive and the more comprehensive. It will tend to cover more than Medicare does, as well as to pick up the deductibles and co-insurance. The low-option plan is cheaper (you still pay the Medicare premiums, deductibles, and co-insurance) and is often merely basic Medicare coverage, leaving the same gaps typical of Medicare coverage. If this is the one you are going to choose, think twice about the advantages and disadvantages it offers over Medicare (outside of the HMO) plus a good supplemental policy. Be sure to compare them in detail.

The convenience of one-stop shopping may appeal to an older person, especially one with limited transportation facilities. On the other hand, if joining an HMO means giving up a long-time relationship with a primary care physician, this may not be a desirable choice. If the only reason for such a move is financial, consider talking the matter over with the physician; more and more doctors are making special arrangements for long-time elderly patients who would otherwise have difficulty meeting their fees. And of course if your family physician accepts the assignment, he or she will also fill out the forms for you (be sure to ask).

A new type of HMO is being tried out in various parts of the country, including Florida. With this setup, health care is free to Medicare beneficiaries. The HMO is paid for by Medicare and charges the beneficiaries nothing. The care is very complete and, so far, the idea seems to be financially viable for the HMO. If you have such an HMO in your area, give it a try. It is certainly an idea worth encouraging.

VII

DISCRETIONARY INCOME— INDEMNITY POLICIES

17

Indemnity—When You Get Paid for Being Sick

WHAT IS INDEMNITY INSURANCE?

Indemnity insurance is a policy that pays you a preset amount of money in cash, regardless of your actual health care costs, usually when you are hospitalized. Indemnity insurance does not pay actual hospital or medical bills. It is considered a form of health insurance because you collect benefits only when you are incurring certain types of health care costs (as when you are hospitalized). If its benefits are linked to hospitalization, it is sometimes called hospital indemnity insurance.

An advertisement in magazines or on television for this type of policy (many of the policies sold by mail order are indemnity policies because they lend themselves best to mail order advertising; they appear easy to understand and sound so enticing) usually tells in big type, in the headline, the cash you can collect. There is no doubt that at first glance, insurance that offers to pay you $1,000 a month when you are in the hospital sounds interesting—especially when the advertisement and literature emphasize that it is your cash to spend any way you please.

A second look, however, dims some of the glow. First of all, $1,000 a month turns out to be approximately $33 a day. It doesn't sound like so much put that way, which is why it isn't put that way. Second, many indemnity policies don't pay from the first day you are hospitalized. There is a waiting period of three, seven, or even more days before the insurance takes effect and starts to pay off. That sounds fair enough until you find out that the average hospital stay is less than a week. You soon realize that your chance of collecting the $1,000 isn't statistically very good; it takes a little longer to realize that most of the time you won't collect so much as a penny.

On the other hand, the longer the waiting period, the lower the premium will probably be. This is where a crystal ball would come in handy, but barring that, your choice of waiting period will probably depend partly on your hospital experience to date and partly on your gambling instincts.

In addition to in-hospital waiting periods, beware of effective date of coverage. A new policy may not cover you for some time after you have started paying premiums; shop for a short—less than six months—waiting period. If you have just bought a policy with a waiting period and will not be compensated for an interim hospitalization, it may be no great inconvenience to put off an optional operation until the policy goes into effect.

No matter how much you may be tempted to buy a hospital indemnity policy, it should not be your first—or only—health insurance purchase. Hospital indemnity policies should not be bought instead of a basic or major medical policy; think of them as supplementary coverage only.

Know Your Nomenclature

It would certainly help the consumer if the insurance industry were required to use standard names to identify the various types of policies. Since this is not presently the case, be sure you ascertain whether the policy you are looking at is the type you have in mind. For instance, indemnity policies are sometimes called indemnity supplement policies, or just a made-up name, such as Group Hospital Cash Plan. Since the benefits also vary widely, from simple daily cash benefits upon hospitalization to far wider coverage through cash benefits, the only sure way of identifying an indemnity policy is by the nature of its benefits. If the benefits are paid, under certain conditions, according to a prefixed dollar amount, generally not related to actual costs, on a daily, weekly, or some such regular basis, it is probably the type of policy known as indemnity. Do not confuse this type of policy with a disability policy, which also pays cash direct to you but is not related to health care costs or hospitalization, and which replaces part of your actual income (disability benefit amounts depend, to some extent, on your salary).

Other Benefits

Originally indemnity policies paid benefits only when you were hospitalized. Recently, as the appeal of ready cash payments proved a potent sales tool, indemnity policies have expanded their coverage into other areas.

Here are some benefits, in addition to the basic cash benefit, that you may find included in your basic indemnity policy.

1. Hospital charges besides room and board. The policy may cover related services (lab tests, drugs, anesthesia, X-rays, and so on) by paying you a specified multiple

of the daily hospital benefit. For instance, if the policy states that it will pay 10 or 20 times for what it calls "ancillary" expenses, and if your hospital indemnity benefit is $33 a day, it will pay up to $330 or $660 for those expenses.

2. Suppose you are hospitalized for maternity and not for illness. If the policy includes a maternity benefit, payment for this will be also a multiple of your daily benefit if there are complications. Maternity benefits are not usually paid for normal childbirth; only for problems arising from complications. Complications of childbirth are either spelled out in specific benefits or described as being covered "just as any other illness."

3. In-hospital doctor visits may be covered for a set amount ($10.00 is usual), with the limit expressed in terms of maximum number of visits. The policy may also have a provision for office visits and even, though very rarely, for house calls. Since very few doctors pay house calls today, this is another item you probably won't collect on but the company looks good offering it.

4. If surgery is covered, it will be paid for according to the company's schedule, which specifies how much will be paid for each procedure, such as gall bladder surgery, prostate surgery, appendectomy, etc. It is usually difficult to get an advance look at this schedule, so you may not know until you file a claim what you will get. As with most other insurance, cosmetic surgery is seldom covered.

NOTE: In all cases, regardless of what you receive the benefits for, the money from indemnity policies is paid directly to you for your unrestricted use; this is the strongest selling point of indemnity policies.

What's Left for You to Pay

Basically health insurance is bought in an effort to cover the major part of health care costs. But no policy that pays a prefixed amount instead of a percentage of the actual costs is going to come anywhere near fulfilling that goal.

Take the hospital room-and-board figure. Hospital rooms are costing around $300 a day, depending on where you live, and they have been going up in cost ten times faster than the annual cost of inflation; obviously $33 a day won't make much of a dent in that figure. Ancillary costs make the day rate look like a bargain and can easily make total daily costs run to $600 or more. Even if you don't need something expensive like a CAT scan, every injection, X-ray, spoonful of medicine, and lab test costs far more than you could possibly imagine. Hospitals have even been known to charge for facial tissues, and it is not impossible that you may be billed over $20 for a spoonful of cough medicine that can be bought at your neighborhood pharmacy for a couple of dollars a bottle. In no time at all, your hospital bill may come to thousands of dollars. Cash you get from even the most generous indemnity insurance policy, far from taking care of your expenses, will be hardly noticeable. And when you get out of the hospital and are confronted with doctor bills or outpatient care expenses, most of the time it won't pay anything.

In an effort to keep the consumer from being too badly hurt by dependence on this type of insurance, many states have passed regulations that require that indemnity policies sold within the state meet certain minimum standards. California, which is not too happy with any health insurance, feels indemnity policies in particular leave too much of the costs for the consumer to pay to be really worthwhile. In an effort to improve this situation, the state has passed the following minimum standards that any indemnity policy sold in the state must meet. If you don't live in California, check out your own state's standards or use California's as a guide.

1. Benefits should be at least $30 a day and be paid for at least 60 days in hospital. Maternity benefits should be at least $75 for a normal birth, $50 for a miscarriage, for the first year. For subsequent years the policy is in effect, coverage should be at least $150 and $75 respectively.
2. Medical benefits should be a minimum of $1,000 for no less than 6 months for an illness or injury. If there is a deductible, it is limited to no more than 10% of the maximum benefits paid.
3. Surgical benefits must be at least $300 for major operations. Lesser operations are, of course, allowed smaller benefits. (With the cost of surgery today, even this leaves a very large amount to pay out-of-pocket.)

Pre-existing Conditions

Indemnity policies, along with other health insurance policies, usually have a pre-existing-conditions clause, which means a waiting period before the policy will pay off on illnesses you now have or have had within a specified period. Compare the policy you are considering with other policies; you will find the waiting period varies; the shorter it is, the better.

IF YOU ALREADY HAVE AN INDEMNITY POLICY

One of the most serious disadvantages of indemnity policies is that they go out of date very quickly. Since health insurance costs are rising so fast, especially hospital costs, you should regularly examine your policy to see whether it needs updating. A policy you bought four years ago, if it is not updated by the company in the meantime, will cover a much smaller percentage of your expenses today, and in addition, the dollar benefits will be much less compared to the benefits offered in the same type of policy bought today. Of course, switching policies may mean incurring another pre-existing-conditions waiting period, so you have to weigh that, as well as the state of your health and the undoubtedly higher premium of the new policy, against the reduced benefits of the older policy. Newer policies will probably offer various kinds of benefits that weren't available when you bought your old policy. On the other hand, the pre-existing condition that is now covered by your old policy may have worsened over the years, and it may be that a new policy will exclude coverage permanently for that illness. Go carefully before giving up the old policy.

SHOULD YOU BUY AN INDEMNITY POLICY?

Even the experts disagree. Many say probably not. You certainly should not buy an indemnity policy as your only health insurance; the false sense of security it may give you will disappear the first time you have occasion to collect benefits.

If you think of this type of policy as supplemental insurance, you may be influenced by the fact, which the ads make a big point of, that you can spend the money any way you please. Of course you can, but when you have gotten through paying the out-of-pocket expenses that the policy didn't cover, it is doubtful that you will have cash left over for Acapulco or the down payment on that new Mercedes. More likely you will add it to the installments you are sending out to try to pay off your doctor bills.

On the other hand, these policies do pay cash, and

nobody can *make* you use that cash to pay health care bills. If being ill is going to put you into a temporary financial bind, paying bills slowly and having some cash coming in might tide you over a bad period. If the premium is not unreasonable in comparison to the benefits and you can afford it without digging into eating money, if the policy is a fair one and gives you a reasonable chance of collecting, and if you don't have a good disability policy to augment your diminished income, an indemnity policy might be a real comfort. Shop extra carefully; the insurance company knows the odds better than you do and will naturally weight the terms of the policy in its favor.

18

Hands-On Experience— Seven Indemnity Policies

There are an almost unbelievable number of variations in the way indemnity policies are written. By their nature they should be the simplest, but in some ways they are among the most confusing of all types of policies, and since they are mostly sold by mail order—through advertisements in magazines and on television—there is no salesperson of whom you can ask questions. Often a free 800 phone number is provided, but you have to know exactly the right questions to ask, and the phone does not encourage the kind of conversation you could have with an in-person sales agent. Most of your information will come from sales literature you receive by mail, and chances are you will probably decide which policy to buy on the basis of the information you garner in this way. Because of this, it is especially important that you learn how to separate the information from the hard sell and not to be misled by a good presentation into buying a poor policy.

Brochures are part of the material you receive when you answer an ad for information about a policy. This chapter will describe and analyze seven brochures and how they describe the policies they offer. The samples were chosen at random. Once you have studied these examples, you will be comfortable with almost any brochure you may be sent.

When you open the envelope and draw out the enclosures, you will find other selling material in addition to the actual brochure. This will include a sales letter, an application blank, and a return envelope. The last two items and the brochure are the ones that are important to you.

Always remember that the brochure is not as complete as the actual policy. If the brochure sounds good to you and you decide to send in your application and check, the law requires that you be given between ten and thirty days (it will specify in the brochure) for you to look at the policy. This is precisely because the brochure may be incomplete. Use this time to good advantage by checking whether the policy offers what you think it does and does not contain any limitations or restrictions of which you were not aware. If you find on consideration that you do not want the policy, your money will be fully refunded, without penalty, providing you notify the company within the stated time. If you decide to cancel the policy at this time, return it with a letter saying so and send it via certified mail with return receipt requested, so that no one can say you didn't return it in time (or at all).

FEATURES MOST POLICIES HAVE IN COMMON

No "coordination of benefits." Unlike other health insurance, an indemnity policy will pay off in addition to and regardless of other coverage.

Cash paid directly to you (or to your hospital or your doctor, but only if you wish). This means the cash benefits come to you in the mail, and no one else has any claim on them. The idea of getting cash is the most appealing part of an indemnity policy. The sales pitch leans heavily on the increasingly high costs of hospitalization and surgery and makes the point that regardless of your coverage from other policies, you will still have to pay something out of your own pocket. The Visa letter, for example, says its policy "helps you meet the unexpected costs of hospitalization and related at-home expenses with cash benefits paid directly to you." This is true; how much it helps is the question you need to ask.

Free-look period. The laws in most states require that you be given a certain length of time after you receive the actual policy to examine it. This period will vary from ten to thirty days.

Descriptive brochure. You must receive a brochure that sets forth the costs, benefits, and restrictions of the policy. Read it carefully, since the explanations are necessarily brief and you may easily miss something important. It is no substitute for the actual policy but can serve as a basis for comparison with other policies.

Unlimited claims. You will usually not be limited to a certain number of claims, although there will usually be a limit to the total dollar amount you can receive.

If, however, the no-limit statement is followed by a phrase such as "except as noted above," look to see what the reference is. Usually the limitation reads something like, "You'll receive benefits for up to twenty-four months as a result of your combined hospital and convalescent home confinements." It is especially important to note these limitations when comparing policies. They may be generous, or they may not.

Pre-existing conditions. All indemnity policies will have a waiting period before they cover pre-existing conditions (illnesses you have had before you took out the policy). As Mutual of Omaha puts it: "During the first 12 months your policy is in force, we will not pay for any injury or sickness that was first manifested or medically treated 12 months or less before your policy went into force. After your policy has been in force 12 months, benefits can begin for old health problems."

Although the number of months can vary, the Mutual terms seem to be fairly standard for this type of policy. What you might not realize is that "medically treated" can mean just the filling of a prescription. If you are taking a prescription medicine regularly—for high blood pressure, for instance—it would be difficult for you ever to be covered for that illness.

Definition of convalescent home. Most of the brochures do not seem to define this term, and the average consumer thinks it means any nursing home. The policy probably explains the term somewhere, in small print, by stating that this benefit applies only to a "skilled nursing facility." An SNF, as it is commonly referred to, is a special, high-level-care facility. In many sections of the country there are very few SNFs, and you might easily end up convalescing in a nursing home that would not qualify for benefits. *Convalescent* is a term that tends to paint a misleading picture for the average consumer, since an SNF is next to a hospital in the level of care it provides and is not needed by most posthospital patients. If all you require is rest and someone to tend to your general needs, an SNF will not be ordered for you. Also, since SNFs are in such short supply, you might not be able to get into one even though you need it, and thus might find yourself in a facility not covered by your policy.

Eligibility. Indemnity policies are often "group" policies and require you to be a member of the group offering the policy before you can join; the group need not be job-related. For instance, group policies are offered by American Express, Visa, the Metropolitan Savings Bank, and the American Association of University Women, among others. There may be an age requirement; in this instance policies are available only to those under (or over) a certain age, such as fifty, fifty-five, or sixty.

Generally indemnity policies guarantee that they are available without a physical examination to anyone who applies.

Not-covered areas. As with all health care policies, certain kinds of illness or accident are seldom covered. The National Group Banking Health Plan sums up these areas as follows: "No benefits are paid for confinements caused by war or any act of war; pregnancy (complications of pregnancy are covered as any other illness); mental diseases and disorders; intentionally self-inflicted injuries; use of alcohol or narcotics."

Policy cancellation or premium raises. Indemnity policies cannot be cancelled or their premiums raised for individuals but only for a group or for all those holding a specific policy.

You may find individual indemnity policies that have additional benefits or that word them somewhat differently, but this gives you an idea of what to look for.

INDEMNITY POLICY BROCHURES EXAMINED

The following specific brochures are examined here:

1. Metropolitan Savings Bank Hospital Cash Insurance

(Underwriter: National Benefit Life Insurance. A subsidiary of American Can Co., Inc., New York, N.Y.)

2. National Group Banking Health Plan (Underwriter: Continental American Life, Wilmington, Del.)

3. American Express Group Hospital Cash Plan, Preferred Risk Version (Underwriter: Fireman's Fund American Life Insurance Company, San Rafael, Calif.)

4. Bank Card Center Visa Hospital Income Plan (Underwriter: AIG Life Insurance Company, Pittsburgh, Pa.)

5. Colonial Penn Franklin Insurance Company Surgical Plus (Philadelphia, Pa.)

6. American Association of University Women Hospital Indemnity Plan (for those ineligible for Medicare) (Underwriters: Hartford Accident & Indemnity Company, Hartford, Conn.)

7. Mutual of Omaha Insurance Company Easy Care Hospital Cash Plan (Omaha, Neb.)

IMPORTANT NOTE: *Policies change often and premiums change at least every year. It is entirely probable, therefore, that none of these policies is any longer offered in this identical form, and it is certain that the premiums will be different from those shown here. They are discussed merely as examples of the kinds of policies and of the range of premiums that the buyer of an indemnity policy may encounter. These actual policies are not meant as an indication of which company has the best policy, since good companies sometimes write poor policies and companies with a less glowing reputation sometimes surprise the critics. This detailed examination will, however, prepare the consumer to make an informed choice from among whatever policies may be encountered.*

Examination of the policies is broken down into (1) premiums, and (2) benefits. The numbers used to identify the policies in each discussion are the same as the numbers in the list of policies beginning on page 219. For fuller description, refer back to that list.

Premiums

Policy #1

MONTHLY PREMIUMS

AGE LAST BIRTHDAY	PLAN A	PLAN B	PLAN C	PLAN D
Under 40	$12.38	$8.25	$7.58	$5.05
40–49	18.53	12.35	11.40	7.60
50–59	22.88	15.25	14.03	9.35
60–64	24.45	16.30	15.00	10.00
65–69*	25.95	17.30	17.63	11.75
70 and over*	27.45	18.30	18.68	12.45
All children*	5.78	3.85	3.23	2.15

* Age 65 and over and all children receive 50% of the cash benefit. The monthly premium covers all children up to age 19 (up to 23 if full-time student). Also the policy is not available to Connecticut and Minnesota residents over age 65.

The four plans referred to differ as follows:

Plan A pays $75 a day for coverage from the first day (day 1) of hospitalization.

Plan B pays $50 a day for coverage from day 1.

Plan C pays $75 a day for coverage from day 4 for an illness, day 1 for an accident.

Plan D pays $50 a day for coverage from day 4 for an illness, day 1 for an accident.

NOTE: The mailing offered coverage for the first month for "you and your entire family" for one dollar.

Comments. Although the policy is age-related, it is different from most age-related policies in that the premium does not increase with your age. "Once you are enrolled at the approximate rate shown here, your monthly premiums will not increase as you enter a new age bracket. You will pay premiums at the same rate for as long as you retain this coverage." You would want to know the meaning of "the approximate rate."

Policy #2

MONTHLY PREMIUMS				
ENTRY AGE	PLAN A	PLAN B	PLAN C	PLAN D
Under 40	$11.04	$7.09	$6.63	$4.25
40–44	13.09	9.00	7.85	5.40
45–49	13.91	9.95	8.34	5.97
50–54	16.02	10.98	9.61	6.59
55–64	17.25	11.59	10.35	6.95
65–74†	19.43	15.75	11.66	9.45
75–79†	24.68	20.93	14.81	12.56
80 and over	42.31	39.95	25.28	23.97
Dependent child*	5.86	3.00	3.52	1.80

* One rate covers all unmarried dependent children from birth to age 21 and pays full benefits.

† All plans provide those 65 and over with 50% of the daily benefit for the first 60 days of continuous hospital confinement, 100% thereafter. Plan is not available to Connecticut residents age 65 and over.

The four plans differ as follows:

> **Plan A** coverage pays $50 a day from day 1, up to age 64. When 65 or older, $25 a day from day 1 for first 60 days, $50 a day from sixty-first day.
>
> **Plan B** coverage pays $50 a day from day 4, up to age 64. When 65 or older, $25 a day from day 1 for first 60 days, $50 a day from the sixty-first day.

Plan C coverage pays $30 a day from day 1, with same reduction in benefits for 65 or over.

Plan D coverage is $30 a day from day 4, with same reduction in benefits for 65 or older.

Plans A and B pay $100 a day for intensive care; $50 a day for confinement in a convalescent facility. Benefits for 65 and over are 50% for first 60 days and 100% thereafter.

Plans C and D pay $60 a day for intensive care; $30 a day for a convalescent facility. Benefits for 65 and over are 50% for the first 60 days, 100% thereafter.

Comments. In comparing age-related policies (where premiums increase as you get older), look at how many years comprise each group (before your premium goes up). Some policies have more of a spread than others. If you can avoid age-related premium rises altogether, you are better off.

Premium rates are for each adult and have to be doubled if husband and wife are to be covered. Although it is hardly a selling point, the brochure describes it as such elsewhere in the text: "Pays you double cash— $200.00 a day, $6,000.00 a month! That's right! If you and your spouse are insured under this plan and both are simultaneously hospitalized from the same accident— you'll receive $200.00 cash a day . . . up to $6,000.00 a month DOUBLE CASH benefits for up to 2 full years when under age 65. If you are age 65 or over, you'll receive $100.00 a day . . . up to $3,000.00 a month DOUBLE CASH BENEFITS!" This is set in somewhat larger type than the note about rates being "per adult."

Generally speaking, I found the brochure confusing and difficult to follow; the layout was busy, with too much display and too many exclamation points. Type sizes (cash was often all caps) seemed to have more to do with hard sell than clarity.

Policy #3

MONTHLY PREMIUMS			
AGE	MAN	WOMAN	EACH CHILD
19–34	$6.50	$8.50	to 19 $5.83
35–44	8.50	11.75	
45–54	10.25	12.25	
55–64	16.50	14.50	
65–69	27.75	22.50	
70–74*	27.75	22.50	

* Renewal only.

Comments. Sex-related premiums are somewhat unusual. They will not be allowed, of course, if the unisex bill now pending in Congress is passed.

The spread in the age groups is so different from that of the policies we have just looked at that one cannot help wondering what basis is used for arriving at the figures.

The "renewal only" restriction is fairly common though not universal. But if one doesn't have one's health insurance needs taken care of by a much younger age than seventy, the pickings are lean in any event.

Policy #4

MONTHLY PREMIUMS			
$30 A DAY BASIC BENEFIT:			
AGE	PLAN A	PLAN B	PLAN C	PLAN D
---	---	---	---	---
Under 35	$4.62	$8.94	$6.37	$10.69
35–44	5.83	11.37	7.59	13.12
45–54	7.86	15.42	9.61	17.17
55–64	9.18	18.06	10.93	19.82
65–69*	15.28	29.81	17.04	31.56

Policy #4 (continued)

MONTHLY PREMIUMS

$60 A DAY BASIC BENEFIT:				
AGE	PLAN A	PLAN B	PLAN C	PLAN D
Under 35	9.23	17.87	12.74	21.38
35–44	11.66	22.73	15.17	26.24
45–54	15.71	30.83	19.22	34.34
55–64	18.36	36.13	21.87	39.64
65–69*	30.56	59.62	34.07	63.13

* Renewal only.

The difference among the four plans is as follows:

> **Plan A** covers one person, "applicant only or spouse only."
>
> **Plan B** covers two people, "applicant and spouse."
>
> **Plan C** covers "applicant or spouse and all children." (This is good for a single-parent family.)
>
> **Plan D** covers "applicant, spouse, and all children," and is the complete family plan.

Comments. The four plans offer a very flexible choice and reflect an understanding of the changing nature of the family. This feature, however, combined with the age-related tables, makes it difficult to compare with the premiums of other policies. To find the policy that is best for you, compare the premium that applies to your age (noting also how much and at what age it will increase) and then, with a checklist, compare the benefits. Your best bet is a favorable combination of the two.

Policy #5

This policy is not comparable to the others we are examining. It has only one premium; it covers surgery, not hospitalization; and it is available to anyone age fifty or over. It is not available to anyone with a Colonial Penn Medicare supplement plan. Surgical procedures covered are described in detail under "A Special Type of Policy."

The monthly premium, per person, was $11.95 at the time the policy was examined and would probably increase each year as the cost of surgery increases.

Policy #6

The AAUW offers various other health insurance plans in addition to this one, which is only for those not eligible for Medicare.

MONTHLY PREMIUMS					
AGE*	PLAN A		PLAN B		PLAN C
	MEMBER *SPOUSE*		*MEMBER* *SPOUSE*		*MEMBER* *SPOUSE*
65–69	$79.75	$100.00	$63.80	$80.00	$31.90	$40.00
70–74	103.25	136.00	82.50	108.80	41.25	54.40
75–79	132.50	179.40	106.00	143.50	53.00	71.75

* Premiums are based on each person's current age. Your premium and that of your spouse, parents and parents-in-law increases on the first premium due date following attainment of age 70 and 75. Plan terminates at age 80.

Plans differ as follows:

Plan A pays $75 a day from day 1.
Plan B pays $60 a day from day 1.
Plan C pays $30 day from day 1.

Comments: This policy is interesting because there are still a number of elderly people not eligible for Medicare (including those relocating from other countries), and they need health insurance even more than Medicare beneficiaries do. Since these people are often parents or in-laws, the plan (which includes them) could be helpful. It is not, however, a plan that will in any way replace Medicare coverage, and basic insurance should still be purchased first. Note that there is no coverage for children.

The explanatory brochure is simple and almost totally lacking in the usual hard sell.

Policy #7

		MONTHLY PREMIUMS		
AGE	PLAN A	PLAN B	PLAN C	PLAN D
Under 35	$7.65	$13.00	$10.25	$15.60
35–49	9.90	17.30	12.50	19.90
50–59	11.65	20.20	14.25	22.80
60–64	13.10	22.85	14.45	24.20
65 and over	15.80	28.45	17.15	29.80

Plans differ as follows:

Plan A is for one person only.
Plan B is for you and your spouse.
Plan C covers one parent and all eligible children.
Plan D covers you, your spouse, and all eligible children.

All plans pay $30 a day, from day 1 for accidents and from day 4 for covered illnesses. Benefits do not change with age.

Comments. The brochure is easy to follow, and benefits are clearly spelled out, providing you understand what "covered illnesses" do not include. Instead of not offering the policy to Connecticut residents, provision is made to add the extra benefits required to make it acceptable under the Connecticut laws (but only to Connecticut residents).

Benefits

Here are the benefits offered by the policies in addition to the basic cash benefits, as gleaned from the brochures.

Length of free-look period

10 days: policies #2, 3, 4
30 days: policies #1, 5, 6, 7

Comments All things being equal, thirty days certainly gives you more time to look over the policy carefully and to seek advice.

Where covered

hospital only: policies #3, 6, 7
hospital and convalescent home: policies #1, 2, 4
in or out of hospital: policy #5
coverage abroad: policies #3, 4

It is no coincidence that the companies offering coverage abroad are those interested in a clientele that travels. If you are a frequent traveler, check your basic health insurance for coverage abroad. If it is not included, consider whether it is important to you. Incidentally, Medicare does not cover you abroad (except in a few instances), but many Medicare supplement policies do. Primarily in countries with a national health plan, you may find medical costs so low (compared to U.S. prices) that it is almost not worth your being insured against them.

Cap on benefits Most benefits are limited; sometimes the limit, or "cap," is expressed in a maximum dollar amount, sometimes in terms of span of time. If no cap is indicated and you are interested in the policy, send for it and see how the policy itself discusses its maximum benefits.

Dollar Amount

- $54,750 maximum; 50% if over 65: policy #1
- $36,000 maximum; $34,500 if 65 or older: policy #2

Length of Benefit Period

- Up to 2 full years. New benefit period starts after 6 months or more between confinements: policy #1
- Up to 2 full years: policy #2
- Up to 500 days. New benefit period begins again after 90 days out of hospital: policy #3
- Up to 365 days. New benefit period begins again after 120 days out of hospital: policy #4
- Up to one year "for a covered accident or illness . . . for each day of confinement for a maximum of one year": policy #6
- "For as long as you're in the hospital." "There's no limit": policy #7

Comments Benefits are a critical area, and failure to understand their limitations is a frequent source of difficulty between subscribers and the insurance company. A poor company can abuse the freedom to interpret its policy; a good one won't play games, but there may still be an honest misunderstanding. The best company in the world isn't going to pay you something it hasn't said it would in the policy. If you have a question, ask it before you send in your check (call an 800 phone number, if one is given). Here are some questions to get your critical faculty warmed up:

"How long can I collect the daily cash benefit for an illness or accidental injury?"

"How do I qualify for a new benefit period?"

"What is the lifetime maximum amount the policy will pay me? Is that for a single illness or the total cash benefit of the policy?"

"How many benefit periods can I have in a year? In a lifetime?"

"Do the answers to any of these questions change as I grow older?"

Pre-existing conditions Pre-existing health conditions are defined as "conditions for which medical advice or treatment was received or recommended by a physician."

- Conditions existing for a twelve-month period before policy inception are covered after a one-year wait under policies #1, 4, 5, 6, and 7.

Comment While this seems to be the most common pre-existing limitation, there are variations.

- **Policy #2:** The brochure reads, "This plan does not provide benefits for the following: Prior health conditions which were medically advised, manifested or treated are not covered for hospitalization beginning in the first 24 months of coverage. . . ."

Comment If it means what it says, any illnesses you have had since the day you were born would not be covered for the first two years the policy is in effect.

For another policy, a letter accompanying the brochure states, "you must be in good health to qualify."

This is a "Preferred Risk Version," but the statement is still ambiguous. If I have had dozens of illnesses during the past twenty years but am now in roaring good health (and medically certified as such), am I eligible for this policy? How recently may I have acquired my good health—yesterday, last week, a year ago? The company urges you to apply without worrying about the answers to such questions. "If you've had a medical condition in the past, you should apply anyway. You may receive a letter that says you have been accepted. . . ."

A look at the application blank provides a clue. It asks two questions relating to your health "within the past five years." Presumably, with maybe some exceptions, that is the period for which you need a relatively clean bill of health.

A third policy has a variation you will encounter fairly frequently. "A pre-existing condition is one for which you have received medical treatment, advice or medication in the 12 months immediately preceding the effective date of your insurance. Such conditions are not covered until you have gone for 12 consecutive months (ending on or after the effective date of your insurance) without further medical advice or treatment, or until you have participated in the Plan for two years." In other words, after two years you are covered—even for an ongoing illness.

Accident and/or illness coverage Many policies differentiate between hospitalization benefits for an illness or for an injury due to an accident. Don't be misled if the brochure says something like, "You are insured for a covered accident or illness." If it does, copy later on may read, "Beginning on the first day of hospitalization due to an accident, after the third day due to illness. . . ." Both these quotes come from the same policy. The reason for the apparent inconsistency is simply that you have a choice of plans, with the higher premium giving better coverage. It would appear that statistics lead the company to believe that you are more liable to be hospitalized due to illness than due to accident.

- **Policy #1:** Both accident and illness coverage with the more expensive plan, and different benefits for the less expensive plan.
- **Policy #2:** More expensive plans start coverage on day 1; the less expensive, with day 4.

Comments You might not, however, be clear about this if you read only the front cover of the brochure for policy #2. It states, "Plan A guarantees to pay you $50.00 cash a day, $1,500.00 cash a month from the very first day up to $36,000.00 cash every time you are hospitalized for any covered accident or illness while under age 65." Plan A actually does exactly what the other plans do not. Read carefully when you are asked to "choose from four economical plans." (Two of these plans pay from day 4.) It is all actually fairly clear if you are used to reading these brochures, but something might be overlooked if you aren't. The cash benefits are clearly printed in large type, black on a light background; the notations as to first- and third-day coverage are printed in much smaller type, white print on a green background. Nowhere in the brochure is this difference printed in one of the larger black types. Putting in zeros for cents (as in *$100.00* rather than *$100*) makes the amount seem larger (most policies do this, but it is still a trick). The facts are there, however, so you have only yourself to blame if you don't sit down and read every word in the brochure when making up your list of benefits and limitations.

- **Policy #3:** Identical coverage for accident and illness.
- **Policy #4:** Same coverage for accident and illness.
- **Policy #5:** Covers surgery only but does not indicate

any difference in coverage for accident or illness.

- **Policy #6:** Same coverage for accident and illness.
- **Policy #7:** The cover of the brochure states it clearly: "Benefits begin the very first day for a covered accident and the fourth day for a covered sickness."

Comments: Policy #7, incidentally, is the only one that says benefits start the fourth day; terminology usually is something like, "coverage begins after the third day due to illness." I find policy #7's wording much clearer.

Mental illness benefits Benefits for mental illness are usually much less generous than for other illnesses. Even Medicare coverage for mental illness is poor. When it is not specifically referred to in the brochure, mental illness may be exempted under the phrase "Benefits apply to covered injury or illness" (mental illness might not be a covered illness). Chances are the policy will go into more detail as to which illnesses are not covered, but if this is a special concern, you might ask.

- **Policy #1:** Brochure does not mention mental illness except to say, "Children who are mentally or physically handicapped and totally dependent (provided disability occurred and their coverage began prior to age 19) may remain insured for half benefits after age 19."

Comments: In line with my working only with the information from the brochure and not going to the actual policy, this appears to be a special feature not offered by the other policies. (It may be in the other policies but it is not in the other brochures).

- **Policy #2:** Under the heading, "Here's what is not covered," the brochure states, "Also, no benefits are paid for confinements caused by war or any act of war; pregnancy (complications of pregnancy are covered as any other illness); mental disease and disorders. . . ."

- **Policy #3:** "EXCLUSIONS . . . THIS IS WHAT IS NOT COVERED. . . . These are the exceptions: intentionally self-inflicted injury or suicide or any attempt thereat, while sane; a mental or nervous disorder. . . ."
- **Policy #4:** No mention of mental illness in the brochure.
- **Policy #5:** Surgical coverage only, does not apply.
- **Policy #6:** No reference to mental illness except that among exclusions, number 2 reads, "acts of intentionally self-inflicted injuries or destruction or attempted suicide while sane or insane." Most of the other policies usually say only "while sane"; however, policy #7 uses this wording.
- **Policy #7:** Same as policy #6.

General Comments

A brochure is not anywhere near as complete as a policy, and only the policy is binding. Do not be intimidated by a policy. Lack of typographic devices (large display type headings, etc.) may make it look less inviting but will also make it easier to concentrate on the actual wording. When it comes to what is covered and what is not, what the policy says will determine to a large extent the benefits you actually receive. What the policy won't tell you is how hard the insurance company will try to find loopholes so that they need not pay off. Some companies have a good claims record and some do not. Ask around and check with your insurance commission.

A Special Type of Policy—Surgical Plus

Policy #5 is different from the other indemnity policies because, although its benefits are paid in cash directly to you, the benefits themselves are not "hospital" benefits but for surgical procedures. It is of interest because it shows what great variations exist among indemnity policies and offers you a chance to decide what kind of coverage you are going to look for.

Surgical Plus is available only to those who are fifty or older. The cover of the brochure says ". . . In or Out of the Hospital . . . Pays you Cash . . . $25.00 to $1,000 for covered surgery. $100.00 increased Benefit for 14 major operations more common to mature Americans. $5,000.00 Benefit for one of four cancer surgeries. Up to $100.00 for covered dental procedures." Before you can evaluate these figures, let's look inside for specific examples.

Among the covered operations listed are:

- $1,000 for heart valve replacement
- $900 for removal of spinal disc with fusion
- $800 for coronary artery bypass graft (single)
- $800 for removal of colon (total)
- $200 for removal of all or part of one breast (simple)
- $200 for surgical repair of inguinal hernia (groin)
- $200 for repair of fractured vertebrae
- $200 for fractured wrist (open reduction)
- $50 for removal of malignant skin lesion(s)

The schedule also says it has added an extra benefit of $100 to certain operations. Total amount paid for certain of these procedures would be:

- $500 for removal of cataract
- $600 for removal of prostate
- $400 for pacemaker implant

The special $5,000 cancer surgery benefit reads, "You can collect a one-time $5,000 benefit for any one of the following when performed for treatment of cancer. This cancer surgery benefit will be paid instead of the lower amount you would otherwise receive." For example, removal of colon (total) would normally receive an $800 benefit but, presumably, if necessitated by cancer would qualify for the $5,000 benefit. Note this is a one-time benefit for cancer surgery and applies only to four specified operations.

Certain dental procedures are covered for amounts from $50 to $100.

There are various limitations spelled out under "Coverage Requirements" and "What is Not Covered," such as, "The maximum amount you can collect for all other surgical procedures during any one 90-day period is $1,000." Preexisting conditions are not covered, in the usual way, "for the first year, for any surgical procedures performed as a result of an illness or injury for which you received medical advice or treatment during the one year period before your coverage goes into effect."

Comments: In deciding whether to buy this type of policy, ask yourself two questions. First, is the annual premium for you and your spouse of $286.80 ($11.95 each per month) buying the most insurance you can get for that money? In other words, compared to other idemnity policies, are you likely to get the same ratio of benefits to premiums? For instance, policy #7 charges $242.20 a year for both husband and wife to pay a hospitalization benefit of $30 a day. Policy #1 charges $366.00 for a $50-a-day benefit for husband and wife. Policy #2 charges $230.64 annually for a husband/wife benefit of $30 a day. (All premiums are in the same age group as policy #5.) To compare the benefits from policy #5, you might, for instance, try to estimate how much you would collect from it and from another policy for the same procedure. A cataract operation for which policy #5 paid $500 in benefits might come out in favor of policy #5, since most cataract operations require no more than one to three days in the hospital. At that rate, the most you would collect from policies #7 and #2 for hospitalization would be $90; from policy #1, $150. And if you had the operation as an outpatient, you might not collect any hospital benefits (some policies specify that hospitalization must be for more than 6 hours in order to qualify for benefits). Today more and more operations are being performed on an outpatient basis, so it is necessary to be clear about whether your policy covers surgery under such conditions.

On the other hand, there are many reasons besides surgery for which you might be hospitalized. If you are an asthmatic, to give just one instance, you might have occasional hospitalizations and none of them would be covered by policy #5.

The second question is whether the amounts paid are realistic in terms of the costs of the operations. You can easily check what surgeons in your area charge for these common procedures. Of course, keep in mind that this is an indemnity policy and that it is meant to provide extra cash, not to pay for your operation. On the other hand, since the policy itself relates its benefits to specific procedures, it is only logical for you to assume some connection. Fifty dollars for removal of malignant skin lesions seems low to me (without checking with a surgeon), since melanoma (presumably included here along with simple skin cancers) usually requires major surgery and costly follow-up treatment. You might want to know, in addition, how often this schedule is updated; the costs associated with these procedures go up much faster than the rate of inflation.

Generally speaking, the more limited a policy is, the more carefully you should look at it. Just as "dread disease" policies are not considered good buys (in fact, they are prohibited for sale in some states), policies that focus on specific operations are not usually as desirable as those that offer broader coverage.

VIII

SEX DISCRIMINATION—
A NEW COMPLICATION
FOR INSURERS

19

Women and Health Insurance—
Three Giant Steps

Wherever women try to remedy sex or, as it is sometimes called, gender discrimination, they meet strong resistance to changing the status quo; nowhere has this resistance been stronger than from the insurance industry. In this instance, however, support has come from the federal government—the White House as well as Congress—and the industry, usually regulated by the states, is finding itself increasingly under examination by Washington.

Unisex insurance is the term that is used to describe insurance that does not, as much insurance presently does, discriminate on the basis of gender. Currently Congress is considering a unisex insurance bill that would eliminate gender as a risk factor in all kinds of insurance. While health insurance is not specifically addressed, it would benefit from across-the-board legislation; life, auto, disability, and health insurance would all be brought under the umbrella of legislation against sex discrimination.

The push for unisex insurance began when women workers first realized that under the then-current contracts, upon retirement they would receive lower pensions than their male co-workers, even though women workers were contributing the same amount to the pension fund. When they questioned the fairness of this, they were told that women as a group, on the average, live about seven years longer than men and, therefore, would tend to receive pension payments over a longer period than would a male co-worker. If women were paid pensions identical to men, the reasoning went, on the average they would end up receiving more total dollars. The insurance companies, using data from their actuarial tables, accordingly prorated the pension money, so that no more would be paid out over the average longer life of a female worker than over the shorter average life of a male worker. The practical result was, of course, smaller monthly pensions for women, including those who died shortly after retiring.

The inequitable pension treatment was not minor. In 1980 the President's Commission on Pension Policy found that only 31 percent of women workers were covered by pension plans during the previous year, as compared with 50 percent of men workers. And the following year the Census Bureau estimated that the average annual pension received by women workers was $2,427, compared with $4,152 a year for men workers. Neither did anyone bother to explain why it was thought that it was possible for women to manage on almost 60 percent less than men did, merely because they were women. Some of this discrepancy was, of course, due to the fact that women were paid less for comparable work and often had their careers interrupted by child-bearing and rearing, with an unfortunate effect on their pension fund. (This latter problem was addressed by the Retirement Equity Act of 1984, which stated that workers could take a one-year maternity—or paternity—leave without it counting as a break in service or against their pension benefits.)

The insurance industry defended this practice by pointing to their actuarial tables, which clearly showed their statistical basis for discrimination to be accurate; women do, on the average, live longer than men. In fact, the industry argued, it wasn't discrimination at all, inasmuch as all insurance rates are based either on experience (as with large groups over a period of time) or on actuarial tables—the traditional way insurance companies assess risks and determine the margin necessary to assure profits.

As it happens, pro-unisex insurance groups were able to question the validity of this argument, inasmuch as actuarial tables also show, for instance, that whites live longer than blacks, Mormons live longer than Episcopalians, and so on; yet because such classifications are not socially acceptable, race and religion are not factors considered in determining pension payments.

THE FIRST GIANT STEP: TITLE VII

Although Title VII had been law since 1964, it had not been operative in many areas to which it theoretically could be applied. Turning the spotlight on sex discrimination in pensions revealed that this already-existing law apparently prohibited it. The wording of Title VII of the 1964 Civil Rights Act, though directed at workers rather than individuals, prohibits employers from discriminating against "any individual with respect to his compensation, terms, conditions or privileges of employment because of such individual's race, color, religion, sex or national origin." Since using statistics to set different rates for women constitutes treating them as a group rather than as individuals, and since the wording of Title VII requires that workers be treated as individuals, this would seem to settle the matter. In addition, Title VII specifically prohibits discrimination on the basis of sex. But clear as all this would seem at first glance, Title VII has turned out to be a law subject to different interpretations depending on which side you are on. Also, as we will see, prohibiting discrimination by sex can apply to men as well as to women.

GIANT STEP TWO: THE MANHART DECISION

So passing Title VII did not end sex discrimination. It remained for the courts to establish precedents that would determine its application. In April 1978 the situation was somewhat clarified in the case of *Los Angeles Department of Water & Power* vs. *Manhart*. Water & Power had tried to require women workers to pay higher contributions to the pension fund to make up for the supposedly longer period for which they would be collecting their pensions. In other words, women workers would receive the same monthly pensions as men but the insurance company would collect more from women's premiums to cover their longer average life expectancy. The Supreme Court ruled against the insurance companies, declaring that higher premiums for women were prohibited by Title VII.

This by no means settled the issue; the Manhart decision was too limited in scope. While it said women could not be compelled to pay more to achieve benefits equal to those of male workers, it did not say specifically whether women could be forced to accept diminished benefits for failure to make the excess payments. In other words, excess payments were illegal, diminished benefits were not. Since diminished benefits are even more of a problem than excess payments, coming as they do at a time when they may constitute a woman's entire income, a new court case inevitably followed the Manhart decision.

GIANT STEP THREE: THE NORRIS CASE

On the day the Supreme Court rendered its decision in the Manhart case, Nathalie Norris, an employee in the Arizona Department of Economic Security, filed a class-action suit against the state of Arizona, whose pension plan provided, in effect, diminished benefits for women workers. Ms. Norris charged that by paying larger annuities to men than to women, Arizona was in violation of Title VII. At issue was a pension plan option by which retirees could choose to defer a portion of current income to after-retirement income. If this option was chosen, employees could then elect to receive either a lump sum, fixed monthly payments over a specified number of years, or an annuity paid by a private insurance company for life. Ms. Norris contended that if she chose the annuity option when she retired, she would, merely because she was a woman, receive only 90 percent as much as a male retiree.

In 1980 she won her case for equal benefits for women in a federal district court, arousing concern in the insurance industry, which marshaled its forces to fight the decision. In spite of industry efforts, however, the Ninth Circuit U.S. Court of Appeals, in March 1982, ruled in Norris's favor. The ruling ordered Arizona to pay retired women who had chosen the annuity option of the pension plan the difference between their payment and that of comparable retired men. Arizona responded creatively to this decision by discontinuing entirely the benefit of the life annuity option, with the result that employees of that state, male and female, could no longer convert deferred compensation to retirement income.

Obviously a suit with such far-reaching consequences would not long remain in the lower courts. On March 28, 1983, the Supreme Court began hearing arguments in the Norris case. On the one hand, the suit was supported by the AFL-CIO, the Civil Liberties Union, and over twenty other women's rights and civil liberties groups. The contention of these groups was that a ruling for the state of Arizona would "perpetuate the second-class status of women workers by guaranteeing that, upon retirement, women will be relegated to a lower standard of living."

On the other side, the state of Arizona was joined by the insurance industry, which realized the issue jeopardized basic assumptions of their entire business.

The specific issues before the justices were twofold: whether insurance companies could legally pay smaller monthly annuities to retired women because the actuarial tables show that as a group they live longer, and whether offering such annuities as one of several retirement plan options was a violation of Title VII.

In question also was the legality of the use of sex-segregated actuarial tables for risk classification.

In a similar case (*Teachers Insurance and Annuity Association and College Retirement Equities Fund* v. *Diana L. Spirt*), filed about six months after the Ninth Circuit appeals court had ruled that the Arizona plan was illegal, the Reagan Administration went unequivocally on record as being of the opinion that using these tables to justify lower retirement benefits for women as a group was already illegal. The administration filed a friend-of-the-court brief arguing that "the use of sex-segregated actuarial tables to calculate employees' retirement benefits is unlawful under Title VII. . . . Whether a woman contributes a greater amount of her compensation than a man for an equal benefit or receives a lesser benefit, the use of sex-based actuarial tables in calculating periodic benefits results in the same discrimination."

In its comments on the Norris case, however, the American Council of Life Insurance (ACLI) said the far-reaching results of such a ruling would mean that "pension plans covering 26.1 million Americans and backed by $165.8 billion in reserves would have to be changed substantially." The ACLI argued further that sex-segregated tables were both economically and statistically sound and legal, inasmuch as the tables are factual. "Use of the long-recognized factual relationship between sex and life expectancy does not result in discrimination on the basis of sex proscribed by Title VII," the ACLI stated.

The state of Arizona disclaimed responsibility for the use of sex-segregated tables but said simply that every insurance carrier in the state used such tables. It stated further that Norris had freely chosen her pension option, and that she could just as easily have opted for deferred compensation in the form of a lump sum upon retirement or the third option of fixed payments for a set number of years. It disputed any relationship between its suit and the Manhart decision on the grounds that Manhart concerned an employer-operated pension fund, whereas Arizona's pension fund was operated by private insurance companies under contract to the state.

Ms. Norris said, on the contrary, that her suit was closely related to Manhart since both plans "discriminate against women as a class; both . . . treat women different than men solely on the basis of their sex." She further contended that since the state controls the overall retirement system, solicits bids from various insurance companies, and selects the company that will administer the retirement program, it could not disassociate itself from the fact that the system it chose was discriminatory.

On June 23, 1983, the Supreme Court, ruling in favor of Ms. Norris, handed down the decision that sex bias in employer-sponsored pension and retirement plans was illegal. The ruling specifically stated that an employer's retirement plan may not provide women workers smaller benefits than comparable men workers.

As Justice Marshall summarized it in writing the majority opinion, "The classification of employees on the basis of sex is no more permissible at the pay-out stage of a retirement plan than at the pay-in stage." (This would seem to be clear enough, but in fact it left a large loophole and several gray areas.) The dissenting justices (Chief

Justice Warren E. Burger, Justices Harry A. Blackmun, Lewis F. Powell, Jr., and William H. Rehnquist) were joined by Justice Sandra Day O'Connor in limiting the application of the decision. They ruled that it should not be applied retroactively; only those making pension contributions after the date of the decision would have retirement benefits calculated on a unisex basis. The effect of this limitation was to phase in the unisex benefits over a number of years rather than making them effective in the immediate future. It did mandate, unless the law is changed in the meantime, that eventually sex as a factor in pension insurance rates and benefits would be eliminated one day. Judging, however, by the mixed reception accorded Title VII (which was supposed to have established the same thing by theoretically doing away with sex discrimination per se in 1964), those in favor of unisex insurance would be wise not to relax just yet.

The Effect of the Norris Case

The effective date of the Norris ruling was August 1, 1983. Since it is not retroactive, it did not apply to women who had already retired or to women workers' contributions that had been made to their retirement plans prior to August 1. The ACLI had argued that including those two groups would have cost the industry between $85 and $676 million a year for at least the next fifteen years, depending on the method used for adjusting benefits.

The Supreme Court decision did not in any way prohibit the "Arizona solution," that of an employer discontinuing employee annuity plans altogether. In addition, the Supreme Court decision left several areas unclear. For instance, a question remained as to whether companies offering annuity plans can comply with the law by reducing the present benefits of the male workers or are required to "top up" the benefits of women workers to equal male benefits.

While the Norris case set a landmark precedent, it had a serious flaw; it applied only to employer-based plans. As Judy Goldsmith, president of the National Organization for Women, pointed out, it left out in the cold all those women who could buy only individual policies; the insurance companies were still free to offer such women sex-based policies that were illegal if offered as group policies. Furthermore, it did not prevent insurance companies from taking into consideration the gender makeup of a company's work force. In drawing up the pension program, the insurance company was free to set higher rates for a company with a workforce that was made up predominantly of women. The ACLI said this ruling, since it was not retroactive, would not have any noticeable effect on most pension plan contracts, since one to three million women and eight million men are already covered by employer-sponsored plans that calculated their benefits on the basis of gender. And of course, the ACLI added, the four million women who have had to purchase individual annuity contracts would not be affected now or in the foreseeable future.

The Employee Benefit Research Institute (EBRI), a nonprofit research group whose members include actuarial firms, insurance companies, and other related groups, disagrees with the ACLI estimates. According to the EBRI, the 25 million people who make up 450,000 pension plans will be more or less affected by the Norris decision. Sophie Korczyk, an EBRI research economist, says that contrary to the general impression, men rather than women will benefit the most. For instance, she points out, a married man who chooses "joint and survivor" benefits presently receives a lower monthly payment than a comparable woman worker, in order to offset the after-death benefits that will go to his wife. This is based on the actuarial assumptions that not only will the female spouse live longer than her worker husband (and thus be more liable to collect spouse benefits), but also she will collect those benefits for a longer period. The Norris ruling makes this kind of discrimination illegal and mandates making men's benefits equal to women's from now on.

In its ruling the court majority said sex may no longer be used to predict longevity, and that doing so "is flatly inconsistent with the basic teaching of Manhart; that Title VII requires employers to treat their employees as individuals, not as 'simply components of a racial, religious, sexual or national class.' " It continues: "The use of sex-segregated actuarial tables to calculate retirement benefits violates Title VII whether or not the tables reflect an accurate prediction of the longevity of women as a class, for under the statute even a true generalization about a class cannot justify class-based treatment." The majority opinion also pointed out that the actuarial tables identified other differences in life expectancy, such as those to be found in comparisons of race and national origin, in addition to sex. If the logic of sex-based life-expectancy statistics is sound, it would be equally sound to use these other factors "as a justification for paying employees of one race lower monthly benefits than employees of another race."

The Supreme Court decision was by no means unanimous, and Justices Powell, Burger, Blackmun, and Rehnquist dissented. In the minority opinion, Justice Powell wrote: "Employers may be forced to discontinue offering life annuities or potentially disruptive changes may be required in long-established methods of calculating insurance and pensions. Either course will work a major change in the way the cost of insurance is determined—to the probable detriment of all employees." The first prediction, evidenced by widespread adoption of the "Arizona solution," has proved accurate.

Justice Powell stated further that Title VII's focus on the individual is contrary to the whole concept of insurance:

> Insurance and life annuities exist because it is impossible to measure accurately how long any one individual will live. Insurance companies cannot make individual determinations of life expectancy; they must consider instead the life expectancy of identifiable groups. . . .
>
> Explicitly sexual classifications, to be sure, require close examination, but they are not automatically invalid. Sex-based mortality tables reflect objective actuarial experience. Because their use does not entail discrimination in any normal understanding of that term, a court should hesitate to invalidate this long-approved practice on the basis of its own policy judgment. Congress may choose to forbid the use of any sexual classifications in insurance, but nothing suggests that it intended to do so in Title VII.

Although Title VII and the Manfred and Norris decisions are considered "landmark" and have had far-reaching effects on the status of women in insurance and pensions, the most important changes are yet to come. Once their attention was turned on the insurance industry, women's groups began to look more closely at all kinds of insurance. It soon became evident that long-established customs needed to be reevaluated and that not all assumptions on which insurance rates are based should continue to go unchallenged. The result, as we shall see in the next chapter, was the clarion call for unisex insurance across the board.

20

The Battle of the Unisex Bills

The Manhart and Norris decisions (see previous chapter) turned the spotlight on the broader aspects of discrimination against women in insurance. True, the matter ostensibly had been settled by Title VII, but putting Title VII into practice had raised questions of interpretation that could be decided only by test cases in the courts.

The first of these had seemed harmless enough. The Manhart case started out as one woman's protest against inequity in one state's pension benefits. What it turned into was an all-out assault on and examination of sexism in all group insurance: auto, health, indemnity, life, and retirement. The insurance industry, not unnaturally, reacted strongly to the threat of having to make from-the-ground-up changes in their whole way of doing business, and once again the federal government found itself involved in an area it had thought was securely under the jurisdiction of the states. Unfortunately, the states have been reluctant to act on the problem; attempts to solve it had been sporadic and very limited. Only Montana had actually passed unisex insurance regulations, and only four other states—Massachusetts, North Carolina, Michigan, and Hawaii—had passed unisex auto insurance regulations by March 1984.

Not that there hadn't been great strides made toward eliminating sex discrimination (usually against women) from insurance policies and rates. First, in 1964, came Title VII with its sweeping reforms (which are becoming less and less sweeping as they are nibbled away at by court interpretations). Then came the Supreme Court's 1978 Manhart decision, which, though limited in scope, affected an area of major interest to women workers by equalizing contributions to the pension funds. The loophole left by Manhart, which allowed insurance companies to pay smaller benefits to women for those equal contributions, was closed by the Norris decision in 1980. And in between, also in 1978, the decision in the case of *General Electric* v. *Gilbert* had improved health insurance coverage for pregnancy by equating it with "other" illnesses and diseases for the purpose of bringing it under the health insurance umbrella. (True, Title VII had already mandated that costs incurred due to pregnancy were to be covered, but the Gilbert case spelled out that the coverage applied to single as well as married women, workers as well as spouses. The fact that these apparently nitpicking distinctions had to be made indicates some of the problems that arise in applying a law in the marketplace.)

Now that Congress had entered the picture, however, it began to examine the very foundation of insurance (and incidentally, health insurance), the industry's use of sex-based actuarial tables as a risk classification factor, and to question whether using these tables to set rates should not be discontinued altogether. The Norris decision certainly seemed to indicate that this was the opinion of many of the Supreme Court justices, but nowhere was it specifically stated that insurance companies had to apply the Norris decision as anything like a basic principle.

Since individual court cases were not achieving the desired result of doing away with sex discrimination and, on the contrary, seemed merely to proliferate lawsuits and countersuits, Congress decided to make another effort (Title VII had been the first) to eliminate sex discrimination in all types of insurance once and for all. To this end the unisex bills were created: S372 in the Senate, sponsored by Senator Robert Packwood (R-Oregon), chairman of the Commerce, Science and Transportation Committee; and HR100 in the House, sponsored by Representative John D. Dingell (D-Michigan), chairman of the House Energy and Commerce Committee. By March 1984 Representative James J. Florio (D-New Jersey), as chairman of the Transportation and Tourism Subcommittee (of the Energy and Commerce Committee) was ready to report out the bill to the full committee. From there it would go to the floor of the House for action.

While congressional committees were slowly guiding these bills through the legislative maze, what was happening outside those hallowed halls? Was the insurance industry sitting placidly by while their sacrosant actuarial tables came under fire? Hardly.

THE INDUSTRY ENTERS THE FRAY

The insurance industry marshaled its forces at the first whisper of unisex legislation. At the best of times the insurance lobby is a force to be reckoned with; in a worst-case scenerio, such as the threatened demise of sex-based actuarial tables, the extent of its activites is awesome.

Certain congressmen were targeted as being most influential and in a position to effect the passage of the unisex bills. These included every single member of the

Commerce Committee (which, of course, has jurisdiction over S372). The only exception was its chairman and sponsor, Bob Packwood, presumably a hopeless case. The House, with forty-two members on the Energy and Commerce Committee, was a little unwieldy, so the lobby selected fifteen representatives with whom it seemed most likely to succeed. (Actually the industry said it would have included the entire House committee but was too short of funds.)

Typical of targeting activity was the mailing put out by the Committee for Fair Insurance Rates (fair to whom? said the women's groups), which was comprised of a number of property and casualty companies and had a war chest of almost $1 million (later lobbying reports showed it was even more than that) that it spent on mailings, public relations activities, and print and radio advertising. The FIR Committee sent about 500,000 letters to voters in key congressional districts. And it is estimated that about 50,000 form letters, neatly printed with the voter's name and address, were sent, in turn, to each targeted congressman. One version was short—only nine lines—simplistic in content, and folksy in style. It started out: "HR100 must be defeated. Lots of folks depend on the steady income from their pensions and annuities for their food and shelter. Now the Congress wants to raise the premiums and change benefits, and a lot of people will be hurt." All the "writer" had to do with this prepared missive was sign it, stamp it, and mail it. Thousands of people did.

In November 1983 the disclosure reports of lobbyist expenditures filed with Congress showed that the insurance industry was among the three top spenders. Through the Committee for Fair Insurance Rates, the industry reported spending $1,370,497 in just the second and third quarters of the year to oppose the unisex bills. The committee said the money had been spent on "grass roots advertising" and mailings to voters in districts represented by lawmakers serving on committees considering the insurance bill. Among the contributors listed were Aetna and Nationwide, $125,000 each; Allstate, Cigna, and St. Paul Fire and Marine, $100,000 each; and Fireman's Fund, Travelers, Phoenix Mutual Life, and U.S. Fidelity and Guaranty, $75,000 each.

Not all insurance groups have looked favorably on the blitz orchestrated by the Committee for Fair Insurance Rates. Some felt it would create ill feeling, leading to an antagonistic rather than a sympathetic response from legislators. And some of the opposition agreed with this point of view. J. Robert Hunter, president of the National Insurance Consumer Organization (NICO), said, "It's the best thing that ever happened to us. It's made so many members of Congress mad that we've made more progress in achieving our goals in the last two months than during the last three years."

There is no doubt it did make some members of Congress mad. Senator Packwood said the Senate "will rise up in wrath against these kind of tactics," and Representative Florio commented, "I categorize what the insurance industry is doing as a propaganda campaign. They're torturing the facts."

The advertisements were cited by many pro-bill organizations for their inaccuracies and slanted approach, and the letter-writing campaign was widely condemned. In all fairness, however, letter-writing campaigns are a popular tactic used today by any cause that can get together money and a group of volunteers to stuff and stamp envelopes. Not everyone, however, has such extensive funds to devote to the cause being promoted.

PRO-UNISEX GROUPS FIGHT BACK

Although unable to raise the funds needed to meet the insurance lobby in an equal fiscal fight, the pro-unisex bills groups have tried to work together to get across their side of the issue. Through statistics, facts, and pointed comparisons, such organizations as NOW, WEAL, and the Leadership Conference of Civil Rights have joined with NICO in a lobbying effort. They have many congressional representatives on their side, and there have even been encouraging pats on the head from the White House. Occasionally the battle takes on more of the aspect of a screaming match than of a battle royal, but contrary to what might be expected, the shrillest voices seem to come from the insurance industry. This may be due partly to worry on the part of the industry that if they make enemies in Congress, the retaliation will be in the form of taxes. Tax reform is always in the wind, and the insurance industry, which has had a somewhat privileged status up until now, is understandably anxious about rocking that particular boat. This puts them between a rock and a hard place: the loss of traditional insurance practices and the costs of changeover vs. the threat of increased taxes.

WHAT'S IT ALL ABOUT?

Okay. So we're talking about a unisex bill that will make it illegal for insurance companies to discriminate on the basis of sex. But what does that mean, how would it work, and why does the thought of it upset the insurance industry so much?

Insurance is a way of sharing the risks of untoward happenings so that the risks (costs) involved are spread among many rather than falling on the shoulders of the person to whom the misfortune occurs. Thus an expensive operation, an automobile accident, or loss of income due to illness all create costs, which the individual involved can mitigate or even cover completely by means of insurance. Obviously, however, no one can predict exactly which misfortune, if any, will actually happen, so insurance premiums may be paid, usually for many years, for an eventuality that the insured fervently hopes will never become a reality. Life insurance is an obvious exception to this rule, but even with life insurance, it is impossible to predict whether the policy will pay off in one year or fifty or more.

Ideally, a person buys insurance for protection against the more expensive misfortunes; each individual's priorities differ, depending on age, life-style, health, and various other factors. But the insured has no way of knowing the future and so can make at best only an educated guess. A person also has to consider what is affordable in the way of premiums, and as a result may not be able to buy all the insurance he or she thinks is necessary.

The insurance company is in a somewhat different situation. It has statistics, constantly accumulated and analyzed, to guide its decisions. And to a large extent it controls both what it charges for covering the risks and whom it will insure. It is sometimes caught in a bind, when, for instance, a natural or man-made catastrophe throws the odds out the window and generates an unusual number of expensive claims that must be paid. War would be an example of this unpredictable high-risk situation, except that companies routinely exclude from coverage conditions resulting from "an act of war." It is only reasonable and fair for companies to consider the odds in writing policies and setting rates; they are, after all, in business to make money and cannot do so if they are constantly paying out more money than they are taking in. As with any gambling situation, the odds have to favor the house and show a profit; even though there may occasionally be a big winner, most of the players are programmed to lose.

Insurance companies could, however, actually pay out more money than they take in in premiums (though this is not supposed to be the way the system works) without going broke, because the bulk of their profits now comes not from excess premiums but from investment income. The investment money, which may originally have accumulated during good years, when premiums far exceeded payouts and no one ever heard of a loss ratio, now has generally grown to the point where it has a life of its own and is more than a comfortable cushion against hard times. In addition, even the premium money eventually paid out in claims generates a certain amount of income from interest and investments before leaving the fold. And a loss ratio of 65 percent—which is considered a good deal for the consumer—leaves a comfortable margin of 35 percent toward operating and other expenses. For example, as Andrew Tobias writes in *The Invisible Bankers,* "The capital underlying the operation of the State Farm Mutual Automobile Insurance Company at year-end 1980, $4.6 billion, was greater than that of either Citicorp or Bank of America, double that of the Chase Manhattan Bank."

Obviously insurance is big business, and like any successful big business, it doesn't want to see the federal government rock the boat with legislated changes. Insurance companies have more clout on the state level, so they would rather see regulation confined as much as possible to the states; Congress is much more unpredictable. Unfortunately for the industry, it is now more under public and federal scrutiny than at any time in its history. There have been other dicey situations, but in spite of its being called an inefficiently run industry with a mind-boggling workforce that Mr. Tobias describes as comprised of "one million eight hundred ninety-five thousand employees, or very nearly as many people as constitute the Armed Forces, twenty times as many as are required to collect all of the nation's federal income and excise taxes, and three times as many people as it takes to run the Postal Service," the most serious charges leveled against it, and the ones that have led to the proposed unisex insurance bills, are based on the way it sets its rates.

Risk Classification— How They Know How Much to Charge

Insurers divide people into "classes," determining these classes according to factors that are supposed to be related to risks. One classification (and the one that has created the current fuss) is sex. Women, just by being female, are presumed to be in a different category of risk than men; sometimes to their advantage, sometimes to their disadvantage. Insurance statistics are, therefore, divided into those for men and those for women. Not so long ago other factors also created classes; among these was race, which has since been dropped as a class. Sex, however, has continued as one of the most persistent classes.

The insurers justify using sex as a class by pointing to their sex-based actuarial tables (the basis for their rate setting) that appear to show distinct differences between the sexes. They point out, also, the instances in which women benefit by being considered as a class and men end up paying higher premiums. (They do not point out the instances in which being a woman buys less insurance for more money.) The industry usually points to life insurance; women today pay between 10 percent and 30 percent lower premiums than men for the same insurance. The statistical basis for this is the actuarial tables that show women live on the average about seven years longer than men and therefore pay premiums for a longer period. Another example is automobile insurance, for which young women get lower rates than young men because, according to the sex-based tables, young men have more accidents.

Opponents say classification is in itself discriminatory, because people are individuals and classifying them discriminates against those who fall above or below the "average." While it is true, this argument goes, that women on the average live longer than men, many individual wives die before their husbands and many individual women die long before many men. The validity of this argument comes into question, says the industry, when it is examined as a principle. Age, for example, is generally accepted as a valid classification. An older person routinely pays a higher premium for life insurance than a younger person because, considered as part of a class, he or she will not live as long. Yet an individual young man may be killed two days later in an automobile accident, and an individual elderly man, leading a quiet life of golf, fishing, and aerobic exercise, may last far beyond his predicted life span. It would be nice to eliminate all classifications, but without some statistical basis, insurance companies could not function in a rational way. In the early days of the industry, insurance companies used to charge flat rates, but they instituted the classification system with actuarial tables as a more sensible method of rate setting.

At present no one is seriously advocating doing away with risk-classification tables entirely. The issue is whether the risk classifications used and the statistics that underlie them are based on correct assumptions, and whether they are being used without prejudice or, rather, are being used selectively to provide a rationale for a predetermined rate-setting action favorable to the industry. The proponents of the unisex bills maintain that the latter is the case.

The insurance industry says their present system not only is fair but that changing it would cost everyone—insured and insurer—a fortune. Even in this area there seems to be a difference of opinion, with no consensus as to just how costly it would be.

According to Richard Schweiker, former secretary of Health and Human Services and currently president of the American Council of Life Insurance, just "topping up pension benefits to make men's and women's equal (and) to equalize existing life insurance policies, would cost more than $15 billion." The ACLI estimates that employees would have to fork over $1.7 billion every year to cover increases for those workers already retired. The Academy of Actuaries told Congress in 1981 that phasing out sex-based actuarial tables would cost women $160 million a year more in life insurance premiums and $700 million a year more in automobile insurance premiums. The *Congressional Quarterly* reported, in a discussion of the unisex bills, that the AAA estimated merely equalizing the pension program would cost perhaps just under $2.5 billion a year. At the same time the Department of Labor disputed this figure, claiming it wouldn't cost more than $1.7 billion.

Basically these figures were being tossed around by the insurance industry to counter the touted benefits that would accrue from a changeover, to indicate the hardship these bills would impose on the industry, and as a scare tactic to win over consumers (who were told they would have to bear the brunt of increased costs) at the same time that women were being told their gains would be small compared to their losses.

In a less strong and somewhat whiny tone, the industry also mentioned in passing that they had always done it this way and why did they suddenly have to change everything.

The unisex bill proponents lost no time in meeting the industry's challenge.

In Favor of Unisex Insurance

WEAL, an acronym for Women's Equity Action League, in a bulletin called *WEAL FACTS* makes many of the points of those who support the unisex insurance bills. Characterizing sex-based discrimination as "the most overt form of unfair treatment insurance companies practice," it continues: "Adequate, affordable and equitable insurance is crucial to the economic security of women, especially for the growing number of women who must support themselves and their families." The marketplace is already unfair to women, since "on the average, a woman working full-time earns 60% of a man's income." And this in spite of the fact that "nearly 10 million of America's families are single-parent families maintained by women," exploding the long-held myth that women work for the fun of it and not because they need the money.

In its bulletin WEAL then details specific discriminatory practices.

Sex and automobile insurance. Young male drivers are charged more than young female drivers, presumably because the tables show they have more accidents. It has been suggested, however, that an erroneous conclusion is being drawn from this statistic and that the determining factor in number of accidents is not sex but mileage. On the basis of mileage, young men, who on the average drive almost twice as many miles a year as young women, do not have appreciably more accidents. According to these statistics, the industry's argument that going the unisex insurance route would cost young women more in automobile insurance premiums would no longer apply. If mileage was used as a basis, young women, driving less, would still be charged less; young men, driving more, would still be charged more.

The credibility of the insurance industry's position in regard to the use of sex-based statistics for automobile rates is further weakened by the lack of consistency in their application. For it is only *young* women who are allowed to reap the benefit of the sex-based actuarial tables. Older women—still unarguably women and still driving less, regardless of age—do not benefit (except with a few companies), even though the argument and conclusion to be drawn from the sex-based tables should logically lead to lower rates for women of all ages, since women as a group have "better driving records." With mileage as the factor, women regardless of age would benefit, since all women, on the average, drive fewer miles than men.

It would appear, therefore, that contrary to the industry's argument that unisex auto insurance would cost women more, it would actually cost them, as a group, less. And extrapolating from this example, proponents of the unisex bill therefore claim that the industry's weak and, as they see it, questionable position and practices in auto insurance call into question the validity of the industry's statistics and risk-classification tables.

Other factors. Supporters of the bill argue that life-style, age, and state of health are more relevant factors than sex for such insurance as life, pension, and disability. Credence has been lent to this point of view by a study at Pennsylvania's Indiana University. Gus Miller, director of Studies in Smoking in Edinboro, Pennsylvania, and Dean Gerstein of the National Research Council, National Academy of Sciences, studied the smoking habits of 4394 people who died in Erie County between 1972 and 1974, and 3916 living residents of the county. Their findings, adjusted for violent deaths (more frequent among males), disputed the statistics that seem to indicate women live longer. They found instead that life expectancy was about the same, with no statistically significant difference between the sexes.

As described in *Public Health Reports,* July-August 1983, the study concluded that "virtually all the increase in the difference between male and female longevity since 1930 is attributable to the effects of cigarette smoking." It is only fair to note that the study has been faulted by some scientists, primarily for using too small a sample for too short a time. The opinion generally held among experts does hold, however, that smoking probably accounts for about half the male-female expectancy differential. Since smoking now appears to be on the increase among women, expectations are that the differences shown by the sex-based expectancy tables may begin to even out, and that perhaps life-style, not sex, is the determining factor in this instance.

Sex and life insurance

1. Certain policies limit the coverage a woman can purchase to a maximum of that held by her husband.
2. Smaller policies (the ones most women can afford) carry a heavy surcharge.
3. Although life-expectancy tables show women live on the averge 7 years longer than men, life insurance policies use a 3-year difference. In other words, a 46-year-old woman would pay the same premium as a 43-year-old man, whereas, according to the tables, she should pay the same premium as a 39-year-old man. This selective use of statistics, of which other instances

can be cited, is one of the reasons critics question the credibility of the industry's arguments in favor of sex-based tables.

Other factors. Life insurance is easier to examine than health insurance because it is less complicated; there are fewer kinds of policies and fewer exclusions, limitations, and options. Some aspects of sex discrimination are, therefore, more readily revealed by examining life rather than health insurance rates.

As we have seen, WEAL claims that the use of sex-related life-expectancy tables results in sex discrimination, not only because the tables are themselves discriminatory but also because they are applied only partially and selectively, and only when they are perceived as advantageous to the industry.

WEAL points out that the industry does not give the whole rate break (7 years greater life expectancy) that women—according to the industry's own system—are entitled to.

The industry's position—which more or less ignores this argument in presenting their defense of sex as a valid risk factor—has been stated at some length on many occasions by various industry spokesmen. On May 19, 1983, Robert N. Houser, chairman of the board of Bankers Life Company, spoke on behalf of the American Council of Life Insurance (ACLI) before the Senate Committee on Commerce, Science and Transportation. He identified ACLI as "a national trade association which represents 572 life insurance companies in the United States and Canada [that] account for more than 95 percent of the life insurance in force in the United States [and] write virtually all of the insured private pension plan business in the United States."

Although his statement was made prior to the decision

in the Norris case, much of it subsequently was repeated, word for word, in the ACLI paper "Gender as a Risk Classification Factor," which was presented at a public hearing in Charleston, West Virginia, the November after the Norris decision.

Both statements characterize the industry's risk classification systems as "traditional," as if that in itself was in its favor. Not only does this lack relevancy, however, it is especially unfortunate in these times when many established traditions—especially the whole area of traditional gender discrimination and discrimination against minorities—are being reexamined and overturned.

As it happens, the use of sex-based tables is not even that old a tradition. Apparently, according to these statements, charging different rates for men and women was first introduced in the 1950s. At a time when much older traditions are under fire, the industry might be wiser not to set too much store on the value of tradition as a persuasive argument.

What the industry might concentrate on instead is the fact that originally the change was made partly in an effort to arrive at a more equitable rate-setting basis than the previous flat-rate method, which gave almost no consumer group a break. True to its knack for putting itself in the worst possible light, the ACLI instead goes on to point out that the change was primarily a sales decision, an attempt to attract a new and practically untapped market. "The lower rates which have been charged for women since then have contributed to the impressive growth in life insurance purchases by women in the last two decades."

They think what they are saying is that giving women a break both encouraged and allowed the fair sex to participate more fully in the advantages of life insurance. What it means to the opposition, however, is that the industry saw sex-based tables as a way of increasing profits.

And the credibility of the industry's position is further weakened by its continuing failure to give women the benefit of the full seven year differential in life expectancy. The selective use of these statistics is even more obvious since the industry justified its unequal retirement benefits treatment of women workers (now prohibited by law) by pointing to exactly this seven-year differential. A now-we-use-them, now-we-don't attitude toward statistics is bound to create a crisis of confidence in the public's perception of the sincerity of the industry.

The industry continues to hand its opponents ammunition with its next argument, that the difference in premiums means "we are able to charge each individual a price that reflects the expected costs of the benefits more accurately than the price we would have to charge if we were obliged to ignore gender." Of course, one of the points of the pro-unisex group is precisely that sex-based tables are unfair to the individual. The industry is trying to make a point but is not being sufficiently sensitive to the aura now surrounding the word *individual* in the unisex vocabulary. To the beleaguered consumer—most often female—familiar with the enormous difference in rates and coverage for policies offered to groups as compared to individual purchasers of health insurance, the industry's claim of being fair to the individual simply doesn't hold water and is not likely to be accepted calmly once that red flag of a word is flown.

Continuing further, the industry statement once again trips over its own feet. "Throughout their history, life insurance companies have added new individual [that word again!] characteristics to their classification system as their relevance became clear, and have discarded old ones that were no longer important." (What happened to tradition?) And further on: "In other areas of risk classification, too, insurance companies are constantly reviewing and updating their classifications. For example, insurers must reflect changing patterns in the mortality associated with various physical impairments, which occur because of progress in medical treatment, public health measures, lifestyles, etc." Which, of course, inevitably leads proponents of the unisex bills to ask, if they have made so many changes in the past, why are they fighting against one more? In modern times change is generally equated with progress; the industry didn't decry the expense of computerizing itself; why fuss about changing a few tables? It may not be quite that simple, but if it is not, the industry is surely failing to communicate the nature of the problem.

Sometimes the statement almost seems to go out of its way to help the other side. In referring to the decision in the Norris case, it says: "the Court ruling made it clear that it was not ruling on sex as a determining factor in all forms of insurance." The industry is right but does not seem to realize that it would be better not to bring that up, since it is exactly that omission that the unisex bills are now attempting to correct.

When one side in an argument tries to make points by using scare tactics, a natural supposition has to be that they are desperate and are falling back on a last resort. On this level the most commonly used scare tactic of this industry is that of cost. It is usually argued that the proposed change will be costly to exactly the group it is meant to benefit. In this instance the insurance industry has a two-pronged approach. On the one hand, it argues that changing from sex-based tables may put some insurance companies out of business. On the other hand, it estimates how much it will cost women, whom the change is supposed to benefit.

If the proponents are considering only the civil rights aspect, neither argument will make a dent. Congress, however, takes money seriously. The industry claims life insurance premiums for women would rise to the level of men's—about 20 percent higher than at present. Presumably, also, although this is not mentioned, if industry costs go up, so will all premiums, in accordance with the modern business custom of passing increased costs right on to the consumer. Direct costs to the industry of the changeover would come primarily in the area of health insurance, pensions, and annuities, but here there is, as has been noted, a discrepancy between the industry's actuarial estimates and that of the Department of Labor. The ACLI explains this by noting that the lower Department of Labor figure (1.7 billion) reflects only the expense of "topping up" pension benefits and does not include the attendant costs for life, automobile, and health insurance, equalization of future retiree benefits, nor the administrative costs of implementation.

Congress has apparently considered that this last argument has some validity, inasmuch as it has offered, as a compromise, not to require "topping up" or to make any of the provisions of the unisex bills retroactive. This will be hard on present retirees, but a line has to be drawn somewhere and perhaps some special provision can be made for that group, as it was for Social Security recipients who would not have been covered under the number-of-quarters requirement that determines eligibility for coverage.

The industry statement contains some encouragement for those who seek to eliminate sex discrimination in insurance practices. It notes that "life insurers [have responded to changes] by liberalizing the availability of life insurance coverage to females, [and] fully support legislation or regulation prohibiting discrimination on the basis of sex in the availability of life insurance coverage, [including] the act of denying benefits or coverage on the basis of sex or marital status." The latter part of the sentence refers to the National Association of Insurance Commissioners'

(NAIC) Model Regulation to Eliminate Unfair Sex Discrimination, which by November 1983 had been adopted or enacted in less than half the states.

Sex and health insurance. Generally when one talks about sex in this context, the feminine sex is the one meant. As we will see in the next chapter, that set is changing rapidly; more and more the issues that affect women also affect men, and what is good for one is often achieved at the expense of the other. For the moment, however, we will talk about how health insurance treats women.

The state of Michigan's Insurance Bureau puts out a number of informative booklets, including one called *Essential Insurance . . . Its Impact on Women.* A glance at the table of contents reveals that auto and home insurance are the only areas covered; there is no mention made of health insurance. This is typical of the kind of problems women have encountered in trying to buy this equally essential kind of insurance.

The problem is especially acute for older women, for women—like men—have increasing health problems as they age, and health insurance (which the industry prefers to sell to the young and healthy) is even harder for an older woman to buy than it is for an older man.

In September 1983, at a hearing conducted by the Task Force on the Status of Older Women of the New York State Assembly Standing Committee on Aging, Adelaide Attard, chairman of the Federal Council on Aging, said action was needed to correct the inequities of the Social Security system, private pension plans, and health insurance coverage which threatened the financial and emotional security of older women. In her testimony she stated that:

1. Four million women, aged 45 to 65, have no health insurance at all.

2. On the average, women retire on less than one-half the fixed income of retired men. (This is not surprising, since a woman working full-time earns on the average 60% as much as a man.) In addition, many women working as domestics and in similar low-level jobs are not eligible for pensions or Social Security most of the time.

The ripple effect of these statistics extends to such coverage as indemnity insurance, in which the amount of benefits is based on one's income. Even if there were no discrimination on the part of the insurance company, the fact that the workplace routinely relegates women to a lower pay status precludes the possibility that they can buy indemnity insurance coverage equal to a man's.

Although some inequities have been prohibited by recent laws or court decisions, the following list will indicate some of the discriminatory practices to which women in search of health insurance have been subjected. And it might be well to note that some of the recent improvements are now being rescinded by even newer decisions or will be in the near future by cases presently in the courts.

1. More women than men must buy individual policies because they are not eligible for group insurance. (Individual policies are not even covered by many of the antidiscriminatory laws.)
2. At present women must pay higher premiums for the same health insurance coverage as men because statistics show they have greater utilization of health care—more hospitalization, more frequent doctor office visits, etc. In a 1972 bulletin issued by Metropolitan Life, the company asserted that the rate for women incurring a disability lasting 8 days or longer in 1972 was 179 per thousand,

whereas it was only 95 per thousand for men.

The following year Casper Weinberger, then secretary of Health, Education and Welfare, said it was a myth that women have more job absenteeism than men. Speaking before a women's conference, he said, "The simple fact is that women are out on sick leave 48 minutes per year longer than men, which is practically insignificant. . . . Actually the amount of sick leave doesn't seem to relate to the sex of the employee but to the employee's length of service and grade level. The longer the service and the higher the grade, the less likely he or she is to be absent." This statement was apparently based on U.S. Department of Labor statistics in which sick days in 1971 were 5.2 for women against 5.1 for men. And the Institute of Life Insurance's Bob Weldron concurred, saying that women on the executive level do not tend to have any greater absenteeism than men.

3. Only recently has pregnancy been covered, regardless of whether it is normal or has complications. And only recently has this coverage applied to both spouses and workers (regardless of marital status). Here again the industry's arguments against coverage rested partly on the notion that pregnancy is a "voluntary" condition (which is certainly often not the case); an argument inconsistent with the fact that coverage already existed for truly voluntary health situations, such as vasectomies. In fact at one point Prudential had a major medical plan that covered male vasectomies but not female sterilization procedures.

4. Women who have health insurance coverage only through their husband's job may lose it if they divorce or are widowed. Also they will find themselves without coverage if their husband should lose his job (unless his policy continues until he finds another job or is

convertible at a premium he can afford).

5. Even with good pregnancy coverage, women may lose seniority and other rights—even their jobs—as a result of taking pregnancy leave. (See next chapter for a discussion of this issue.)

6. Coverage for maternity benefits, when provided, can be inadequate compared to coverage for other "illnesses." There is often a dollar limit to the benefits, and this can be as little as $500 for a normal delivery. Some policies allowed five days of medical care, with cash benefits of up to $300 for female workers, but provided wives of male employees up to 10 days of hospital care and a maximum of $1,000 for medical costs. It would still have been discriminatory if it had been the other way around, but at least it wouldn't have been so blatantly sexist.

A similar example of this peculiar kind of discrimination against women is a group plan that was offered by Aetna to small businesses, which did not provide maternity benefits for women workers but did cover the spouses of male workers. Of course, this is not as whimsical as it might seem; small businesses probably have an overabundance of women employees, in which case this provision is a simple way of reducing payouts. This conjecture would seem to be borne out by the fact that companies that employ a high percentage of women routinely pay higher health insurance premiums.

Another example, in a different area, is to be found in survivors' pensions. In 1983 more than half of the pension plans paid widows smaller monthly incomes than they paid the widowers who survived a similarly situated female worker. The unisex bill would, of course, change all that; both widows and widowers would collect on the same basis.

7. Although nearly 10 million of America's families are single-parent families headed by women, their dependents may be denied benefits from the mother's policy.
8. Disability insurance is generally not available to part-time workers (two-thirds of whom are women) or to women not employed outside the home.

THE LAST WORD

Since it is "traditional" for women to have the last word, it seemed only fitting that the final comment on the use of sex-based actuarial tables as a risk classification factor be a comment by Mary Gray, president of WEAL: "I have one life expectancy as an American, a longer one as a woman, a shorter one as a worker in Washington, a longer one as a nonsmoker, and a shorter one as an overweight person. Why use just my sex?"

21

The Other Side of the Coin— Reverse Discrimination

It should come as no surprise to anyone that as soon as discrimination against women begins to be addressed, men perceive the resulting changes as discriminating against and unfair to them. After all, a similar situation exists as a result of the effort to afford blacks equal opportunity: soon white workers question whether blacks have been given an unfair advantage merely because of the color of their skin. In every field, whether it is admission to medical school or allotment of scarce jobs, instituting a quota system rather than a merit system seems to solve one problem only to create another.

The insurance companies can thank their lucky stars that their rate setting is not based on race—as it well might be if race-based actuarial tables (which do show differences between whites and blacks) had been used— and that they are not, therefore, involved in this controversy. When they, quite innocently, switched to sex-based tables, the status of women was not nearly so much in the news; although since these tables came into use as late as the 1950s, futurists in the industry might well have predicted the 1980s explosion of the demand for equality of the sexes.

Once women realized they were being discriminated

against by the insurance industry—as well as by practically every other industry—it became a target for both civil rights and equal rights groups. But no sooner had these groups achieved a few gains in a few isolated areas than reverse discrimination reared its masculine head. The current brouhaha over the "pregnancy issue" is a case in point.

HEALTH INSURANCE AND PREGNANCY

Although there were many inequalities in the health insurance coverage available to women, most were not so obvious as that of pregnancy coverage. First of all, it was clear that when a woman took maternity leave, her group health disability policy did not offer her the same benefits as those given to a male worker on disability, under the same policy by which a male worker taking sick leave was covered. When the costs of pregnancies ran only a few hundred dollars, this could be dismissed—except as a matter of principle—as a minor irritation. But as health care costs rose and the costs of pregnancy crept up into the thousands, the matter became more serious.

As we have noted, the employer (who faced higher premiums) and the insurance company (who faced an increase in claims) both justified denying pregnancy coverage on the grounds that it was a "voluntary" act. Since pregnancy and maternity leave were issues that affected a large percentage of the workforce—both female workers and spouses of male workers—it inevitably ended up in the courts.

General Electric v. Gilbert

As is usual with this type of issue, which concerns equally those workers who want to have that kind of coverage and those who not only don't want it but also don't want to pay for someone else to have it, the matter was hard fought until it reached the Supreme Court. In 1976 the *General Electric Company* v. *Gilbert* and *Gilbert* v. *General Electric Company* were heard. At issue was whether an employer was violating the sex-discrimination ban (good old Title VII) by excluding pregnancy and pregnancy-related disabilities from the group disability plan. The justices, with Justice Rehnquist writing the majority opinion, ruled that the employer was not in violation. Justice Rehnquist took the position that the GE plan was not unequal in coverage because there was no risk from which one sex was protected and the other was not; in other words, it was not as if one sex was covered for pregnancy and the other was not. Since coverage was, therefore, equal, the employer was free to choose whether to cover the disability of pregnancy, just as the employer was free to choose whether to cover any other disability. Justices Brennan, Marshall, and Stevens dissented. This was on December 7. On December 13 the Supreme Court again ruled against unisex in *Mathews* v. *de Castro,* deciding Congress had not acted unconstitutionally when it denied spouse insurance benefits to divorced wives under sixty-two years of age and with dependent children, but provided those benefits for wives under sixty-two who were still married (to a worker covered by the policy). Though this ruling did not deal directly with the area of reverse discrimination, it led to a case that did.

Califano v. *Goldfarb*

Bringing spouses into the picture pointed up the fact that a spouse can be either male or female. This led to the case of *Califano* v. *Goldfarb.* At issue was the difference in coverage between male and female spouses; this time the female spouses were said to be receiving preferential treatment in that widows who had been receiving one-half of their support from their spouse at the time of his death were eligible for survivor's benefits: widowers, in a similar situation due to deceased wives, were not. On March 2 the Supreme Court ruled that in this instance Congress had indeed acted unconstitutionally. The question was, was this a case of discrimination against women or of reverse discrimination? If you find this confusing, so did the justices. Justices Brennan, Power, Marshall, and White took the position that it was discrimination against women because they paid the same premiums as male workers yet obtained less protection for their spouses. Justice Stevens regarded it as discrimination against widowers (reverse discrimination). It came to the same thing in the end, inasmuch as both sides agreed that Congress had acted unconstitutionally in having different requirements for widows and widowers in regard to survivor benefits; reverse or not, it clearly came under the heading of sex discrimination (even though it wasn't clear which sex was being discriminated against).

Congress Gets into the Act

During this period many minor cases of sex discrimination were decided by the Court, but none was of the importance of *General Electric* v. *Gilbert*. Every time a worker or a worker's spouse became pregnant, it came to mind and could not help but be a constant irritant, both to women and men workers and their spouses. On the other hand, a great deal of money in benefits was at stake, and neither employers nor insurance companies were eager to take on the additional costs.

Indignant over the *Gilbert* decision, a coalition of labor, civil rights, and women's groups met in Philadelphia to work toward a change in legislation. More than fifty organizations sent representatives, including the American Citizens Concerned for Life (ACCL), an antiabortion organization that felt the *Gilbert* decision would increase abortions among those workers who needed the financial support of disability coverage.

On March 15, 1976, legislation was introduced, and hearings began the following month. All the usual arguments, pro and con, surfaced.

- Con: Disability coverage for pregnancy would reduce equal employment opportunities for women (employers would think twice about hiring a nubile female).
- Pro: Disability pregnancy coverage would dispel myths about working women that kept them in inferior jobs (because, theoretically, they weren't as serious about working as about raising a family).
- Pro: An adequate income (disability payments) during pregnancy would help cover medical costs and living expenses, just as during any illness.
- Pro: The bills would give women the same fringe benefits and seniority rights that men already received during disability.
- Con: Increased costs would be passed on to the already beleaguered consumer.
- Con: Employers without disability plans would be less likely to institute one because of the increased cost.
- Con: It would be difficult to assess the extent of disability and to separate disability due to pregnancy from that due to the needs of the child. (For example: how long should disability leave be—for an uneventful delivery, a cesarean delivery, or for one with complications?)
- Con: G. Brockwel Heylin, speaking for the Chamber of Commerce, testified that about half of women who take maternity leave do not come back to work. In

such a case they would receive both leave and disability benefits or, in effect, severance pay. Men workers quitting a job would not get an equally fair shake. These figures were disputed by both Ethel Bent Walsh, chairman of the EEOC, and Ethel Censor Rubin, an actuary, who testified that not only do nearly two-thirds of women who work do so from need, but also that the number of women returning after maternity leave is steadily increasing—from 46 percent in 1973 to 69 percent in 1975.

One of the major problems was predicting the costs involved in viewing pregnancy as an illness and thus bringing it under the classification of disability and health benefits. As usual, there was total disagreement among the factions involved as to how much these costs would amount to. The Health Insurance Association of America (HIAA) estimated that cost to employers, based on an 11.3-week average leave, would be $611 million in disability payments and $1 billion in increased coverage of hospital and medical expenses. Those in favor of the bill disputed these figures and presented their own. Ms. Rubin estimated the increased cost to employers at only $320 million in disability payments. The lower estimate was due partly to Ms. Rubin's determination that average leave time would be 8 rather than 11.3 weeks, with a longer period needed by only 5 percent to 10 percent of those taking maternity leave.

During the House hearings, subsequently, the Labor Department estimated that the bill would cost about $191 million (about 20¢ a week per worker), assuming the average disability payment of $80 a week for an average disability leave of 7.5 weeks. The AFL-CIO had even more optimistically estimated the cost at $130 million. With a spread of $481 million between the highest and lowest cost-increase figures, the estimates began to look more like guesstimates, with each faction's point of view perhaps influencing its projections. But instead of puzzling out the reason for this discrepancy, it was possible to look at a situation where this kind of coverage was already in place.

In Hawaii, where most employees have had this kind of coverage since 1970, under the Hawaii Temporary Disability Insurance Plan, experience has been that temporary disability insurance rates actually have decreased, in spite of covering women workers for pregnancy. While this experience might not necessarily hold true for other states, Hawaii's experience does seem to indicate that perhaps cost should not be a primary consideration.

The Senate Human Resources Committee reported out on the bill (S995) in July, stating that the issue was covered under Title VII and that discrimination based on pregnancy, childbirth, and related medical conditions was therefore sex discrimination. The committee further found that the *Gilbert* decision "threatens to undermine the central purpose of sex discrimination prohibitions of Title VII," and characterized as sex stereotyping the assumption that women workers were more or less inevitably bound to become pregnant and could justifiably receive disparate treatment in the workplace. "A failure to address discrimination based on pregnancy, in fringe benefits or in any other employment practice, would prevent the elimination of sex discrimination in employment."

The report continued:

It would be difficult to overstate the importance of removing this barrier to equal employment opportunity for women. Currently about 46 per cent of all women over the age of 16 are in the labor force. There are now 39 million women who are working or seeking work. Since 1950, the greatest gains anywhere in the labor force have registered among women 25 to 54 years of age.

Most of these women work out of hard economic necessity. Seventy per cent, or over 25 million of the women who work, are either their family's sole wage earner, are married to husbands who earn less than $7,000 per year or are single, divorced or widowed. . . . One of every 10 babies is born to a woman who is divorced, widowed, or single and who thus can be expected to have no income other than her own.

Under this bill, the treatment of pregnant women in covered employment must focus not on their condition alone but on the actual effects of that condition on their ability to work. Pregnant women who are able to work must be permitted to work on the same conditions as other employees; and when they are not able to work for medical reasons, they must be accorded the same rights, leave privileges, and other benefits, as other workers who are disabled. . . .

After considerable discussion, including the question of coverage of abortions and the length of time to be allowed for leave, S995 was passed in September 1977 by the Senate, and finally HR6075, its counterpart, cleared the House. The ninety-fifth Congress, in passing the legislation, agreed to a compromise version in which the Senate agreed to modified antiabortion language that had been desired by the House.

The final legislation amended Title VII, making discrimination on the basis of pregnancy, childbirth, or related medical conditions illegal in all matters of employment, including hiring, promotion, and seniority rights as well as receipts of benefits under fringe benefits programs. It did not prevent employers from refusing to cover pregnancy if incurred before the worker was hired, since this fell under the preexisting conditions clause that the employer was free to specify.

The bill also gave employers a choice as to whether the benefits would apply to elective abortions, except if the life of the mother would be endangered without the abortion, but required coverage for medical complications resulting from abortions, including disability and sick leave benefits. This gave the employers the right to grant or withhold benefits depending on their personal attitude toward abortion.

Predictably, the abortion amendment was unhappily received by those who viewed it as proabortion. On the other hand, women's rights groups concurred with Ted Weiss (D-NY) in viewing it as a new form of discrimination against women employees.

In 1978, when the bill was passed, it was considered an important milestone in women's rights. But lest you should think that the issue of pregnancy and the working woman (or spouse) was now settled once and for all, read on.

BACK TO SQUARE ONE—THE GARLAND CASE

By the spring of 1982 the seesaw of sex discrimination was once again in motion. And again the issue was reverse discrimination, pitting men's rights against women's.

The Garland case started out as a typical working woman's quest for equal treatment. Lillian Garland, a receptionist, filed a complaint with the California Fair Employment Agency against her employer, California Federal Savings and Loan. Her complaint was based on her employer's action in connection with maternity leave from her job in May 1982.

She had taken disability leave to have a baby by

cesarean section, and when she returned, the bank would not give her back her job. It had never occurred to her that she might lose her job by taking maternity leave, and she had apparently not been so informed by her employer. Seven months later, when a vacancy in a similar position occurred, the bank hired her back, but in the meantime, with no money coming in, she had been evicted from her apartment and had lost custody of her baby.

In desperation she had finally turned to the state department of Fair Employment and Housing. They told her that under the state law, she was legally entitled to up to four months' leave without pay and that she had been fired illegally. She filed suit, but Cal Fed decided to fight it, saying the state law was contrary to the federal law and discriminated against men, who were not guaranteed reinstatement after disability. The bank was joined in its suit by the California Chamber of Commerce and the Merchants and Manufacturers Association.

As usual, the case wended its leisurely way through the legal system until, in March 1984, a California court ruling on the case overturned the 1979 state law that required reinstatement for women returning after maternity leave.

Judge Manuel Real, of the United States District Court, ruled that the California state law violated federal law because it required preferential treatment for women disabled by pregnancy, childbirth, or related conditions. His point was that the state law requires employers to grant up to four months of unpaid maternity leave and then to reinstate the woman worker upon her return, whereas the federal law requires such reinstatement only from employers who provide the same leave benefits, with reinstatement, to the disabled male worker. In other words, his ruling was that the state law was reverse discrimination, favoring the female over the male worker.

The Garland case has attracted nationwide attention. It is now awaiting a ruling from the United States Court of Appeals for the Ninth Circuit but is almost certain to end up in the Supreme Court. Meanwhile there are over two hundred similar cases in California alone awaiting a final decision.

Love and Work

Among those commenting publicly on the Garland case is Carol Snow, publisher of *Scientific American Medicine*. In a letter to the editors (*New York Times,* August 5, 1984) she wrote:

> ... This law is indeed discriminatory. The solution, however, is not to penalize pregnant women, but rather to take the stigma of disability away from pregnancy. ...
>
> It is important to remember that the environment in which the conditions of disability are defined is a workplace whose labor schedules have long been established for the convenience of working men, not working women. ...
>
> [Feminism] has created a two-gender society— persons and mothers. Persons are that androgynous and narcissistic combination of men and women, who are creating the current power structure. But there are still mothers around, and they are still poor and still women. ... If we want the success of the women's movement to continue beyond our own generation, then we must strive for the more perfect integration of the processes of love and work.

The feminist point of view is that Ms. Garland is in the wrong. As reported in *The New York Times,* Mayor Dianne Feinstein of San Francisco praised Judge Real's ruling. "What we women have been saying all along is we want to be treated equally. Now we have to put our money where our mouth is. What we were asking was to create a special group of workers that in essence is pregnant women and new mothers. I just don't happen to agree with that."

Those in favor of the bill, such as Carole Ward-Allen, chairman of the state Commission on the Status of Women, feel: "In essence it [the law] says women have a choice: 'You can choose to work or you can have children. But you can't have both.'" Mayor Feinstein looks upon it as just another one of the problems that confront women who work. "I believe that women have the choice. If they make the choice for career and children, there is no question there are problems. But I don't think the work market has to accommodate itself to women having children."

On the other hand, there is no doubt that nature herself discriminates, through pregnancy, against the female but not the male parent; and society, through custom, goes even further by putting the burden of early parenthood largely on the woman. In spite of movies like *Kramer vs. Kramer,* it is still the mother who is usually considered the primary parent in the care of young children. In more primitive societies this was not the hardship it is today, since mothers could take their children along with them, whether into the fields, the factory, or the household. Even today, in much of the Far East, as in Taiwan, whole families move into the "factory" to accompany the worker, and babies are tended and meals are prepared on the spot.

Of course, the ruling could conceivably be applied also to the creation of day-care centers and other support facilities that are necessary if many mothers are to be able to work. Since, as we have seen, most women work not from choice but from financial necessity—often as sole head of household or sole support—they cannot chose not to work, and since working women are increasingly working mothers, the problem isn't going to go away. As quoted in a *New York Times* editorial, "Who'll Mind America's Children?" (March 29, 1984), "The Congressional Budget Office estimates that by 1990 the majority of America's mothers will hold jobs outside the home, including more than half those with children under 6. One of four children under 10 will be living in a single-parent household and most of their parents will be working, or would be if they could afford child care."

The Garland case, with its strange alignment of feminists on the side of the employers, must obviously be decided on a much more complex basis than the simplistic black-and-white of Title VII. It is not enough to say that men and women are equal when nature itself says differently. This kind of inequality will not disappear with equal treatment; it is inherent in the fact that women bear children and men do not.

As has often been the case with antidiscrimination laws, the focus has been too narrow. In an effort to deal with maternity benefits, they have been put under the disability umbrella. This simply does not work; pregnancy is not a disability, and equating it with disability has led to the confusion that now underlies all approaches to maternity/paternity benefits. Now that we have recognized the problem of discrimination, we need to go one step further and deal with exceptions; pregnancy is an exception. As Linda Kreig, an attorney with the Employment Law Center in San Francisco, says, "We are the only industrialized nation that doesn't provide paid maternity leave as a matter of national policy. I don't see why it should be illegal sex discrimination to fire a woman because she gets pregnant, but acceptable to tell her she loses her job if she takes off a few weeks for childbirth. In the real world, it's the same thing. The point isn't that men and women must be treated alike, it's that they must have equal opportunities. When it comes to pregnancy, equal treatment means inequality for women."

To equate the desire for children—a desire essential to the survival of the race—with other less basic needs would seem somewhat lacking in a sense of the proper priorities. Up to the point of overpopulation, the country as a whole benefits from its children; it would not be in the interests of society if children were to be considered a luxury. Also, if a woman cannot work and have children, it would appear we are depriving her of her basic rights as a person as well as arbitrarily limiting the freedom to have children to those women who either have someone else to support them or are independently wealthy or to men who are gainfully employed and have a woman to bear their children. And once we grant that children are necessary to society and that women are "entitled" to have them, it hardly seems consistent to deny mothers the ability to feed those children by making it impossible for the mothers to work. If this requires certain support facilities, it seems only logical that in the interests of society they should be provided (and numerous studies have shown that helping people work is much less costly than taking care of them on welfare). As long as these facilities are also available to working fathers, it would seem to meet the test of fairness. Also, those who argue that men should not have to pay for pregnancy coverage because they do not get pregnant would surely not like to see purely male diseases eliminated from coverage simply because women workers cannot get them.

On the other hand, as long as pregnancy is considered, under the law, the same as any other disability, it would appear fair enough to require that benefits for it conform to whatever the employer offers for other types of disability. Although men and women are subject to certain "diseases" peculiar to their sex—women get pregnant, men get prostate problems—disability is theoretically not supposed to differentiate by type. In any case, California Assemblywoman Maxine Waters, who was co-author of the state law, does not intend to let the ruling go without a fight. She plans either to appeal in the courts or to work through the state legislature by amending a bill now under consideration. In the long run, creating a situation that works is going to require some major rethinking of the whole problem of discrimination.

22

Auto Insurance— Young Men Join the Fray

Auto insurance may not at first appear relevant to a discussion of health insurance, but it has generated sex-discrimination lawsuits that may have direct impact on the unisex bill. The most important, and presently ongoing, litigation is the Mattes case.

Families who own cars know that the most expensive part of their automobile insurance is the coverage for their young male drivers. Young females of the same age and situation pay premiums that are considerably lower. But almost no policyholder knows why.

The insurance companies explain the difference in premiums by pointing to their sex-based tables, which appear to show irrefutably that young men have more accidents than young women. Once the unisex bill had raised the consciousness of men as well as women, however, it was only a matter of time before a young male driver cried foul and filed a complaint alleging sex discrimination in auto insurance rates.

THE MATTES CASE

In this case the complainant was a twenty-six-year-old man, Philip Mattes, who availed himself of a state of Pennsylvania statute that said any insured person had a right to seek an administrative hearing from the insurance commission if he had a complaint against an insurance company. Mr. Mattes was fortunate that he lived in Pennsylvania, since not all states have this statute. His complaint was, quite simply, that the Hartford Accident and Indemnity Company had violated his rights by charging him, a male, a higher premium on his automobile insurance than it charged a female in like circumstances. In 1979 he was duly granted a hearing during which the insurance commissioner, David O. Maxwell, agreed that sex was an unfairly discriminatory way to classify risk. The adjudication said, in part:

> Under its rating plan, Hartford uses a combination of classification factors in determining the premium of the insured. These include the insured's age, sex, marital status, status as principal or occasional operator, and driving record, as well as the use and type of vehicle and the territory in which his vehicle is garaged. . . . For drivers under 30, the rate for a male is always higher than for a female, all other circumstances being the same. . . .
>
> While Hartford presented evidence that as a group males have more accidents than females, ISO's rating plan, adopted by Hartford, does not use this data in establishing the automobile rate differentials for men and women. ISO's statistics show, for example, that where a policy lists the insured as an unmarried male, age category 25–29, as a principal operator, the average loss is $228 per vehicle per accident but where

a policy indicates an unmarried female in that category (where she is lumped into what is called the adult class) the average loss is $118 per accident. It is important to emphasize, however, that these figures are not based on who was responsible for the accident or who was driving the insured vehicle at the time. Instead, these insurance losses are correlated to the one sexual classification listed on the particular policy insuring the vehicle. If a policy, for example, specifically covers both an unmarried male and unmarried female, both between ages 17 and 20, and both non-principal operators, the accident for rate-making purposes will be arbitrarily attributed to the male, even though the female was driving or caused the loss. Thus, Hartford's higher premiums for men result not from statistics that men actually cause more expensive accidents but from the rate classifications (including sex) listed on the insurance policy of the car involved in any accident.

As more and more careful drivers who happen to be young men become aware of how these statistics are collected, it is easy to imagine a scenario in which the young male driver will crack down on his girlfriend or sister and refuse to give her the car keys unless she agrees to drive very, very carefully.

Having so decided, the commissioner declared such risk classification unlawful and required the Hartford Accident and Indemnity Company to file a new rate, eliminating the bias of sex-based tables. Instead Hartford promptly filed an appeal and obtained a stay of the commissioner's order from the appellate court.

The Commonwealth Court, as it is called, affirmed the commissioner's order. As we have seen, this is seldom the end of the matter, and sure enough, three years later, in 1982, the case ended up in the Pennsylvania Supreme Court—where it still was in April 1984.

By this time five states had already passed unisex auto insurance laws, but the insurance industry marshaled its forces to prevent Pennsylvania from joining their ranks. In addition to Hartford, briefs were filed by State Farm, the American Insurance Association, the Insurance Federation of Pennsylvania, Nationwide, and Allstate. With the unisex bills already under consideration by Congress, the industry possibly felt it could allow no more unfortunate precedents. The appellee was the Insurance Commission of the Commonwealth of Pennsylvania.

In court the insurance companies stood by their sex-based actuarial tables, which showed a higher rate of accidents for young male drivers compared to young female drivers. They also claimed that unisex premiums would penalize young women drivers, increasing their premiums by a sizable amount.

The premium paid by Mr. Mattes, who had no record of suspension, revocation of license, or any traffic violation, was $360 a year; a similarly situated female paid $212 a year for the same insurance protection. The premium difference of $148 a year admittedly was due entirely to the Hartford's rate classification system. Hartford was, of course, perfectly within its rights in using this system since it previously had been approved for use in Pennsylvania by the commission. Now, however, the commission was examining the validity of using sex as a rate classification factor. It is easy to see why the insurance industry was concerned; a decision against the use of these tables was liable to open a Pandora's box of court cases around the country in connection not only with auto but with many other kinds of insurance.

The commission's examination of the statistics on which the tables are based, both in connection with the original hearing and in subsequent proceedings, as set forth in the brief submitted by Hannah Leavitt, chief of litigation and counsel for the Insurance Department, Commonwealth of Pennsylvania, on June 27, 1983, led to the following conclusions:

1. That in any given year over 90% of both males and females in the complainant's age group do not have accidents. . . . The accident-free males must pay a rate, however, twice that of the accident-free females.
2. Loss data on automobile policies is collected in such a way that the sex of the driver that actually caused or was involved in the accident is not indicated. For example, the loss experience on family policies that include a youthful female operator is compared to those family policies that include a youthful male operator. If the loss experience on the second type of policy is higher, it will be used to justify a higher premium for families that include a youthful male. The actual losses of the family policy with a youthful male, however, may have been caused by any other member of the family, including a youthful female.

If, for instance, a young man's mother is a poor driver given to fender benders in shopping malls, and if he is insured on the same family policy that covers her, all her accidents will be counted against him statistically. As the brief points out, because of the way the statistics are gathered, he will be blamed for accidents that

> may have been caused by any other member of the family, including a youthful female. . . . If a youthful male operator loans his car to his girlfriend, who is involved in an accident, that loss will be charged to the male insured, and then be used to justify a higher premium for all youthful males applying for insurance.

This would seem to indicate that the statistics are not meaningful and, contrary to appearances, do not show sex-related differences at all. If the brother is invariably assigned the sister's (or mother's or girlfriend's) accidents, one can hardly say who in the family is a good or bad driver—at least not from the tables. In a sense, it is really the car that is insured, not the driver; the young male driver is simply arbitrarily assigned the losses. If valid, this would mean that both the young male driver and any family containing a young male driver is arbitrarily required to pay a higher premium, even though the family's personal loss record may be exemplary.

3. Expert testimony by Hartford's own witness conceded at the hearing that there is no causal relationship between an insured's and his or her accident records. "The Department of Transportation found no basic difference in driving ability, rather in the situations which playing the role of the male in society will expose one to." According to the Hartford's expert witnesses, males expose themselves more to driving under the influence of alcohol than females and "more at those risky hours when there are more accidents happening when the roads are more congested and . . . more dangerous."

   "Since Section 3 (c) of the Rate Act requires that 'differences among risk' demonstrate 'a probable effect upon losses,' " the brief states, "a person's sex does not have a probable effect upon losses; it is rather how, where, and under what conditions a person drives that creates the 'probable effect.' "

The point would seem to be especially well taken inasmuch as male role-playing may be seen as part of overall sex stereotyping. As women increasingly enter the business world and engage in the same occupations as men, many of the differences that have been considered sex related appear to be disappearing. Even life expectancy seems less sex related than we had thought, with life-style playing a more important role. If complete equality is ever fully achieved, a great many statistics may prove invalid and without solid basis. In a curious way, discrimination seems to breed discrimination. The question as to which characteristics are inherent and which are due to social conditioning is being debated not only on campuses among psychologists and social scientists but also by consumers who are concerned with and perhaps penalized by actuarial tables.

The Hartford argued, as is usual in most unisex controversies, that eliminating sex-based tables would result in unfair discrimination against women because it would mean that insurance companies would have to level "the current rate structure between males and females." In other words, it raised the specter of increased cost. In its brief, the commission counters this argument by saying

> There are . . . many ways to approach the problem of assessing risks and differentiating between them fairly. As the record shows, sex is presently used as a primary rating factor, which is then adjusted according to secondary factors such as how the automobile is used and number of miles driven. By making the secondary factors primary and adjusting those factors by age or experience in driving, for example, the resulting rates could be quite different from those realized under the current structure and impossible to predict by gender.

Since it has been claimed by unisex proponents that premiums based on mileage would still mean lower rates for females, because they drive less than males, the industry argument would not seem to hold water. Women would, in fact, benefit, since women of all ages, not only young women, would qualify for lower rates. (There is no apparent reason why they do not even under the present system, but currently only young women benefit.)

The inconsistency (already noted) with which the Hartford (and other auto insurers) apply their statistics is pointed up in the commission's brief. "Taken to its logical conclusion, Hartford's position would require rates based on religion, race, hair color, S.A.T. scores, or on any other basis for which a difference in loss experience could be shown. Its own rate system would be invalid because it ceases to exact a premium differential for males over 30 years even though its evidence indicates males over 30 continue to have a higher rate of accident involvement."

To understand the case it is necessary to know that the Rate Act requires that "rating factors be supported by actuarial justification and demonstrate fairness. . . . The statutory scheme thus restrains insurers from attempting, for example, to correlate loss experience with an individual's earned income to establish rates, or from differentiating on some equally inappropriate basis such as race or religion . . . [prohibiting] those rating factors that are against public policy." And sex as a rating factor was determined to be against public policy—just as are race and religion.

Further, "The record indicated that it is not sex per se that has a causal relationship to the risk of loss, but rather that it was other factors, such as drinking habits, mileage, and the use of a car at rush hours, that relate to driving hazards. These factors are only coincidentally related more to males than to females."

The insurance industry clearly perceives ruling out sex as a risk classification factor as a threat. It rightfully realizes that sweeping changes, but most especially in health and auto insurance, would follow. It argues increased cost, both to the consumer and the industry; decreased benefits or at least insufficient improvement relative to cost; and breaking with tradition. In addition, it argues that there is no alternative. Bob Hunter of NICO is among those arguing that as regards auto insurance, mileage is not only an alternative but would be both accurate and fairer to all policyholders. The next chapter gives you a chance to hear both sides of the argument.

23

Mileage As a Risk Classification Factor—Two Views

If sex is ruled out as a risk classification factor, what other basis could the industry use? The alternative that has been offered is the gender-neutral factor of mileage. The Pennsylvania Insurance Commission is not the only proponent of eliminating sex-based tables in favor of mileage tables as a risk classification factor for automobile insurance. Many groups, including the National Insurance Consumer Organization (NICO), are strongly in favor of it.

J. Robert Hunter, president of NICO (which he organized in 1980) and federal insurance administrator under presidents Ford and Carter, was also an automobile insurance actuary for ten years, in charge of setting rates for auto insurance for the largest rating bureau representing hundreds of insurance companies. In view of his background, his opinion on the subject is certainly authoritative and well worth listening to. In a way, the insurance industry thinks so, too, since it has gone to a great deal of trouble to refute Mr. Hunter's arguments. An Insurance Services Office paper, "Mileage is not a Valid Substitute for Gender in Determining Fair Insurance Rates," takes issue with Mr. Hunter in considerable detail.

Mr. Hunter, on the other hand, says that the argument

that such a change (using mileage instead of sex) would mean a sharp increase in premiums to women is simply not so. In a March 4, 1983, letter to Representative Florio, chairman of the House Subcommittee on Commerce, Transportation and Tourism, Hunter wrote, "If mileage were used at all ages, premiums would fall significantly (by about 25%) for cars driven by women over the age of 25."

Insurance companies claim that using rates based on unisex tables would increase premiums paid by young women by $700 million. But according to a NICO study, if actuarially sound mileage experience is used in setting unisex rates, rates for young women would remain "essentially unchanged."

Later, in a press conference at the Capitol in Washington, D.C., on April 12, 1983, Mr. Hunter reiterated that gender classifications should be abolished. They are "surrogates for mileage and driving records. I used the data the industry itself put into the record in recent Congressional hearings to prove this and to show that women, as a class, pay too much for auto insurance under today's unfairly discriminatory sex-based rating approaches."

In his March 4 letter Mr. Hunter wrote that a preliminary actuarial review of mileage, based on statistics presented by the National Association of Independent Insurers (February 22, 1983, hearing before the subcommittee) showed that on a unisex basis, "driving record deteriorates as mileage increases." In his letter to Representative Florio, Mr. Hunter enclosed a table (shown on p. 302) showing that annual mileage up to 2,499 miles has a three-year accident record of .101. As the mileage increases, the accident record rises; at 50,000 miles and up it is .556

Calculations of Indicated Rate Differentials
Based upon Annual Mileage

ANNUAL MILEAGE	NO.	AVERAGE MILEAGE	3 YEAR ACCI-DENT RECORD	USE FOR RATES	DIFFER-ENTIAL (5) ÷ .249
Up to 2,499	840	1491	.101	.100	.40
2,500–4,999	1416	3355	.146	.150	.60
5,000–7,499	2610	5666	.176	.175	.70
7,500–9,999	1156	8231	.205	.200	.80
10,000–14,999	3645	11,185	.264	.250	1.00
15,000–19,999	1677	15,830	.309	.300	1.20
20,000–24,999	1150	20,660	.340	.325	1.30
25,000–29,999	527	25,446	.347	.350	1.40
30,000–39,999	651	31,985	.346	.400	1.60
40,000–49,999	252	41,621	.425	.450	1.80
50,000 and up	455	70,282	.556	.550	2.20
Total	14,379	13,776	.252	.249	1.000

SOURCE: Exhibit VII, page 1 of Statement of Galen R. Barns of National Association of Independent Insurers, February 22, 1983, before the Subcommittee on Commerce, Transportation and Tourism.

Since geography is also a factor in rate setting, Mr. Hunter also presented a table that shows what would happen in the various states to the premiums of a twenty-three-year-old woman whose rates were determined by a unisex/mileage combination. The three insurance companies whose rates are used are identified by the insurance industry only as A, B, and C, but Mr. Hunter theorizes:

It looks to me that Companies A and B are Allstate and State Farm and that Company C is either a substandard writer or at or above ISO rates (in any event Company C is noncompetitive). Company A (if it is Allstate) has a below and above 7,500 mileage class today. Typically, it is a $10 charge every six months, or about 5%. State Farm has a 10% surcharge for over 7,500 miles in many places. I have not adjusted my analysis for this effect (since I can't be sure that these are the right companies) but such adjustment would not alter my conclusions significantly. Company C probably has no mileage split. . . .

In conclusion he wrote, "Overall, abolition of sex rating coupled with introduction of meaningful mileage rating will lower women's premiums fairly substantially."

By the following fall NICO had completed a major study, "Women and Auto Insurance," that showed women's auto insurance premiums would drop by $1 billion if gender was replaced by a mileage classification. Again Bob Hunter was the spokesman. "The insurance industry has been maintaining that auto insurance premiums would rise by $700 million if gender classification were eliminated. Their study is fatally flawed in that it ignores the impact of the introduction of mileage classification certain to accompany the gender change," Hunter asserted. "When this is considered, women's rates drop sharply, by over $1 billion, or by 15%—and that's a $1.7 billion misunderstanding."

WHY NOT MILEAGE-BASED TABLES? THE INDUSTRY'S VIEWPOINT

We have seen that the insurance industry argues that dropping unisex-based tables would be costly to the consumer, especially to women. Since both sides support their respective positions with statistics, the question arises, which estimate is accurate? In the absence of a crystal ball that would allow us to visualize actual statistical experience several years from now, we are thrown back on a consideration of the principle involved: can sex-based actuarial tables be justified from a civil rights or sex discrimination standpoint? When the insurance industry says yes, they explain they mean because not using them "would cost more."

In the first place, that sounds suspiciously like use of scare tactics to influence the consumer against the idea. In "Myth and Reality: Getting to the Bottom Line in the Unisex Insurance Legislation Debate," Mavis A. Walters, senior vice-president of Insurance Services Office, says: "A recent poll conducted by Yankelovich, Skelly and White found that more than 80 percent of American women say it would be unfair to charge young women the same rates for auto insurance as young men." But in other material on the subject, the results are described: "81 percent of the women thought it unfair to increase premiums of young women by even as much as $100 a year." Which cannot help but make you wonder how the question was worded; without knowing the exact wording, it is impossible to evaluate the answer.

It is difficult to determine the merits of the industry's position when it makes sweeping statements that are open to question. This same paper, for instance, says: "Despite all the rhetoric to the contrary, women benefit under today's insurance system. . . . Women today pay lower insurance prices and consumers should be aware of that fact." Well, yes and no. Not all women and not all insurance. For instance, women on the whole pay more for health insurance, less for life insurance. And younger women pay less for auto insurance but older women do not (though according to the industry's own system, they should). This is a sensitive area, and the industry ought perhaps to approach it more candidly or not at all.

Second, cost is not really a response to the question asked: cost is not a matter of principal but of pragmatism. The pro-unisex arguments, while refuting that there would be an inevitable rise in rates, say that as a matter of principle—even if rates were to rise (and they say they would not)—there is no other fair way, and that society as a whole will benefit from unisex laws in the long run. The anti-unisex contingent may dispute this, but they cannot do so by using rates instead of principles as their argument.

When mileage tables are offered as an alternative to sex-based tables, and when statistics show that this would quite possibly be a fairer classification, insurers argue that all other considerations aside, mileage is unreliable and difficult for them to verify.

NICO, while recognizing the reality of the problem, offers some possible solutions.

> Certainly it requires more effort than gender, but we believe effective methods of control can be put in place for minimal cost (any cost would be more than offset by the savings due to people choosing to drive less to save premium dollars, we think). Several control methods are available to insurers. Insurers can look at all odometers or sample enough to control the universe. They can require self-certification, or certification via service stations. (They could offer larger discounts for service station certified odometers to give an incentive to insureds to go that route.) They can pick it up (in some states) from the Motor Vehicle Department. They can penalize, at claims time, those who have falsified their miles driven. They could even deny claims if the mileage representations were material misrepresentations.

The industry undoubtedly has a point that verification of mileage might be difficult, but it would be helpful if it at least discussed some of the possible ways that have been suggested.

There is no doubt that the industry weakens its case by appearing to hold sacrosanct tables that it uses so selectively. As we have seen, the industry offers only young women lower premiums than young men, even though women of all ages, if industry statistics are valid, should be offered this same benefit.

Another example of selective use, pointed out by pro–unisex groups, is the special auto insurance policies offered by some companies to the elderly. The stereotype of the elderly driver proclaims them a greater-than-average risk on the grounds that they don't see well, don't hear well, and are unsteady. It is true that their driving habits are not generally as good as those of younger drivers, but in spite of all this, some companies offer them especially low auto insurance rates because, as one expert put it, "the mileage tables show that their miles driven per year are so low that it is possible to offer a substantial discount to this group and still make a handsome profit." This would seem to indicate that the industry uses mileage as a risk classification factor when it is advantageous to do so, which leads to the further thought that whatever actuarial tables are used, the industry should be required to apply them consistently and not be allowed to pick and choose, use or not, according to whether it is profitable.

It will be helpful, also, when the industry explains either the rationale or the flaw in the basic point made in the Mattes case as to how the statistics on young male drivers are gathered. As long as they are penalized, statistically speaking, for accidents on policies covering them no matter who actually incurs them, it is hard to see how these statistics can be meaningful. Undoubtedly sometime in the prolonged litigation this matter will be addressed, but until it is, it cannot help but count on the unisex side of the argument.

24

What's Ahead for Unisex Insurance?

Is unisex a fad that will just go away? If, as seems likely, it will soon be here to stay, get ready for some important changes in what insurance costs and how its benefits will work. Some costs will go down, some will undoubtedly rise; the only thing you can be sure of in this area is that you can't trust any predictions at present. The industry will raise the specter of enormous increases in premiums; the proponents will counter with somewhat more optimistic figures. When the smoke clears and the last case has been decided in the courts, it may be that sex will at last have been legislated out of the insurance marketplace.

Meanwhile you might find it interesting to follow the course of the battle. The media find insurance newsworthy, and you will see an item in your paper, on radio, even on television at least once or twice a week.

Watch the news whenever major union contracts are being negotiated; health insurance is always a key issue and may well be a bone of contention; and, as we have seen, the unisex bills will impact strongly on health insurance. The importance of health insurance as a fringe benefit was shown, for example, in August 1984; General Motors, in its very first formal proposal for a new contract, asked for a major revision in health care benefits.

At this time General Motors provides benefits for 2.1 million employees at a cost of $2.2 billion a year—$5,000 on the average for each worker or $430 per car sold (passed on to the consumer). GM is understandably nervous about rising costs in the years to come, especially since its workforce is five years older than the national average age and older people have, generally, higher health care costs.

What GM is proposing, in order to reduce its costs by 10 percent, is a choice of three options: (1) use of preferred providers; (2) an HMO; (3) its present medical insurance system, somewhat revised. The first option refers to a network of hospitals and clinics that agreed to a preset price schedule. This is somewhat new, although it is similar to the sort of arrangement that has made Blue Cross so successful.

You will want to note in reading about union negotiations, occasional references to nonunion workers; they are sure to lose out on many of the goodies and to pay more for what they get. Often when a manufacturer picks up all or the major share of premiums of union workers, it demands high deductibles and co-insurance from its nonunion workers.

In tracking the news, look also for feminist organization activities. At the same time that GM was gingerly approaching a new contract, the National Organization of Women was filing a $2 million lawsuit against Mutual of Omaha, charging the insurance company with illegally overcharging women for health insurance. Mutual has responded with a "Why me?" kind of comment, but since it sells more health insurance than any other company in the District of Columbia, its high visibility makes it a natural target. The suit is clearly related to the unisex bills and is probably typical of the kind of pressure these groups will be putting on the government and the industry to get their act together on sex discrimination in insurance.

I asked Bob Hunter what chance the unisex bills had of passing. He said, "Insurance is a major part of the economy; 4 percent of the disposable income goes into insurance premiums. [With all the changes going on in the economy and given the feeling against discrimination], unisex insurance is inevitable, as certain as night follows day."

Index

311